THE DOOR

90 DAY DEVOTIONAL EMBRACING TRANSITIONS, OPPORTUNITIES, AND DIVINE ENCOUNTERS

STEPHENIE BROWN

Copyright @ 2023 by Stephenie Brown

All rights reserved. This book or parts thereof may not be reproduced in any form, stored in a retrieval system, or transmitted in any form, stored in a retrieval system, or transmitted in any form by any means - electronic, mechanical, photocopy, recording, or otherwise - without prior written permission of the publisher, except as provided by United States of America copyright law.

The Door: 90 Day Devotional Embracing Transitions, Opportunities, and Divine Encounters

ISBN: 979-8-9894816-0-6 (paper)

"Scripture quotations are from the ESV® Bible (The Holy Bible, English Standard Version®), © 2001 by Crossway, a publishing ministry of Good News Publishers. Used by permission. All rights reserved. The ESV text may not be quoted in any publication made available to the public by a Creative Commons license. The ESV may not be translated in whole or in part into any other language."

Scripture quotations marked (NLT) are taken from the Holy Bible, New Living Translation, copyright ©1996, 2004, 2015 by Tyndale House Foundation. Used by permission of Tyndale House Publishers, Carol Stream, Illinois 60188. All rights reserved.

Scripture quotations taken from The Holy Bible, New International Version® NIV®, Copyright © 1973, 1978, 1984, 2011 by Biblica, Inc. Used with permission. All rights reserved worldwide.

Scripture quotations marked KJV are from the King James Version of the Bible.

Printed in the United States of America

INTRODUCTION

Welcome to "The Door: 90 Day Devotional Embracing Transitions, Opportunities and Divine Encounters" a book designed to accompany you on this journey of transformation. Within these pages, you will find a collection of heartfelt reflections, biblical wisdom, and uplifting messages that aim to brighten your days, enlighten your soul, and ignite a sense of purpose within you.

Life can be a magnificent adventure, filled with both joyous moments and unexpected challenges. It often takes us through winding paths, where we navigate through peaks and valleys, seeking meaning and fulfillment. In this devotional, we embark on a shared journey to explore our hearts, find comfort in the present moment, and discover the extraordinary in the ordinary.

Each day, you will be greeted with a carefully crafted devotion that relates with the complexities of life. Drawing from various spiritual traditions, timeless philosophies, and biblical anecdotes, the aim is to provide you with a diverse selection of wisdom that goes beyond boundaries and embraces our shared humanity. These devotions will empower you to embrace your unique gifts, cultivate gratitude, and nurture a sense of inner peace.

Whether you are seeking comfort during challenging times, inspiration to pursue your dreams, or simply a moment of reflection in your busy day, "The Door: 90 Day Devotional Embracing Transitions, Opportunities and Divine Encounters" is here to accompany you. You will find encouragement to face life's uncertainties with courage and grace, reminders to cherish the simple joys, and gentle nudges to embrace self-discovery and personal growth.

Let this devotional be your daily companion, a guiding light that illuminates your path and reminds you of the infinite possibilities that lie within. May it inspire you, uplift your spirit, and awaken a deep sense of purpose as you navigate the triumphs and tribulations of life.

Remember, you are never alone on this journey. Together, let's embark on this adventure of self-discovery, growth, and embrace the abundance of life's blessings. Open your heart, open your mind, and let the light within you shine brightly as we embark on this transformative journey together.

DOOR TO THE ABUNDANT LIFE

DAY 1

*J*ohn 10:7 (ESV) - So Jesus again said to them, "Truly, truly, I say to you, I am the door of the sheep."

In today's verse, Jesus presents a profound revelation about Himself: He is the gate or door through which we enter into a life of abundant blessings and eternal security. This visual metaphor of Jesus as the gate is not only beautiful but also holds deep spiritual truths that can transform our lives.

Imagine for a moment a sheepfold, a place of refuge and safety for the sheep. The shepherd carefully constructs a strong gate to protect the flock from harm, keeping predators out and the sheep within. Similarly, Jesus, our Good Shepherd, provides us with a secure and loving environment in which we can find rest, peace, and fulfillment.

Jesus declares, "I am the door of the sheep." He is the exclusive entrance to the abundant life He desires to offer us. It is through a personal relationship with Him that we can experience true contentment and purpose. He invites us to walk with Him, making Him the center of our lives.

As the gate, Jesus provides protection and guidance. He shields us from the snares of the enemy, leading us away from harm and towards green pastures of spiritual nourishment. By following Him, we gain access to the abundant life He promises, filled with His grace, love, and provision.

Furthermore, Jesus as the gate signifies inclusivity. He opens the door to all who seek Him, regardless of their backgrounds, past mistakes, or social status. Through Him, we find acceptance, forgiveness, and a new beginning. He invites each one of us to enter into a life-transforming relationship with Him, where we can experience true freedom and restoration.

Therefore, let us approach Jesus, the door, with faith and trust. Embrace His teachings, follow His footsteps, and surrender our lives to His loving care. As we enter through Him, we will discover the abundant life He promises – a life marked by joy, peace, purpose, and eternal salvation.

Take a moment today to reflect on Jesus as the gate of your life. Are you seeking His guidance and protection? Have you fully surrendered your life to Him? Let us open our hearts wide to Jesus, allowing Him to lead us towards the abundant life that only He can provide.

Prayer: Lord Jesus, thank You for being the door to the abundant life. Help me to fully surrender my life to You and walk in the path You have set before me. Guide me, protect me, and lead me into the fullness of Your blessings. In Jesus' name, I pray, Amen.

Remember, Jesus is the door to abundant life. May you find peace, joy, and fulfillment as you walk through Him today and every day.

TRANSITION. OPPORTUNITY.
DIVINE ENCOUNTER.

THE DOOR OF FAITH

DAY 2

*A*cts 14:27 (ESV) - "And when they arrived and gathered the church together, they declared all that God had done with them, and how he had opened a door of faith to the Gentiles."

I hope this day finds you well and filled with the grace of our Lord. Today, let us journey together into the profound message hidden behind the metaphorical "door of faith." In the book of Acts, we witness how God opened this door, not only to the Jews but also to the Gentiles, forever changing the landscape of Christianity.

1. A Door of Opportunity:

Just as doors allow us to enter new spaces, the door of faith presents us with remarkable opportunities. As believers, we are invited to step through this doorway, leaving behind our doubts, fears, and limited perspectives. Beyond the door lies a realm of limitless possibilities, where God's power and transformative love abound.

2. A Door of Inclusion:

In Acts 14:27, we see how God extended His invitation to the Gentiles, breaking barriers that once separated people based on their background or ethnicity. Through this open door, God demonstrated His heart for inclusion and His desire for all to come to know Him. It reminds us that faith is not limited to a select few but encompasses every person willing to enter through this door and embrace God's love.

3. A Door of Transformation:

Stepping through the door of faith enables us to experience true transformation. It is an invitation to leave behind our old ways and walk in the light of God's truth. As we surrender our lives to Him, His Spirit works within us, molding us into the image of Christ. Through this transformative process, we are no longer bound by our past mistakes but are freed to live a life of purpose and joy.

4. A Door of Assurance:

One of the beautiful aspects of the door of faith is the assurance it provides. When we enter through this door, we find solace in knowing that our faith is not based on our own strength, but on the unchanging character of God. Through the ups and downs of life, we can lean on Him, trusting that He will guide our steps and provide for our needs.

Take a moment to reflect on your own journey through the door of faith. How has God opened doors of opportunity, inclusion, and transformation in your life? In what ways has your faith brought assurance and peace during challenging times?

As we embrace the door of faith, let us be mindful of the doors we can open for others. Just as God opened the door to the Gentiles, we have the privilege and responsibility to extend the love and grace of Christ to all those around us. Let us be a living testimony of the transformative power found behind the door of faith.

Prayer: Father God, thank You for opening the door of faith to us, inviting us into a deeper relationship with You. Help us to embrace the opportunities, inclusion, and transformation that lie beyond this door.

May our faith be a shining light, guiding others towards You. In Jesus' name, we pray. Amen.

May you continue to walk through the door of faith, experiencing the abundant blessings and grace our loving God has prepared for you

TRANSITION. OPPORTUNITY.
DIVINE ENCOUNTER.

_____

_____

_____

_____

_____

_____

_____

_____

_____

_____

GATES AND ANCIENT DOORS

DAY 3

Today, let's examine the profound words of Psalm 24:7 (ESV), which reminds us of the majesty and sovereignty of our God. This verse serves as a beautiful reminder of the exalted nature of our Heavenly Father, the King of Glory.

Imagine for a moment the breathtaking scene described in this verse:

"Lift up your heads, O gates! And be lifted up, O ancient doors, that the King of glory may come in." Picture ancient gates and doors opening wide, welcoming the arrival of a majestic and glorious King. This imagery presents a powerful invitation for us to embrace the presence of God in our lives.

In our daily lives, we often face challenges, uncertainties, and burdens that can weigh us down. It is during these moments that we need to remember that we serve a God who is greater than any problem we may encounter. He is the King of Glory, and His presence is a source of strength and hope for us.

When we lift up our heads and open the doors of our hearts to the King of Glory, we invite His power and grace to enter. As believers, we have the privilege of experiencing the presence of God in our lives, knowing that no situation is too big for Him to handle. We can approach Him confidently, knowing that He is always ready to guide, comfort, and strengthen us.

Furthermore, this verse reminds us that our God is not only a King, but also the King of Glory. His glory is beyond measure, shining brightly in every aspect of His creation. When we recognize and acknowledge His glory, we are reminded of His greatness and the wonders He can work in our lives.

So, let us, like the gates and ancient doors, lift up our heads and be ready to welcome the King of Glory into our lives each day. Let us open our hearts and minds to His presence, allowing Him to transform us, uplift our spirits, and lead us in His perfect ways.

As we journey through each day, may we always remember that we serve a God who is not only mighty and powerful, but also loving and compassionate. He is the King of Glory who desires to walk alongside us, guiding us with His wisdom and filling our lives with hope and joy.

Prayer: Lord Jesus, we thank You for being the King of Glory, the mighty and majestic God who reigns over all. Help us to open our hearts and minds to Your presence each day. Teach us to lift up our heads, welcoming Your power and grace into our lives. May Your glory shine brightly in and through us, as we seek to honor You in all we do. In Jesus' name, Amen.

Takeaway: Today, take a moment to reflect on the majesty and glory of God. Open your heart and invite Him into every aspect of your life. Allow His presence to transform you and give you strength to face any challenge that comes your way. Remember, you serve the King of Glory, and His power is at work within you.

TRANSITION. OPPORTUNITY.
DIVINE ENCOUNTER.

THE OPEN DOOR OF REVELATION

DAY 4

Revelation 4:1 (ESV) - "After this I looked, and behold, a door standing open in heaven! And the first voice, which I had heard speaking to me like a trumpet, said, 'Come up here, and I will show you what must take place after this.'"

Today, let us embark on a journey into the book of Revelation, a captivating vision that John received on the island of Patmos. In this supernatural encounter, John's eyes are opened to the glorious realm of heaven, revealing profound insights into things yet to come.

Imagine for a moment standing alongside John, as he gazes upon an open door in heaven. This door represents an invitation to enter into an extraordinary encounter with God, where divine revelations are unveiled and mysteries unfold. As we reflect on this verse, three key aspects come to light.

1. Divine Invitation: Notice that the voice John hears is not just any voice but the voice of authority, resounding like a trumpet. It is the voice of the Almighty, extending a personal invitation to John, saying, "Come up here!" Likewise, God extends the same invitation to us today. He invites us to draw near to Him, to seek His presence, and to dive into His Word.

The Lord desires to reveal His plans, purposes, and wisdom to those who seek Him wholeheartedly.

2. Heavenly Perspective: As John accepts the invitation and steps through the open door, he gains a heavenly perspective. The things he witnesses and the truths he encounters surpass the limits of earthly understanding. In the same way, when we draw closer to God, our perspective shifts. We begin to see our circumstances, challenges, and even the world around us through the lens of God's eternal kingdom. This heavenly perspective brings hope, comfort, and clarity in the midst of uncertainty.

3. Unveiling of the Future: Lastly, the voice promises John that he will be shown what must take place after the present time. Through the book of Revelation, God unveils His redemptive plan and provides glimpses into the future. This reassurance reminds us that God holds the ultimate authority over all creation and that His divine purposes will prevail. As we read and meditate on Revelation, let us remember that God's sovereignty grants us confidence and peace, knowing that He is in control, even when the world may seem chaotic.

Today, let us respond to the divine invitation to draw near to God, seeking His presence and desiring a heavenly perspective. As we do, may God graciously unveil His wisdom and truth, giving us hope, guidance, and assurance in every season of life.

Prayer: Lord Jesus, thank You for extending an open invitation for us to draw near to You. Help us to respond with open hearts, seeking Your presence and desiring a heavenly perspective. As we journey through the book of Revelation, grant us wisdom, understanding, and peace. May Your Word illuminate our paths and deepen our faith. In Jesus' name, we pray. Amen.

TRANSITION. OPPORTUNITY.
DIVINE ENCOUNTER.

THE DOOR OF DIVINE COMMUNION

DAY 5

M atthew 6:6 (ESV) - "But when you pray, go into your room and shut the door and pray to your Father who is in secret. And your Father who sees in secret will reward you."

Today, let's reflect upon the significance of the door as a symbol of our intimate connection with God. In Matthew 6:6, Jesus invites us to enter into a private space, shutting the door behind us, and commune with our Heavenly Father in secret. This act of prayer and solitude holds great spiritual significance for our lives.

1. A Threshold of Solitude:

Imagine yourself standing before a door, ready to enter into a sacred space. As you close the door behind you, a sense of solitude envelops you. In this solitude, you can truly let go of the distractions and noise of the world. It is here, in the stillness, that you can encounter God in a deeply personal and transformative way. Embrace this moment of solitude, knowing that you are entering into a divine exchange with your Creator.

2. A Gateway of Connection:

The door represents a gateway that leads us into an intimate connection with God. Behind this door, we can pour out our hearts, share our joys and burdens, and seek guidance and wisdom from our Heavenly Father. It is a safe space where we can be vulnerable, knowing that God sees and hears us, even in the secret places of our hearts. Through this connection, we experience His love, comfort, and guidance, strengthening our faith and transforming our lives.

3. A Portal of Rewards:

Our loving Father promises rewards to those who seek Him in secret. As we faithfully enter through the door of divine communion, our relationship with God deepens. He graciously rewards us with His presence, peace, and joy that surpasses understanding. These rewards may also manifest as answers to our prayers, spiritual growth, renewed strength, and a closer walk with Him. Remember, God longs to bless His children who diligently seek Him in the secret place.

Prayer: Father God, thank you for the privilege of entering into your presence through the door of divine communion. Help us to embrace the solitude that allows us to connect with you intimately. As we seek you in secret, may we experience the rewards of your presence, peace, and guidance in our lives. In Jesus' name, we pray. Amen.

Take a moment today to reflect on the door as a symbol of divine communion. May this passage encourage you to create a sacred space for prayer and solitude, deepening your connection with God. Remember, behind the door lies the transformative power of His love and the rewards of seeking Him in secret. May your journey through this door be filled with abundant blessings and a growing relationship with your Heavenly Father.

TRANSITION. OPPORTUNITY.
DIVINE ENCOUNTER.

_____

_____

_____

_____

_____

_____

_____

_____

_____

THE PRECIOUS BLOOD: A MARK OF DELIVERANCE

DAY 6

Exodus 12:22-23 (ESV) - "Take a bunch of hyssop and dip it in the blood that is in the basin, and touch the lintel and the two doorposts with the blood that is in the basin. None of you shall go out of the door of his house until the morning. For the Lord will pass through to strike the Egyptians, and when he sees the blood on the lintel and on the two doorposts, the Lord will pass over the door and will not allow the destroyer to enter your houses to strike you."

Today, let us reflect on the powerful story of the Passover found in the book of Exodus. In this account, God instructed the Israelites to take the blood of a lamb and mark their doorposts with it as a sign of protection. This act of faith would spare their households from the final plague: the death of the firstborn.

Imagine the scene: families huddled together inside their homes, anxiously awaiting the Lord's judgment. But as the destroyer passed through the land, he saw the blood on the doorposts and passed over those dwellings, leaving them untouched. The blood became a mark of deliverance, a symbol of God's faithfulness and redemption.

In a similar way, the blood of Jesus Christ, shed on the cross, became the ultimate mark of deliverance for all humanity. Just as the Israelites were saved from physical death, we are saved from eternal separation from God through the blood of Jesus. His sacrifice covers our sins, paving the way for forgiveness, restoration, and abundant life.

As we reflect on this ancient story, let us remember the significance of the blood of Jesus in our lives. It is a constant reminder of God's love, grace, and power. It is a mark that sets us apart as His redeemed children, protected from the enemy's attacks. It is a symbol of the ultimate deliverance we have received through Christ.

Today, take a moment to thank God for the precious blood of Jesus that covers you. Trust in His faithfulness, knowing that His mark of deliverance is upon you. Embrace the forgiveness and freedom that His blood provides, and live each day in the joy and confidence of your salvation.

Prayer: Lord, thank you for the blood of Jesus that marks us as Your redeemed children. Help us to fully grasp the magnitude of Your sacrifice and the deliverance it brings. May we live each day in the power of Your blood, knowing that we are protected, forgiven, and set free. In Jesus' name, Amen.

Remember, you are loved, cherished, and protected by the power of the blood of Jesus Christ. May His mark of deliverance be your source of hope and strength today and always.

TRANSITION. OPPORTUNITY.
DIVINE ENCOUNTER.

_____

_____

_____

_____

_____

_____

_____

_____

_____

_____

EMBRACING OPPORTUNITIES WITH FAITH

DAY 7

Colossians 4:3 (ESV) - "At the same time, pray also for us, that God may open to us a door for the word, to declare the mystery of Christ, on account of which I am in prison."

In today's verse, the apostle Paul shares his heartfelt plea for believers to pray for an open door to proclaim the gospel. Although written from a prison cell, Paul's focus remains on the opportunities to share the life-transforming message of Christ. This verse reminds us of the incredible power that prayer holds in our lives, not only for ourselves but also for those who are called to spread God's word.

1. Recognizing Divine Appointments:

Paul's request for prayer highlights the importance of recognizing the divine appointments that God orchestrates in our lives. Each day presents us with opportunities to share the love of Christ with those around us. Whether it is through a conversation, an act of kindness, or even a simple smile, let us approach each encounter with an open heart and a willingness to be used by God.

2. Praying for Open Doors:

Just as Paul asked for prayers, we too should continuously

seek God's guidance and favor in opening doors for His word. Through prayer, we invite God into our situations and ask Him to provide us with opportunities to speak His truth boldly and effectively. Let us remember to pray not only for our own lives but also for fellow believers who are actively engaged in spreading the Gospel.

3. Trusting God's Timing:

Although Paul was in prison, his focus remained on the mission of sharing the mystery of Christ. This reveals his unwavering trust in God's perfect timing. Often, we may find ourselves in challenging circumstances, seemingly hindering our ability to share the Gospel. However, let us remember that God can use any situation to bring about His purposes. Trust in His divine timing and have faith that He will open doors in His perfect plan.

4. The Mystery of Christ:

Lastly, we are reminded that the message we carry is the mystery of Christ. The gospel is not merely a historical account or a set of rules, but a mystery of God's love and salvation revealed through Jesus Christ. As we embrace opportunities to share this mystery, let us do so with joy, gratitude, and a deep understanding of its life-changing power.

Prayer: Father God, we thank You for the opportunities You provide us each day to share the mystery of Christ. Open our eyes to recognize divine appointments and grant us the courage and boldness to speak Your truth. We pray for open doors to proclaim Your message, trusting in Your perfect timing. In Jesus' name, we pray. Amen.

Take a moment today to reflect on the divine appointments God has placed in your life. Embrace each opportunity with faith and joy, knowing that you have the privilege of sharing the mystery of Christ with those around you. May God bless you abundantly as you walk in obedience to His call.

TRANSITION. OPPORTUNITY.
DIVINE ENCOUNTER.

_____

_____

_____

_____

_____

_____

_____

_____

_____

HOPE IN THE WILDERNESS

DAY 8

"*And there I will give her her vineyards and make the Valley of Achor a door of hope. And there she shall answer as in the days of her youth, as at the time when she came out of the land of Egypt.*" - Hosea 2:15 (ESV)

Today, let us take a moment to reflect on Hosea 2:15 and find encouragement in its profound message. These words carry a promise of restoration, redemption, and a renewed sense of hope.

In this verse, the Valley of Achor, which means "trouble" or "troubling," is transformed into a door of hope. It is a reminder that even in the midst of our most challenging seasons, God is at work, bringing forth beauty from the ashes. He is the master of turning our trials into stepping stones towards a brighter future.

Just as the Israelites journeyed through the wilderness after leaving Egypt, we face our own wilderness experiences. These wilderness seasons can be filled with uncertainty, loneliness, and even pain. However, it is in these very moments that God often draws us closer to Him, molding our character, and revealing His faithfulness.

When we find ourselves in the wilderness, let us not lose heart. Instead, let us trust that God is working behind the scenes, preparing us for the blessings that lie ahead. In the midst of the wilderness, God promises to provide us with spiritual nourishment, just as He provided vineyards to His people. These vineyards symbolize His abundant grace, love, and provision in our lives.

As we embrace the wilderness, may we also long to answer God's calling with the same zeal and passion as when we first encountered His love. Let us remember the days of our youth, when our hearts were unburdened by the weight of the world, and our trust in Him was unwavering. In returning to that childlike faith, we can experience a renewed sense of joy, wonder, and intimacy with our Heavenly Father.

Today, let us hold onto the promise that God can transform our valleys of trouble into doors of hope. He is with us in every season, guiding us, comforting us, and leading us towards a future filled with His goodness. Embrace the wilderness, knowing that it is through these very trials that our faith is strengthened, our character refined, and our hope restored.

May you find comfort and encouragement in God's promises today. Remember, you are never alone, for the Creator of the universe walks beside you every step of the way.

Prayer: Lord, thank You for Your promise of hope in the midst of our wilderness seasons. Help us to trust in Your faithfulness, knowing that You are working all things together for our good. Grant us the grace to embrace the challenges we face, knowing that You will turn them into opportunities for growth and blessing. In Jesus' name, we pray. Amen.

Take some time today to meditate on this verse and allow God's truth to bring you peace and hope.

TRANSITION. OPPORTUNITY.
DIVINE ENCOUNTER.

_____

_____

_____

_____

_____

_____

_____

_____

_____

ASK, SEEK, AND KNOCK

DAY 9

*T*oday, we dive into the powerful words of Matthew 7:7-8 (ESV) - *"Ask, and it will be given to you; seek, and you will find; knock, and it will be opened to you. For everyone who asks receives, and the one who seeks finds, and to the one who knocks it will be opened.*

Let us explore the significance of these verses and how they can inspire us in our daily walk with God.

In this passage, Jesus invites us to embark on a journey of asking, seeking and knocking. These actions are not mere suggestions but powerful invitations to engage with our heavenly Father. They reflect a deep desire within us to connect with God, to seek His wisdom, guidance, and provision.

Ask: The first step is to ask. Our heavenly Father delights in our prayers, and He eagerly waits for us to come before Him with our needs, desires, and concerns. Through prayer, we engage in a conversation with the Almighty, expressing our dependence on Him and acknowledging His sovereignty. As we present our requests, let us remember to align our desires with God's will, trusting that He knows what is best for us.

Seek: The second step in this journey is seeking. Jesus

encourages us to actively pursue a relationship with God, to seek His presence, truth, and will. Our seeking should be earnest, born out of a genuine hunger for spiritual growth and a longing for a deeper understanding of God's character. As we seek Him diligently, we open our hearts to the countless blessings He has in store for us.

Knock: Lastly, Jesus invites us to knock. The act of knocking signifies our persistence and determination in seeking God's intervention. It reminds us not to grow weary or discouraged in our journey of faith. When we encounter closed doors or obstacles, let us not give up but rather knock, trusting that God's timing and purposes are perfect. He promises that when we persist, the door will be opened.

Today, let us embrace the call to ask, seek and knock, confident that our heavenly Father is always ready to respond. May we approach Him with childlike faith, knowing that He is our loving Creator, a faithful provider, and a wise guide. As we seek His presence, ask for His grace, and persistently knock on the doors, we will experience His unfailing love, provision, and guidance.

Take a moment now to reflect on what requests you need to bring before Him, how you can actively seek God's presence in your life, and what doors you need to persistently knock on. May this devotion inspire you to draw closer to our heavenly Father, who eagerly awaits your asking, seeking, and knocking.

Remember, you are not alone on this journey. God is with you every step of the way, ready to extend His hand and guide you. May His love and wisdom surround you today and always.

Prayer: Lord Jesus, thank You for the invitation to ask, seek, and knock. Help me to actively pursue a deeper relationship with You, aligning my desires with Your will. Grant me the courage to persistently knock on the doors of life, trusting in Your perfect timing. In Jesus' name, I pray. Amen.

TRANSITION. OPPORTUNITY. DIVINE ENCOUNTER.

_____

_____

_____

_____

_____

_____

_____

_____

_____

EMBRACING THE POWER OF CHOICE

DAY 10

Scripture: Genesis 4:7 (ESV) - "If you do well, will you not be accepted? And if you do not do well, sin is crouching at the door. Its desire is contrary to you, but you must rule over it."

In this verse from the book of Genesis, we find a powerful reminder of the significance of our choices and the impact they have on our lives. As we navigate through each day, we are faced with countless decisions and opportunities to either align ourselves with God's will or succumb to the temptations of sin.

God's words to Cain in this verse are not meant to discourage or condemn, but rather to reveal the inherent power of choice that He has graciously bestowed upon us. With this power comes great responsibility, for our choices can shape the course of our lives and influence those around us.

The first part of verse 7 reminds us that if we choose to do well, to live in obedience to God's commandments, we will find acceptance in His sight. Our actions, motivated by love, compassion, and righteousness, become a pleasing offering to our Heavenly Father. Each day, we have the opportunity to make choices that reflect our commitment to doing what is right in God's eyes.

However, the second part of the verse warns us of the lurking presence of sin. Sin is portrayed as a predator, crouching at the door of our hearts, seeking to entice and ensnare us. It goes against our very nature as children of God and seeks to lead us astray from His perfect plan for our lives.

Yet, the good news is that we have been given the power to rule over sin. Through the indwelling of the Holy Spirit and the transformative work of Christ in our lives, we have the ability to resist temptation, overcome our sinful inclinations, and walk in victory. It is through this power that we can make choices that honor God and bring about blessings and fulfillment.

Today, let us approach each decision with intentionality and prayer, seeking God's guidance and wisdom. Let us be mindful of the power of our choices, recognizing that they have the potential to shape our character, relationships, and ultimately, our eternal destiny.

May we be encouraged to choose well, embracing the abundant life that God has prepared for us. And when sin seeks to entangle us, let us rely on the strength and grace of our Heavenly Father to overcome and rule over it. With His help, we can navigate this journey of faith, making choices that reflect His love, and experiencing the joy and peace that comes from walking in obedience to Him.

Prayer: Father God, thank you for the power of choice that you have given us. Help us to be intentional in our decisions, seeking your guidance and wisdom. Grant us the strength to resist sin's allure and to walk in obedience to your commands. May our choices reflect your love and bring glory to your name. In Jesus' name, we pray, Amen.

TRANSITION. OPPORTUNITY.
DIVINE ENCOUNTER.

EMBRACING GOD'S OPEN DOORS

DAY 11

1 Corinthians 16:8-9 (ESV) - "But I will stay in Ephesus until Pentecost, for a wide door for effective work has opened to me, and there are many adversaries."

In our journey of faith, we often encounter both open doors and adversaries. Sometimes, it may seem easier to focus on the adversaries and let them discourage us. However, today's scripture reminds us of the importance of recognizing and embracing the open doors that God places before us.

The apostle Paul, in his letter to the Corinthians, expressed his decision to stay in Ephesus until Pentecost because a wide door for effective work had opened for him. Despite the presence of adversaries, Paul understood that God was leading him through this open door, providing him with an opportunity to make a significant impact.

Just like Paul, we face various doors in our lives. Some doors may be open wide, while others may be barely cracked. It is crucial for us to seek God's guidance and discern which doors He wants us to walk through. Often, the doors He opens may not be the easiest or most comfortable, but they are the ones that lead to growth, transformation, and purpose.

When we encounter open doors, it's important to remember three things:

1. Prayerful Discernment: Seek God's wisdom through prayer and His Word. Ask Him to reveal His will and guide your steps as you evaluate the opportunities before you. Trust that He will provide clarity and confirmation.

2. Courageous Action: Embrace the open doors with courage and faith, even if they come with challenges or uncertainties. Remember that God equips us for the tasks He calls us to, and He promises to be with us every step of the way.

3. Perseverance: Recognize that open doors do not guarantee a smooth journey. Adversaries may arise, obstacles may appear, and doubts may creep in. However, stand firm in your faith, knowing that God's strength and grace will sustain you. Keep pressing forward, trusting in His power to overcome every obstacle.

Today, let us prayerfully reflect on the open doors God has placed before us. Instead of focusing on the adversaries or potential difficulties, let us embrace these opportunities with courage and trust. Remember that when God opens a door, He goes before us, preparing the way.

May we step through these doors with confidence, knowing that God will accomplish His purposes in and through us. As we walk in obedience, may we experience the joy and fulfillment that comes from aligning our lives with His perfect plan.

Prayer: Lord, thank You for the open doors that You place before us. Give us the wisdom to discern Your will and the courage to step through those doors, even when challenges arise. Help us to trust in Your guidance and provision, knowing that You are always with us. Strengthen us to persevere when faced with adversaries, and fill us with Your peace and joy as we walk in obedience. In Jesus' name, Amen.

TRANSITION. OPPORTUNITY.
DIVINE ENCOUNTER.

_____

_____

_____

_____

_____

_____

_____

_____

_____

DOORS OF DEPARTURE AND FORGIVENESS

DAY 12

2 Chronicles 28:24 (ESV) - "And Ahaz gathered together the vessels of the house of God and cut in pieces the vessels of the house of God, and he shut up the doors of the house of the Lord, and he made himself altars in every corner of Jerusalem."

Today, let's reflect on a verse from the book of 2 Chronicles that teaches us important lessons about the consequences of straying away from God's will. The story revolves around King Ahaz, a ruler who turned his back on the Lord's commands and indulged in idolatrous practices.

Ahaz's actions were not only disrespectful but also destructive. He gathered the sacred vessels from the house of God and broke them. Moreover, he closed the doors of the Lord's temple and erected altars to false gods throughout Jerusalem. His actions represented a departure from the faith and a rejection of God's guidance.

This verse serves as a reminder for us to evaluate the state of our own hearts. Are we honoring God with our actions and choices, or are we straying away from His will? It's crucial to regularly examine our lives and ensure that we are walking in alignment with His Word.

While Ahaz's actions were disappointing, we can find hope in the fact that God's love is unfailing. Even when we make mistakes or turn away from Him, He patiently waits for us to return. His love is not conditional on our perfect obedience but rather on His unchanging character.

If you find yourself in a place of spiritual distance, remember that God is always ready to forgive and restore. Take a moment to reflect on your relationship with Him. Are there any areas where you have shut the doors of your heart to His presence? Are there altars of distractions or false gods that have taken priority in your life?

Today, let us seek to restore our connection with the Lord. Open the doors of your heart and invite Him in. Remove any idols that have taken His rightful place. Embrace His forgiveness and grace, knowing that His love is always available to you.

Prayer: Father God, forgive us for the times we have strayed away from Your will and pursued our own desires. Help us to recognize any idols or distractions in our lives that hinder our relationship with You. We open our hearts to Your presence and ask for Your forgiveness and guidance. May Your unfailing love lead us back to the path of righteousness. In Jesus' name, we pray, Amen.

Remember, God's love is always waiting for you with open arms. May you find comfort and encouragement in His presence as you journey through each day. Stay blessed, and know that you are never alone.

TRANSITION. OPPORTUNITY.
DIVINE ENCOUNTER.

SIGNS OF THE TIMES

DAY 13

Scripture: Matthew 24:33 (NLT) - "In the same way, when you see all these things, you can know his return is very near, right at the door."

Have you ever wondered about the signs that indicate the nearness of Christ's return? In Matthew 24, Jesus spoke to His disciples about the signs that would point to the end of the age. It's essential for us as believers to pay attention to these signs, as they give us hope, encouragement, and a sense of urgency to live for Christ.

In this verse, Jesus encourages His followers to be attentive to the signs around them. He uses the analogy of a door, emphasizing that when all these signs converge, His return will be imminent, just like when someone is standing right outside a door, ready to enter. How exciting is that?

As we observe the world around us today, we can't help but notice many of these signs coming to pass. Wars and conflicts, natural disasters, moral decline, a rise in false prophets, and an increasing disregard for God's Word are just a few indicators. However, rather than being fearful or disheartened, Jesus calls us to be wise and discerning.

Rather than being consumed by fear or speculation, let us be people of hope and faith. We can be confident that our Savior is indeed coming back. These signs serve as a reminder that our time on this earth is limited, and we have a mission to fulfill. We are called to share the good news, love others, and live out our faith boldly.

In light of these signs, let us not grow complacent or indifferent. Instead, let us be diligent in seeking God, knowing His Word, and staying rooted in prayer. Let us live with an eternal perspective, investing our time, resources, and talents in things that matter for eternity.

Remember, the Lord's return is nearer than ever before. Let this truth ignite a passion within us to impact lives for Jesus, to love unconditionally, and to share the hope we have in Him. May we be found faithful when He returns, eagerly awaiting His arrival, with hearts full of joy and anticipation.

Prayer: Dear Lord, thank You for the signs You have given us that remind us of Your imminent return. Help us to be wise, discerning, and faithful in these times. Fill us with boldness to share Your love and the hope we have in You. May we live each day with an eternal perspective, knowing that our time is limited. In Jesus' name, we pray. Amen.

May your day be filled with the assurance of Christ's return and the hope that it brings. God bless you!

TRANSITION. OPPORTUNITY.
DIVINE ENCOUNTER.

_____

_____

_____

_____

_____

_____

_____

_____

_____

EMBRACING GOD'S GUIDING PRESENCE

DAY 14

"*Now when I went to Troas to preach the gospel of Christ and found that the Lord had opened a door for me.*" - 2 Corinthians 2:12 (ESV)

Today, let us reflect on the profound truth found in 2 Corinthians 2:12. As we dive into this verse, we discover Paul's journey to Troas and the incredible door the Lord opened for him to preach the gospel. This verse serves as a reminder of God's guiding presence in our lives and the doors He opens for us when we surrender to His will.

In life, we often face various doors of opportunity. Some doors may lead us to success, while others may lead to uncertainty or even closed doors. But as followers of Christ, we have the assurance that God is with us, guiding our steps and leading us towards His purposes.

Just like Paul, we are called to be attentive to the doors God opens for us. These doors may come in the form of new relationships, career opportunities, or even moments to share the love of Christ with someone in need. It is crucial that we remain open to the leading of the Holy Spirit and aware of God's voice, for He is the one who orchestrates these divine encounters.

Sometimes, the doors God opens may not align with our own plans or expectations. It is in those moments that we must trust His wisdom and step out in faith. As we do so, we may discover that the doors God opens lead to unexpected blessings, growth, and transformation.

Moreover, let us not forget that the open doors are not solely for our benefit but for the expansion of God's kingdom. Each opportunity we embrace becomes a platform to share the good news of Christ, bring healing and restoration, and offer hope to a world in need.

As we embark on this journey of faith, let us pray for discernment to recognize the doors God opens before us. May we have the courage to step through those doors, trusting that God's guiding presence will be with us every step of the way. Let us embrace each open door as an invitation to participate in God's divine plan and to be His vessels of love and grace.

Remember, God is faithful. He knows what is best for us. So, let us surrender our plans and desires to Him, seeking His will, and trusting that the doors He opens will lead us to immeasurable blessings and abundant life.

Prayer: Father God, thank you for your guiding presence in my life. Help me to recognize the doors you open before me and to step out in faith, trusting your wisdom and perfect timing. Give me discernment to understand your will and the courage to embrace the opportunities you provide. May each open door be an opportunity to share your love and bring glory to your name. In Jesus' name, I pray. Amen.

May you be blessed as you walk through the doors God opens for you, guided by His unwavering love and grace.

TRANSITION. OPPORTUNITY.
DIVINE ENCOUNTER.

_____

_____

_____

_____

_____

_____

_____

_____

THE DOOR OF WISDOM

DAY 15

*G*ood morning! Today, let's dive into the beautiful words of Proverbs 8:34 (ESV), which says, "Blessed is the one who listens to me, watching daily at my gates, waiting beside my doors."

Imagine yourself standing at the threshold of a magnificent door labeled "Wisdom." As you approach, you can feel a sense of anticipation and wonder. This door represents the gateway to greater understanding, discernment, and a blessed life.

1. Openness to Listening: The first key to unlocking the door of wisdom is a willingness to listen. Just as the verse says, "Blessed is the one who listens to me." Cultivate an open heart and attentive ears, ready to receive the gentle whispers of wisdom that can guide your steps.

2. Daily Watchfulness: The verse encourages us to "watch daily at my gates." Wisdom is not a one-time event but a lifelong journey. Make it a daily practice to seek wisdom, observing the world around you with curiosity and a desire to learn. In doing so, you position yourself to recognize wisdom's arrival and embrace its guidance.

3. Patient Waiting: "Waiting beside my doors" highlights the

importance of patience. Wisdom often requires us to exercise patience, trusting that the answers and insights we seek will come in due time. As you wait, embrace the present moment, knowing that wisdom will open the door when the time is right.

4. The Blessing of Wisdom: The ultimate reward for listening, watching, and waiting at the door of wisdom is the blessing that follows. Wisdom can bring clarity in times of confusion, peace amidst chaos, and direction when we feel lost. It equips us to make informed decisions, cultivate healthy relationships, and live with purpose.

Today, my friend, let us embark on a journey of seeking wisdom. Open your heart, be watchful, and patiently wait for the door to open. Remember, wisdom is not a destination but a lifelong pursuit. May you be blessed as you listen, watch, and wait at the door of wisdom.

Prayer: Lord, thank you for the gift of wisdom. Help me to have an open heart and attentive ears, ready to receive the wisdom you offer. Grant me the patience to wait for your guidance and the discernment to recognize it when it comes. May the blessings that flow from wisdom enrich my life and the lives of those around me. In Jesus' name, Amen.

Remember, each day brings new opportunities to seek wisdom. May you find joy in this pursuit and be richly blessed as you journey through life's open doors.

TRANSITION. OPPORTUNITY.
DIVINE ENCOUNTER.

_____

_____

_____

_____

_____

_____

_____

_____

_____

_____

UNLOCKING DOORS: GOD'S MASTER KEY

DAY 16

Isaiah 22:22 (NLT) - "I will give him the key to the house of David—the highest position in the royal court. When he opens doors, no one will be able to close them; when he closes doors, no one will be able to open them."

Have you ever found yourself facing closed doors in your life? Doors that seem impossible to open, opportunities that seem out of reach, or even circumstances that leave you feeling trapped? We all encounter such situations at various points in our lives. However, today's verse from Isaiah offers us a beautiful promise and a powerful reminder of God's faithfulness in unlocking doors for us.

In this verse, God speaks through the prophet Isaiah, promising to give someone the key to the house of David. Symbolically, this key represents authority and access to positions of influence and power. It signifies divine favor and the ability to open doors that no one else can. What a remarkable promise!

Through this verse, we can draw valuable insights into how God works in our lives. Firstly, God holds the key. He alone has the authority to unlock doors and open new pathways for us.

Sometimes, we may feel overwhelmed or discouraged by closed doors, but we can find comfort in knowing that God is in control.

Secondly, when God opens a door, no one can close it. His plans for us are unshakeable. We may face challenges or opposition, but if God has opened a door, nothing can stand against it. His timing is perfect, and He will make a way for us even when it seems impossible.

On the other hand, when God closes a door, no one can open it. There may be times when we desperately want a door to remain open, or we struggle to understand why it has closed. In these moments, we must trust in God's wisdom and believe that He knows what is best for us. Sometimes, closed doors redirect us to better opportunities or protect us from harm.

Lastly, God's promise of the key to the house of David reminds us that He desires to bless us and elevate us to places of influence. As we faithfully follow Him, He will grant us access to positions where we can make a difference, bring about positive change, and reflect His love and grace to others.

So, if you find yourself facing closed doors today, I encourage you to remember Isaiah 22:22. Trust in God's sovereignty and allow Him to unlock the doors in your life. Seek His guidance and be open to the new paths He may lead you towards. His plans are far greater than we can imagine, and He will always provide a way for those who trust in Him.

May your day be filled with the assurance of God's master key unlocking the doors of opportunity, blessings, and divine favor in your life.

TRANSITION. OPPORTUNITY.
DIVINE ENCOUNTER.

_____

_____

_____

_____

_____

_____

_____

_____

_____

THE DOOR OF PATIENCE

DAY 17

In our fast-paced world, patience is a virtue that often feels in short supply. We live in an age where everything is instant, and waiting can be seen as a burden rather than an opportunity for growth. However, in the book of James, we are reminded of the importance of patience and the blessings that come from embracing it.

James 5:9 (ESV) says, "Do not grumble against one another, brothers, so that you may not be judged; behold, the Judge is standing at the door." This verse serves as a gentle reminder to resist the temptation to complain or become impatient with others. Instead, we are encouraged to extend grace, understanding, and kindness towards one another, knowing that God is the ultimate judge of all.

Patience is not just about waiting for something to happen; it's about how we navigate the waiting period. It's about preparing a heart that is willing to trust in God's timing, even when it seems slow or uncertain. Patience allows us to grow in character, empathy, and perseverance, while also fostering healthier relationships with those around us.

Prayer: Father God, Thank you for your Word that guides and instructs us in all aspects of life. Today, we come before you, seeking your wisdom and strength to embrace patience in our daily lives. Help us, Lord, to resist the urge to grumble or become impatient with others, but instead, grant us a heart of understanding, empathy, and kindness.

Father, we acknowledge that waiting can be challenging, especially when we desire quick results. But we trust in your perfect timing and surrender our anxious thoughts and desires into your hands. Teach us to find contentment in the present moment, knowing that you are working all things together for our good.

Grant us the strength to persevere in times of waiting, and let patience shape our character as we grow closer to you. Help us to be a reflection of your love and grace to those around us, showing kindness and understanding even in the face of difficult circumstances. In Jesus' precious name, we pray, Amen.

TRANSITION. OPPORTUNITY. DIVINE ENCOUNTER.

_____

_____

_____

_____

_____

_____

_____

_____

_____

GUARDING OUR WORDS

DAY 18

*P*salm 141:3 (ESV) says, "Set a guard, O Lord, over my mouth; keep watch over the door of my lips." In this powerful verse, we are reminded of the importance of guarding our words and the impact they have on ourselves and others. Let us take a moment to reflect on this verse and its practical application in our daily lives.

1. Recognizing the Power of Words:

Words possess incredible power. They have the ability to build up or tear down, to encourage or discourage. Our words can shape our relationships, influence our emotions, and impact our own self-perception. Acknowledging this power is the first step towards creating a mindful and intentional approach to our speech.

2. Seeking Divine Guidance:

The psalmist's plea for God's intervention reflects our need for divine guidance in our speech. By inviting the Lord to set a guard over our mouths, we demonstrate humility and recognize our own limitations. When we seek God's guidance, we invite Him to shape our words, ensuring that our speech aligns with His will.

3. Reflecting on the Source:

In order to guard our mouths effectively, we must also examine the source of our words. Jesus teaches us that "out of the abundance of the heart the mouth speaks" (Luke 6:45 ESV). Therefore, it is crucial to nurture a heart filled with love, kindness, and compassion. By growing these qualities within ourselves, we can ensure that our words are always uplifting and edifying.

4. Practicing Mindful Speech:

Guarding our words requires intentional effort. We must strive to be mindful of what we say, considering the potential impact before we speak. This involves pausing before responding, actively listening to others, and choosing our words wisely. By doing so, we foster healthier communication and build stronger relationships.

5. Choosing Words of Grace:

As followers of Christ, we are called to be imitators of His love and grace. Ephesians 4:29 (ESV) reminds us, "Let no corrupting talk come out of your mouths, but only such as is good for building up, as fits the occasion, that it may give grace to those who hear." Let us strive to use our words to encourage, uplift, and inspire others, allowing God's grace to flow through us.

Today, let's reflect on the profound message of Psalm 141:3. As we seek to guard our mouths, let us remember that our words have the power to shape our lives and the lives of those around us. By seeking divine guidance, reflecting on the source of our words, practicing mindful speech, and choosing words of grace, we can become beacons of love and encouragement in a world that desperately needs it. May we continually strive to honor God with our speech, allowing His light to shine through us and bring hope to others.

Remember, each day is an opportunity to grow in the way we communicate. Let us embrace this challenge and allow God's transformative power to shape our words, making us instruments of love and kindness in the world.

TRANSITION. OPPORTUNITY. DIVINE ENCOUNTER.

_____

_____

_____

_____

_____

_____

_____

_____

_____

EMBRACING DIVINE OPPORTUNITIES

DAY 19

*A*cts 5:19 (ESV) - "*But during the night an angel of the Lord opened the prison doors and brought them out, and said, 'Go and stand in the temple and speak to the people all the words of this Life.'*"

In the book of Acts, we witness the incredible faith and courage of the early disciples of Jesus. Despite facing persecution and opposition, they remained steadfast in their commitment to share the life-transforming message of the Gospel. Acts 5:19 presents an extraordinary event where an angel of the Lord miraculously released Peter and the apostles from prison, giving them specific instructions to continue preaching in the temple.

This passage teaches us several valuable lessons about embracing divine opportunities in our lives. Let us explore them together:

1. Trust in God's Timing: The angel's intervention occurred during the night, at a time when the disciples were likely feeling hopeless and uncertain about their future. Yet, God's perfect timing is always at work behind the scenes. He knows the right moment to step in and open doors that no one can shut. There-

fore, even in the darkest of times, trust that God is orchestrating events for your ultimate good.

2. Be Open to Divine Interventions: The angel not only freed the disciples from prison but also provided them with clear instructions. Sometimes, God may use extraordinary means to guide and direct us. Remain open to His interventions, whether through dreams, visions, or unexpected circumstances. He will make a way where there seems to be no way.

3. Step into Opportunities with Courage: The angel's command to "go and stand in the temple" was no small task. It required courage for the disciples to boldly proclaim the message of Jesus, knowing the risks involved. Similarly, we are often presented with opportunities to share our faith, extend love, or make a difference in someone's life. Let us not shrink back in fear but step forward with courage, trusting that God will equip us for every task He sets before us.

4. Share the Words of Life: The angel specifically instructed the disciples to share "all the words of this Life." The message of the Gospel is a message of hope, forgiveness, and eternal life found in Jesus Christ. As followers of Christ, we are called to share this life-giving message with others. Let us be intentional about speaking words of life, encouragement, and truth to those around us, pointing them towards the source of everlasting hope.

Today, embrace the divine opportunities that come your way. Trust in God's perfect timing, be open to His interventions, and step forward with courage to share the words of life. Remember, you are not alone on this journey. The same God who opened prison doors for the disciples is with you, guiding and empowering you every step of the way.

May God's grace and peace be with you always.

TRANSITION. OPPORTUNITY.
DIVINE ENCOUNTER.

RESTORING THE HOUSE OF GOD

DAY 20

2 Chronicles 29:3 (NLT) - "*In the very first month of the first year of his reign, Hezekiah reopened the doors of the Temple of the Lord and repaired them.*"

Welcome to today's devotional! Today, we dive into the inspiring story of King Hezekiah and the restoration of the Temple of the Lord. In this verse, we witness an incredible act of faith and obedience that can teach us valuable lessons for our own lives.

Hezekiah, a young and righteous king, wasted no time in prioritizing the restoration of God's dwelling place. In the first month of his reign, he took it upon himself to reopen the doors of the Temple and commence the much-needed repairs. His actions display a heart that longs for the presence of God and a desire to honor Him.

Similarly, in our lives, we may find areas that need restoration. It could be broken relationships, spiritual dryness, or even neglected areas of our faith. Just as Hezekiah looked at the Temple and recognized the need for repair, we too can take a moment to reflect on the state of our hearts and lives.

Restoration requires effort and a willingness to address the areas that need healing. Like Hezekiah, let us not delay in taking the necessary steps to reopen the doors and restore what may have been broken. It may involve seeking forgiveness, extending grace, or simply reconnecting with God through prayer and His Word.

As we embark on this journey of restoration, it is essential to remember that we are not alone. God, our ever-present Helper, is right beside us, ready to guide and support us every step of the way. His love and grace are always available, empowering us to bring healing and renewal to our lives.

Today, let us be inspired by Hezekiah's example of faith and obedience. Take a moment to reflect on areas in your life that may need restoration. Invite God into those spaces and trust Him to guide you through the process. Remember, His desire is to see you flourish and experience the fullness of life in His presence.

Prayer: Father God, thank You for Your unwavering love and grace. Help me to recognize areas in my life that need restoration and give me the courage to address them. Guide me through the process, Lord, and fill me with Your strength and wisdom. I trust that with Your help, I can experience true restoration and walk in the fullness of Your presence. In Jesus' name, I pray, Amen.

Remember, God is with you every step of the way. May your day be blessed with restoration and peace as you seek to honor Him in all that you do.

TRANSITION. OPPORTUNITY. DIVINE ENCOUNTER.

_____

_____

_____

_____

_____

_____

_____

_____

_____

THE RIVER OF LIFE

DAY 21

*W*elcome to today's reflection on Ezekiel 47:1 (ESV) - *Then he brought me back to the door of the temple, and behold, water was issuing from below the threshold of the temple toward the east (for the temple faced east). The water was flowing down from below the south end of the threshold of the temple, south of the altar.*

This verse takes us on a journey alongside the prophet Ezekiel, where he witnesses a beautiful vision of a river flowing from the temple of God. As we explore the significance of this imagery, let us open our hearts and minds to the wisdom and encouragement it holds for us.

Imagine standing with Ezekiel, gazing at this river as it trickles out from under the temple's threshold, gradually growing deeper and wider. This river symbolizes the abundant life that God desires for His people. It represents His provision, grace, and the refreshing power of His Spirit.

Just as the river flowed from the temple, so too does the source of our spiritual nourishment and sustenance come from God. It is in His presence that we find true fulfillment, purpose, and blessings beyond measure. The river reminds us that God's blessings are not limited; they overflow generously, inviting us to partake and share with others.

As the river expands, Ezekiel notices something remarkable: trees lining its banks, bearing fruit every month. These trees symbolize the continuous growth and fruitfulness that God desires for our lives. Through His Spirit, we are empowered to produce spiritual fruits such as love, joy, peace, patience, kindness, goodness, faithfulness, gentleness, and self-control (Galatians 5:22-23).

Moreover, these trees provide healing leaves, ensuring that nothing is wasted in God's kingdom. Our lives, too, can bring healing to those around us through acts of compassion, encouragement, and forgiveness. We are called to be vessels of God's love, extending His grace and healing touch to a broken world.

So, how can we apply this beautiful vision to our daily lives? Let us recognize that God's desire is for us to experience His abundant life and to be a source of blessing to others. As we spend time in His presence, reading His Word, and communing with Him in prayer, we allow the river of His Spirit to flow through us.

Let us also remember the importance of continuously growing in our faith and character. Just as the trees along the riverbanks bear fruit every month, let us seek to bear fruits of righteousness consistently. Through our words, actions, and attitudes, may we reflect God's love and bring healing to those we encounter.

Today, let us embrace the vision of Ezekiel's river of life. May it inspire us to seek God's presence, experience His abundant blessings, and become vessels of His healing and love. Remember, you are a valuable part of God's beautiful plan, and He desires to work through you to bring hope and transformation to the world around you.

Prayer: Lord, thank You for the beautiful imagery found in Ezekiel's vision. Help us to remember that You are the source of life and blessing. May Your Spirit flow through us, enabling us to bear fruit and bring healing to those in need. Guide us each day to live in the abundance of Your love. In Jesus' name, Amen.

TRANSITION. OPPORTUNITY.
DIVINE ENCOUNTER.

_____

_____

_____

_____

_____

_____

_____

_____

_____

THE STATE OF OUR HEARTS

DAY 22

*L*et's dive into Revelation 3:20 (ESV) - "Behold, I stand at the door and knock. If anyone hears my voice and opens the door, I will come in to him and eat with him, and he with me."

This verse from the book of Revelation holds a powerful message that speaks to our hearts and souls. It reminds us of God's unwavering presence in our lives and His desire for a deep and personal relationship with us.

Imagine the scene: Jesus stands at the door of our hearts, gently knocking, patiently waiting for us to invite Him in. He doesn't force His way in or demand our attention; instead, He patiently seeks a genuine connection with us.

When we hear His voice, whether through scripture, prayer, or the gentle whisper of our conscience, we have a choice to make. We can either open the door of our hearts and welcome Him in or ignore His call and remain distant.

When we choose to open the door, something extraordinary happens. Jesus enters into our lives, wanting to dine with us. This symbolic act of sharing a meal represents intimacy, communion, and fellowship. It signifies a deep bond and a desire for mutual presence.

By accepting Jesus into our lives, we experience the incredible privilege of sharing a table with the King of Kings. In His presence, we find comfort, guidance, wisdom, and unending love. We can pour out our hearts, joys, and struggles, knowing that He understands and cares deeply for us.

Today, let us reflect on Revelation 3:20 and consider the state of our own hearts. Are we opening the door and inviting Jesus in, or are we shutting Him out? Are we making space for Him to dine with us and commune intimately with Him?

Prayer: Lord, thank you for seeking genuine connection with us. Help us to listen for your gentle whisper, guidance, and wisdom in our quiet times with you. Guide us to open our hearts and minds as you move and make your presence known. We welcome you into our lives. In Jesus' name, Amen.

Remember, Jesus is a gentle and patient friend who longs for a relationship with us. Let's take a moment to pause, listen for His voice, and open the door of our hearts. As we do so, may our lives be transformed by the loving presence of our Savior, who desires nothing more than to commune with us.

TRANSITION. OPPORTUNITY.
DIVINE ENCOUNTER.

_____

_____

_____

_____

_____

_____

_____

_____

_____

THE OVERFLOWING JAR OF OIL

DAY 23

2 Kings 4:4 ESV - *"Then go in and shut the door behind yourself and your sons and pour into all these vessels. And when one is full, set it aside."*

Today, let's reflect on a remarkable story from the book of 2 Kings that teaches us about God's generosity and the power of faith. In 2 Kings 4:1-7, we encounter a widow who was left with nothing but a jar of oil and a debt that she could not repay. In her desperation, she sought the help of the prophet Elisha.

Elisha, being led by God, instructed the widow to gather empty vessels from her neighbors and pour the oil she had into those vessels. It was a perplexing command, but the widow chose to trust in the prophet's words and in the faithfulness of God.

As she began to pour the oil, a remarkable miracle unfolded before her eyes. The oil did not stop flowing until every single vessel was filled to the brim. The widow's obedience and faith led to an abundant provision that not only satisfied her immediate need but also allowed her to sell the oil and pay off her debts.

This story serves as a beautiful reminder that God is not

limited by our circumstances or the resources we possess. Just like the widow, we may find ourselves in situations where we feel overwhelmed, lacking, or uncertain about the future. However, it is precisely in these moments that God invites us to step out in faith and trust Him.

God's provision often comes in unexpected ways and through unconventional means. He is not confined to human limitations but is able to multiply what we have when we surrender it to Him. We must be willing to offer our little, just like the widow's jar of oil, and watch as God multiplies it beyond our wildest imagination.

Today, let us remember that God is our loving Father who delights in providing for His children. Let us have faith like the widow, trusting that God will meet our needs according to His perfect plan. May we be willing vessels, ready to pour out what we have and witness the overflow of His blessings in our lives.

Take a moment to reflect: Are there areas in your life where you feel lacking or in need of God's provision? How can you step out in faith and surrender what you have to Him, trusting that He will multiply it for His glory?

Prayer: Lord Jesus, thank You for being our provider and for your faithfulness in meeting our needs. Help us to have unwavering faith like the widow in 2 Kings, knowing that You are able to do exceedingly abundantly above all that we ask or think. Give us the courage to surrender what we have, trusting that You will multiply it for Your glory. In Jesus' name, we pray. Amen.

May you experience the overflowing blessings of God's provision as you trust Him today and always.

TRANSITION. OPPORTUNITY.
DIVINE ENCOUNTER.

_____

_____

_____

_____

_____

_____

_____

_____

_____

THE DOORS OF OPPORTUNITY

DAY 24

Scripture: Acts 16:26 ESV - "and suddenly there was a great earthquake, so that the foundations of the prison were shaken. And immediately all the doors were opened, and everyone's bonds were unfastened."

Have you ever found yourself standing in front of a closed door, uncertain of what lies beyond it? Doors can be symbolic of new beginnings, opportunities, and even challenges in our lives. As we explore the significance of doors in our spiritual journey, let us reflect on Acts 16:26 and the powerful message it holds for us.

1. Closed Doors:

Sometimes, we encounter closed doors in our lives that seem to hinder our progress or prevent us from pursuing our dreams. These closed doors may appear as obstacles or disappointments, but it's essential to remember that God can work even in these situations. Just as the prison doors were shut in Acts 16, God can use closed doors to protect us, redirect us, or teach us valuable lessons. Trust that God's plans are far greater than our own.

2. Unexpected Open Doors:

The earthquake in Acts 16 was not only a physical event but also a spiritual one. It represented God's power and intervention in the lives of His people. In the same way, God can create sudden shifts in our circumstances, opening doors we never imagined possible. These unexpected open doors can lead us towards new opportunities, relationships, and experiences that align with God's purpose for our lives. Let us be open and receptive to God's leading.

3. Freedom and Boundlessness:

Acts 16:26 tells us that not only were the doors opened, but everyone's bonds were unfastened. This signifies the freedom and liberation that God brings into our lives. Through His grace and love, God breaks the chains that bind us, setting us free from sin, fear, and limitations. As we walk through the doors He opens, we are invited to embrace the boundless possibilities, knowing that we are no longer slaves to our past, but rather children of a loving and limitless God.

Prayer: Father God, thank You for being the God of open doors and boundless opportunities. Help us to trust in Your plans, even when faced with closed doors. Grant us the wisdom and discernment to recognize the doors You open and the courage to step through them. May we experience the freedom that comes from surrendering to Your will. In Jesus' name, we pray, Amen.

Take a moment to reflect upon the doors in your life today. Trust that God is working behind the scenes, guiding you towards His perfect will. Embrace the closed doors as opportunities for growth, and be ready to step through the doors of unexpected blessings. May your journey be filled with God's grace and favor.

TRANSITION. OPPORTUNITY.
DIVINE ENCOUNTER.

_____

_____

_____

_____

_____

_____

_____

_____

_____

EMBRACING THE OPEN DOOR

DAY 25

*R*evelation 3:7-8 ESV - "And to the angel of the church in Philadelphia write: 'The words of the holy one, the true one, who has the key of David, who opens and no one will shut, who shuts and no one opens. "'I know your works. Behold, I have set before you an open door, which no one is able to shut. I know that you have but little power, and yet you have kept my word and have not denied my name."

Have you ever stood before an open door, unsure of what lies beyond it? Perhaps it was a door leading to a new opportunity, a fresh start, or a chance to make a difference. In Revelation 3:7-8, we find encouragement and hope in the promise of an open door set before us by our loving Savior.

The church in Philadelphia, despite facing trials and having limited resources, was commended by Jesus for their faithfulness and unwavering commitment to His Word. In the midst of their challenges, Jesus assured them of an open door that no one could shut.

Just like the believers in Philadelphia, we too may find ourselves feeling small in our abilities and resources. We might wonder if we have what it takes to step through the open doors placed before us. Yet, let us remember that it is not our own strength that determines the outcome, but the One who opens and shuts doors according to His perfect plan.

The open door represents countless possibilities and opportunities that come our way. It may be a door leading to a new career path, a chance to serve others, or an invitation to share the love of Christ with those around us. The key lies in recognizing and embracing these open doors, even if they seem daunting or uncertain.

As we face these open doors, let us remember three essential truths:

1. God's Timing: Our heavenly Father knows the perfect timing for each door to be opened or closed. Trust in His divine wisdom and guidance. Seek His counsel through prayer and His Word, and allow Him to lead you through the open doors according to His plan.

2. God's Provision: When God opens a door, He equips us with everything we need to fulfill His purpose. Though we may feel inadequate or lacking, remember that His strength is made perfect in our weakness. Rely on His provision, knowing that He will provide the necessary resources, wisdom, and courage to walk through the open door.

3. God's Presence: Never forget that as you step through the open door, Jesus walks alongside you. He promises to be with us always, empowering us and guiding us every step of the way. Trust in His unfailing love and lean on Him for strength and direction.

Today, let us embrace the open doors set before us, knowing that with faith in God's timing, provision, and presence, we can boldly step into the opportunities He has prepared for us. Though challenges may arise, we can walk forward with confidence, for the One who holds the key is faithful and true.

Prayer: Lord, thank you for the promise of open doors in our lives. Help us to trust in Your timing, provision, and presence as we navigate through them. Grant us the wisdom to recognize the opportunities You place before us and the courage to step through them. May our lives be a reflection of Your love and grace as we walk in faith. In Jesus' name, Amen.

TRANSITION. OPPORTUNITY.
DIVINE ENCOUNTER.

REFLECTION ON LOCKED DOORS

DAY 26

Judges 3:25 ESV - "And they waited till they were embarrassed. But when he still did not open the doors of the roof chamber, they took the key and opened them, and there lay their lord dead on the floor."

Welcome to today's devotional reflection! Today, we turn our attention to an intriguing passage from the book of Judges. It tells the story of Ehud, a judge of Israel, who was sent by God to deliver His people from the oppressive Moabite rule. In this particular verse, we witness an unexpected turn of events that holds a valuable lesson for our lives.

Imagine the scene: Ehud had just assassinated King Eglon of Moab with a hidden dagger. As he made his escape, he locked the doors of the roof chamber to buy himself some time. The Moabite guards, however, were reluctant to disturb their king, waiting until their embarrassment grew overwhelming. Finally, they took the key, opened the doors, and discovered their lord dead on the floor.

Now, let's apply this story to our own lives. The doors in this passage symbolize the opportunities that come our way. Sometimes, we lock them because we fear the unknown, doubt our

REFLECTION ON LOCKED DOORS

abilities, or simply hesitate to step out of our comfort zones. We may find ourselves waiting, just like those guards, until our embarrassment or regret becomes too great.

But what if behind those locked doors lies something extraordinary? What if it is an opportunity for growth, success, or even a chance to make a positive impact in the lives of others? In order to uncover the blessings that await us, we must be willing to take a leap of faith and open those doors.

It is natural to feel unsure or hesitant when faced with uncertainty. However, we shouldn't let fear hold us back from experiencing the abundant life God has planned for us. We must remember that God is always with us, guiding and equipping us for the journey ahead. He will never leave us alone in our pursuit of new doors to open.

Today, let us reflect on the locked doors in our lives. Have we been avoiding opportunities due to fear or uncertainty? Are we waiting for the perfect moment, or are we willing to trust God and step forward in faith? Remember that God's plans and purposes often lie behind the doors we are hesitant to open.

Prayer: Lord Jesus, thank you for the reminder that You are always with us, guiding us through life's uncertainties. Help us to break free from our fear and hesitations, and empower us to embrace the opportunities You place before us. Grant us the courage and wisdom to open the doors that lead to growth, blessings, and a closer relationship with You. In Jesus' name, we pray, Amen.

Take a moment to ponder the doors in your life today. May you find the strength and faith to step forward and embrace the opportunities that await you. Remember, with God by your side, doors that were once locked can become gateways to incredible blessings. Stay encouraged and have a blessed day!

TRANSITION. OPPORTUNITY. DIVINE ENCOUNTER.

_____

_____

_____

_____

_____

_____

_____

_____

_____

EMBRACING THE NARROW DOOR

DAY 27

*L*uke 13:24 (ESV) - "Strive to enter through the narrow door. For many, I tell you, will seek to enter and will not be able."

Today, let us reflect on the profound message Jesus shared about the narrow door. In this passage, Jesus urges us to strive to enter through this door, for many will attempt to enter but will not be able to. This teaching carries a vital lesson for our daily lives as followers of Christ.

Imagine a door that is narrow, not in a restrictive sense, but in its exclusivity. This narrow door symbolizes the path to eternal life, a journey that requires our utmost dedication and sincere commitment. It is not a path for the faint-hearted, but rather for those who wholeheartedly seek God's kingdom.

Firstly, it is essential to recognize that the narrow door represents Jesus Himself. He boldly proclaimed, "I am the way, and the truth, and the life. No one comes to the Father except through me" (John 14:6 ESV). Jesus is the exclusive gateway to eternal life, and it is only through faith in Him that we can enter into a deep and meaningful relationship with God.

Striving to enter through the narrow door involves intentional choices and actions. It calls for a genuine desire to live in accordance with Christ's teachings. We are invited to daily surrender our lives, align our thoughts and actions with His Word, and cultivate a heart that seeks after God's will. It may mean making sacrifices, letting go of worldly desires, and living a life of obedience and love for God and others.

While the wide path may seem more alluring and convenient, leading to temporary pleasures and self-indulgence, it ultimately leads to destruction. The narrow door, though challenging and counter-cultural, leads to life abundant and eternal. It is an invitation to experience the true joy, peace, and fulfillment that can only be found in Christ.

In our journey towards the narrow door, we may encounter obstacles, doubts, and temptations. But take heart, dear friend, for the Lord is faithful and will guide us every step of the way. He promises to be with us, strengthening us in times of weakness and providing the wisdom we need to navigate life's challenges.

Today, let us renew our commitment to strive towards the narrow door. Let us fix our eyes on Jesus, the author and perfecter of our faith, and trust in His never-failing love and grace. May we be inspired to live with purpose, embracing the exclusivity of the narrow door, and inviting others to join us on this incredible journey of faith.

Prayer: Father God, thank you for the gift of salvation through Jesus Christ. Help us strive to enter through the narrow door, even when the world tempts us with its wide paths. Strengthen us, guide us, and grant us the wisdom to discern and follow Your will. In Jesus' name, we pray, amen.

Remember, the narrow door may seem daunting at times, but its rewards are immeasurable. Keep pressing on, and may God's abundant blessings be upon you as you walk this path of faith.

TRANSITION. OPPORTUNITY.
DIVINE ENCOUNTER.

THE DOORWAY OF BLESSINGS

DAY 28

Scripture: 2 Kings 4:15 ESV - "He said, 'Call her.' And when he had called her, she stood in the doorway."

Have you ever stopped to think about the significance of a doorway? Often, we pass through them without giving them a second thought. However, the doorway mentioned in 2 Kings 4:15 holds a beautiful lesson for us today, reminding us of the blessings that can enter our lives through a simple act of obedience.

In this passage, we find the story of the Shunammite woman who had shown great kindness to the prophet Elisha, providing him a room in her home whenever he passed by. Touched by her generosity, Elisha desired to bless her in return. He called her and, as she stood in the doorway, he prophesied that she would embrace the joy of motherhood, despite her previous barrenness.

The doorway symbolizes a threshold between the outside world and the intimate space of our homes. It also represents a place of transition, where we leave behind what is known and step into the unknown. In the case of the Shunammite woman, it became a place where her life was forever altered by the power of God's blessing.

Just like the Shunammite woman, we too have doorways in our lives. These doorways may not be physical, but they represent moments of decision, opportunity, and change. They can be as simple as saying "yes" to a new friendship, pursuing a dream, or even accepting God's calling in our lives. When we embrace these doorways with faith and obedience, incredible blessings can enter our lives.

God desires to bless His children abundantly, but often He waits for us to take that step of faith in obedience. He invites us to stand in the doorway of His divine purpose for our lives, trusting that He will bring forth blessings beyond our imagination.

So, as you go about your day, be attentive to the doorways that appear before you. Seek God's guidance, and when He calls you to step forward, do so with faith and courage. Embrace the unknown, knowing that behind these doorways lie blessings, growth, and a deeper experience of His love.

Prayer: Gracious Father, thank You for the reminder that obedience and faith can open doors to blessings beyond our wildest dreams. Help us to recognize the doorways You place before us and give us the courage to step through them, trusting in Your perfect plan for our lives. May we always find ourselves standing in the doorway of Your presence, ready to receive Your abundant blessings. In Jesus' name, we pray. Amen.

Remember, as you walk through the doorways of life, God is with you, guiding and blessing your every step. May your day be filled with His favor and grace.

Blessings and peace to you!

TRANSITION. OPPORTUNITY.
DIVINE ENCOUNTER.

_____

_____

_____

_____

_____

_____

_____

_____

_____

EMBRACING CLOSED DOORS WITH FAITH

DAY 29

"*And while they were going to buy, the bridegroom came, and those who were ready went in with him to the marriage feast, and the door was shut.*" - Matthew 25:10 ESV

Today, let's reflect on the concept of closed doors and how they can impact our lives. Throughout our journey, we often encounter moments when doors close, opportunities fade away, and plans seem to crumble. It can be disheartening and leave us feeling lost or discouraged. However, let us remember that even in those moments, there is hope, purpose, and guidance from above.

In the parable of the ten virgins, Jesus shares a profound message about the importance of being prepared and watchful for His return. Five of the virgins were ready, had their lamps filled with oil, and entered the marriage feast with the bridegroom. Meanwhile, the other five, who were unprepared, found themselves knocking on a shut door.

Closed doors can represent various things in our lives. They may symbolize missed opportunities, dashed dreams, or even protection from harmful paths. It is crucial to remember that God's plans for us are far greater than we can imagine, and

EMBRACING CLOSED DOORS WITH FAITH

sometimes what appears to be a closed door is actually His way of directing us towards something better.

When facing a closed door, our initial response might be frustration or disappointment. However, let us shift our perspective and embrace these moments with faith. Rather than dwelling on what we may have lost, let us seek to discover what God might be revealing to us in this season.

Closed doors can serve as reminders to seek God's guidance, wisdom, and timing. They provide us with an opportunity to reevaluate our desires, priorities, and paths. Instead of forcing open a door that is shut, let us trust that God is working behind the scenes, orchestrating circumstances according to His perfect plan.

During these times, it is vital to seek God's will through prayer and scripture. He promises to guide us and open doors that align with His purpose for our lives. While waiting for new doors to open, let us focus on growing spiritually, cultivating patience, and nurturing our relationship with Him.

Remember, closed doors are not the end of our story but rather an invitation to trust in God's unfailing love and His desire to lead us on the right path. As we surrender our plans to Him, He will guide us through the open doors that will lead us to His blessings and fulfillment.

Prayer: Lord God, thank You for Your guidance and wisdom. Help us to trust in Your perfect timing when faced with closed doors. Give us the strength to surrender our desires to You and to seek Your will above all else. Open our eyes to the new opportunities and blessings You have in store for us. In Jesus' name, we pray, Amen.

Take a moment today to reflect on any closed doors in your life. Trust in God's plan and have faith that He is leading you towards something even greater. May His peace and assurance fill your heart as you embrace the journey ahead. Remember, closed doors do not define you; they simply redirect you towards the path that aligns with God's perfect will.

TRANSITION. OPPORTUNITY.
DIVINE ENCOUNTER.

_____

_____

_____

_____

_____

_____

_____

_____

_____

THE SYMBOLISM OF DOORS

DAY 30

1 Kings 6:32 (ESV) - "The two doors were of olive wood, and he carved on them carvings of cherubim, palm trees, and open flowers, and overlaid them with gold; and he spread gold on the cherubim and on the palm trees."

Stop and think about the significance of doors in our lives. Doors are not merely physical barriers; they hold a deeper symbolism that can guide our spiritual understanding. In the Bible, doors are often used to represent opportunities, transitions, and encounters with God. Let's explore the beautiful symbolism of doors and how they can impact our daily journey of faith.

1. Doors as Opportunities:

Just as doors open up to new spaces and possibilities, they also represent the opportunities God places in our lives. Sometimes, we hesitate to step through a door that God has opened before us due to fear or uncertainty. However, when we trust in His guidance, we can embrace the open doors with faith and anticipation. God's plans for us often lie beyond those doors, and stepping through them can lead to growth, blessings, and fulfilling His purpose for our lives.

2. Doors as Transitions:

Doors also symbolize transitions in our lives. They mark the boundary between one season and another, whether it's entering a new job, starting a family, or embarking on a spiritual journey. These transitions can sometimes be challenging, as we leave behind what is familiar and step into the unknown. However, just as God was present with Solomon as he built the doors adorned with cherubim, palm trees, and open flowers, He is also with us in every transition. Trust that He will guide and protect you as you move through each door, leading you to new levels of spiritual growth and understanding.

3. Doors as Encounters with God:

In the Bible, doors often serve as gateways to encounters with God Himself. Jesus declared in John 10:9, "I am the door. If anyone enters by me, he will be saved and will go in and out and find pasture." Through faith in Jesus Christ, we find salvation and a profound connection with our Heavenly Father. By walking through the door of faith, we enter into a personal relationship with God, experiencing His love, grace, and transformative power. Every encounter with God is an invitation to draw closer to Him, to abide in His presence, and to experience the abundant life He offers.

As we reflect on the intricate carvings on the doors of the temple in 1 Kings, let us remember that God's craftsmanship is not limited to physical structures. He intricately designs the doors of opportunity, transitions, and encounters in our lives. Today, let us seek His guidance, trust His leading, and boldly step through the doors He presents before us. Embrace the symbolism of doors as a reminder of His faithfulness and the abundant blessings that await us on the other side.

Prayer: Father God, thank You for the symbolism of doors in our lives. Help us to trust in Your guidance and embrace the opportunities and transitions You present before us. May we have the courage to step through the doors that lead us closer to You and Your purpose for our lives. In Jesus' name, Amen.

Remember, God holds the keys to the doors of your life. Trust Him, and He will lead you into a future filled with hope and blessings.

TRANSITION. OPPORTUNITY.
DIVINE ENCOUNTER.

DOORS OF CHANGE

DAY 31

*G*reetings! Today, let's dive into a fascinating proverb that offers us a valuable life lesson. Proverbs 26:14 (ESV) beautifully states, "As a door turns on its hinges, so does a sluggard on his bed." While this verse primarily highlights the folly of laziness, let's take a moment to explore the metaphorical significance of a door turning on its hinges and uncover the deeper message it holds for our lives.

1. Hinges and Movement:

Imagine a door without hinges. It would be rendered useless, unable to fulfill its purpose. Similarly, our lives rely on movement, growth, and progress. Just as a door needs hinges to open and close, we must embrace change, adapt to challenges, and continually strive to improve ourselves. By doing so, we allow ourselves to experience new opportunities and discover the fullness of life that awaits us.

2. Consistency and Faithfulness:

A door turns on its hinges effortlessly, consistently, and reliably. This teaches us the importance of consistency and faithfulness in our own lives. To achieve our goals and dreams, we must commit to daily habits, disciplines, and responsibilities. By remaining faithful in our pursuits, we can overcome obstacles and unlock doors of success that may have seemed impossible.

3. Perseverance and Endurance:

Consider the significance of a door's ability to swing open and shut countless times throughout its lifespan. It withstands the test of time, enduring the elements and countless interactions. Similarly, we are called to persevere in the face of challenges, setbacks, and disappointments. When we encounter closed doors, let us remember that they are not permanent barriers but opportunities for growth and redirection. By trusting in God's guidance and leaning on His strength, we can find the perseverance to overcome any obstacle that lies before us.

4. Welcoming New Beginnings:

A door that turns on its hinges signifies the possibility of new beginnings and fresh starts. It welcomes both familiar faces and strangers alike. In our own lives, let us embrace change with open hearts and minds. Each day presents an opportunity to embark on a new journey, to learn, to grow, and to impact the lives of those around us positively. Just as a door stands ready to welcome whatever lies beyond, let us approach each day with hope, openness, and a willingness to seize every moment.

Prayer: God, thank you for the wisdom found in Your Word. Help us to remember that, just as a door turns on its hinges, our lives are meant to move, grow, and embrace change. Grant us the strength to persevere, the faithfulness to remain consistent, and the courage to welcome new beginnings. May we always trust in Your guidance and find joy in the journey. In Your precious name, we pray. Amen.

Remember, you hold the key to unlock the doors of your potential. Embrace the lessons taught by the simple act of a door turning on its hinges, and may your life be filled with purpose, perseverance, and endless blessings.

TRANSITION. OPPORTUNITY.
DIVINE ENCOUNTER.

_____

_____

_____

_____

_____

_____

_____

_____

DOORS OF SERVICE

DAY 32

1 Samuel 3:15 ESV - "Samuel lay until morning; then he opened the doors of the house of the Lord."

Doors hold a special significance in our lives. They serve as passageways, separating one space from another, offering privacy, security, and even new opportunities. In 1 Samuel 3:15, we witness a profound moment as Samuel, the young servant of the Lord, opens the doors of the house of the Lord. This simple act symbolizes an invitation to explore the open doors of opportunity that God places before us.

1. Doors of Revelation:

Just as God revealed Himself to Samuel within the walls of the house of the Lord, He desires to reveal Himself to us through open doors of revelation. When we seek God's wisdom and guidance through prayer, studying His Word, and listening in silence, we open ourselves to divine insight. God's revelation can come in various forms, such as a scripture verse that speaks to our hearts, godly counsel from a friend, or a gentle nudge from the Holy Spirit. Let us be attentive and sensitive to the doors of revelation that God opens for us.

2. Doors of Service:

When Samuel opened the doors of the house of the Lord, he was preparing to serve God faithfully. We, too, have opportunities for service behind the doors God opens for us. These doors may lead us to serve our families, communities, or even strangers in need. Through acts of kindness, compassion, and selflessness, we can bring God's love and light into the lives of others. Let us embrace the doors of service that God presents, knowing that our humble acts of obedience can have a significant impact on those we encounter.

3. Doors of Growth:

As Samuel stepped through the doors of the house of the Lord, he embarked on a journey of personal growth and spiritual development. Similarly, God often opens doors that lead us to new experiences and challenges, ultimately fostering our growth. These doors might include opportunities for learning, personal development, or stepping out of our comfort zones. Though they may seem intimidating at first, let us trust that God equips us for the path He sets before us, guiding us towards our full potential.

4. Doors of Encouragement:

Lastly, opening the doors of the house of the Lord symbolizes an act of encouragement. Just as Samuel encouraged others in their relationship with God, we too can open doors of encouragement for those around us. By offering a listening ear, a word of affirmation, or a helping hand, we can uplift and inspire others in their faith journey. Let us be intentional in creating a welcoming and supportive environment for those who cross our paths.

Prayer: Lord Jesus, we thank You for the doors of opportunity that You place before us. Give us discernment and courage to step through these doors, trusting in Your guidance and provision. May we faithfully serve You and others, grow in our relationship with You, and encourage those around us. In Jesus' name, we pray, Amen.

Remember, doors are not mere barriers, but gateways to

new possibilities. As we trust in God's leading, let us embrace the doors of opportunity, knowing that He walks with us, guiding our every step.

TRANSITION. OPPORTUNITY. DIVINE ENCOUNTER.

_____

_____

_____

_____

_____

_____

_____

_____

_____

THE DOOR OF HOSPITALITY

DAY 33

"*But Lot went out to the men at the entrance, shut the door after him, and said, 'I beg you, my brothers, do not act so wickedly.'*" - Genesis 19:6 ESV

In this verse, we find Lot, a righteous man, demonstrating an extraordinary act of hospitality. The events leading up to this moment involve two angels who had arrived in Sodom, where Lot resided. Unaware of their divine nature, the people of Sodom gathered around Lot's door, demanding to have their way with these visitors. However, instead of turning a blind eye or succumbing to the wickedness around him, Lot took a stand and offered his guests his utmost protection.

Hospitality is a virtue that runs deep within the heart of God. It involves opening our homes, our hearts, and our lives to others, embracing them with warmth and kindness. Lot's actions remind us of the importance of extending hospitality, even in the face of adversity or temptation.

In our fast-paced world today, where individualism often takes precedence, it can be easy to neglect the practice of genuine hospitality. Yet, when we welcome others into our lives, we create space for God's love and grace to flow in unimaginable ways.

Consider the doors in your life. Are they open or closed to those around you? Are you willing to go the extra mile, like Lot, to ensure the safety and well-being of others? Hospitality isn't limited to inviting people into our homes; it's about inviting them into our lives, offering a listening ear, a helping hand, or a word of encouragement.

As followers of Christ, we are called to be a reflection of His love to the world. Jesus Himself demonstrated radical hospitality throughout His ministry, welcoming all, regardless of their background or reputation. He ate with sinners, healed the sick, and comforted the brokenhearted. He showed us that true hospitality transcends societal norms and calls us to see the inherent worth and dignity of every person.

Today, let us reflect on our own practice of hospitality. Are there areas of our lives where we can extend a helping hand? Can we be more intentional in creating a welcoming space for others? Let us pray for the wisdom and compassion to follow in the footsteps of Christ, offering the gift of hospitality to those who cross our paths.

Remember, even the smallest acts of kindness can have a profound impact on someone's life. Let us be known as people who embrace others with open hearts, just as God has embraced us.

Prayer: Lord, thank you for the example of Lot, who demonstrated extraordinary hospitality even in the face of wickedness. Help us to cultivate a spirit of genuine hospitality in our lives. Open our eyes to opportunities where we can extend a helping hand, a listening ear, or a word of encouragement. Teach us to love and embrace others just as You have loved and embraced us. In Jesus' name, we pray. Amen.

May you be blessed with countless opportunities to extend hospitality and experience the joy of welcoming others into your life.

TRANSITION. OPPORTUNITY. DIVINE ENCOUNTER.

_____

_____

_____

_____

_____

_____

_____

_____

_____

THE SIGNIFICANCE OF DOORPOSTS

DAY 34

*D*euteronomy 11:20 (ESV) *"You shall write them on the doorposts of your house and on your gates."*

Today, let us explore the profound significance of the doorposts, as instructed in Deuteronomy 11:20. In this verse, we are reminded of the importance of surrounding ourselves with reminders of God's teachings and commandments. Just as the doorposts serve as a physical reminder, let us consider how we can apply this concept in our daily lives.

1. Establishing Boundaries: Our doorposts mark the entrance and exit points of our homes, symbolizing the boundaries of our personal sanctuaries. They remind us of the need to establish boundaries in our lives, guarding our hearts and minds against harmful influences. By surrounding ourselves with reminders of God's truth, we create a spiritual boundary, protecting our faith from being diluted or compromised.

2. Proclaiming Identity: The doorposts also serve as a statement of identity. They distinguish our homes from others and declare our commitment to God's ways. Similarly, our lives should be a proclamation of our faith, reflecting our identity as children of God. By embracing God's commandments, we

declare to the world that our lives are guided by His love and wisdom. Let our words, actions, and even the atmosphere in our homes reflect our identity as followers of Christ.

3. Guiding Direction: Doorposts often serve as a guide, helping us find our way and preventing us from getting lost. Likewise, the teachings of God's Word act as guiding principles for our lives. When we write His commandments on our hearts and post them in our homes, we ensure that we are constantly reminded of the path we should walk. As we encounter life's challenges and decisions, may we turn to the Word of God, allowing it to guide our steps and keep us on the right track.

4. Inspiring Conversation: Doorposts are often a focal point of conversation among visitors to our homes. Similarly, when we display reminders of God's truth, it can spark meaningful conversations with others. Let our homes become places where faith is discussed, questions are asked, and spiritual growth is nurtured. By sharing our faith and the wisdom we have gained, we have the opportunity to inspire and encourage others on their own spiritual journeys.

Prayer: God, help us to internalize the significance of the doorposts and apply it to our lives. May we establish boundaries, proclaim our identity, seek Your guidance, and inspire others through the reminders of Your truth. We desire to live faithfully and intentionally, reflecting Your love and grace to the world. In Jesus' name, Amen.

Takeaway: As we reflect on Deuteronomy 11:20, let us consider how we can incorporate the concept of doorposts into our lives. By establishing boundaries, proclaiming our identity, seeking God's guidance, and inspiring others, we can create an environment that nurtures our faith and draws others closer to Him. Let the doorposts of our hearts and homes be a constant reminder of God's love and truth.

TRANSITION. OPPORTUNITY.
DIVINE ENCOUNTER.

_____

_____

_____

_____

_____

_____

_____

_____

THE DOORWAY OF HOPE

DAY 35

Judges 19:27 ESV - "And her master rose up in the morning, and when he opened the doors of the house and went out to go on his way, behold, there was his concubine lying at the door of the house, with her hands on the threshold."

Today, let's explore the significance of doors in our lives and the lessons we can draw from them. In Judges 19:27, we encounter a tragic scene where a woman is found lying at the door of a house. While this passage may depict a distressing event, it also invites us to reflect on the symbolic meaning of doors in our spiritual journey.

1. The Door as a Threshold:

Doors represent thresholds, separating what is within from what is outside. In our lives, they can symbolize the boundaries we establish to protect ourselves physically, emotionally, and spiritually. Just as the door in the passage marks the boundary between the woman's safety inside the house and the dangers beyond, we too must discern what we allow into our lives. Let us prayerfully consider the influences, relationships, and thoughts we allow to cross the threshold of our hearts.

2. The Door as an Invitation:

Doors are also invitations, beckoning us to enter new spaces and experiences. They represent opportunities for growth, change, and transformation. Just as the door in the passage called the master to venture out into the world, doors in our lives often present chances to step out in faith and embrace new possibilities. As we encounter these doors, let us remember to seek God's guidance and be open to the adventures He has in store for us.

3. The Door as an Exit:

Lastly, doors can be paths to liberation and freedom. In the story of the woman lying at the door, we witness the need for rescue and deliverance from the darkness outside. Similarly, there may be times in our lives when we find ourselves trapped in difficult circumstances or unhealthy patterns. In those moments, God can provide an exit door, leading us to divine restoration, healing, and renewed hope.

As we journey through life, let us be attentive to the doors we encounter. May we discern what we allow into our hearts, embrace the opportunities that come our way, and trust in God's guidance to lead us towards freedom and abundant life.

Prayer: Lord God, thank You for the doors in our lives that symbolize thresholds, invitations, and exits. Grant us discernment to safeguard our hearts, courage to embrace new opportunities, and the wisdom to recognize the doors You open for our deliverance. In Jesus' name, we pray. Amen.

Takeaway: Today, let us reflect on the doors in our lives. Are there any boundaries we need to establish or protect? Are there doors of opportunity we need to step through in faith? Are there areas in our lives where we need God's deliverance? Let us trust in His guidance and seek His wisdom as we navigate the doors before us. Remember, God is the ultimate Doorkeeper, and through Him, we find the pathway to hope, freedom, and abundant life.

TRANSITION. OPPORTUNITY. DIVINE ENCOUNTER.

_____

_____

_____

_____

_____

_____

_____

_____

_____

A HEART THAT OPENS DOORS

DAY 36

Job 31:32 ESV - "The sojourner has not lodged in the street; I have opened my doors to the traveler."

In the book of Job, we find a man who exemplified righteousness and integrity in the face of immense suffering and loss. Job's life serves as an inspiration and a reminder of the importance of extending hospitality and kindness to those around us, even amidst our own trials.

Job's words in Job 31:32 reveal his commitment to offering refuge and shelter to the traveler, refusing to let them lodge in the street. This act of compassion demonstrates Job's deep understanding of the value of human connection and his willingness to go above and beyond to meet the needs of others.

Hospitality is not merely a social courtesy; it is a reflection of the heart. Opening our doors to others, both physically and metaphorically, signifies our readiness to embrace and support those who cross our paths. It is an opportunity to show the love of Christ by providing comfort, nourishment, and a place of belonging.

While we may not always encounter literal travelers, there are countless individuals who journey through life burdened with loneliness, pain, or despair. As followers of Christ, we are called to be mindful of these sojourners and to offer them a safe haven amidst their struggles.

Consider how you can extend hospitality in your own life. It may involve opening your home to someone in need, inviting a friend for a meal, or simply lending a listening ear. Small acts of kindness can make a significant impact on someone's journey, reminding them that they are seen, valued, and loved.

Let us also remember that hospitality extends beyond physical spaces. We can create an atmosphere of warmth and acceptance wherever we go, embracing the opportunity to show God's love through our words and actions. A friendly smile, a kind word, or a helping hand can transform someone's day and leave a lasting impression.

As we reflect on Job's example, may we be inspired to emulate his heart for hospitality. Let us be a people who open our doors, both literally and metaphorically, to those in need. By extending love, compassion, and understanding, we become vessels of God's grace, bringing light into a world that often feels cold and unwelcoming.

Prayer: Lord, thank you for the example of Job and his commitment to hospitality. Help us to cultivate hearts that are open and welcoming, ready to extend love and care to those who cross our paths. Show us practical ways to demonstrate hospitality, both in our homes and in our daily interactions. May our lives reflect your love and bring comfort to those who need it most. In Jesus' name, we pray, Amen.

TRANSITION. OPPORTUNITY. DIVINE ENCOUNTER.

_____

_____

_____

_____

_____

_____

_____

_____

_____

UNITED IN PURPOSE

DAY 37

Scripture: Nehemiah 3:1 ESV - "Then Eliashib the high priest rose up with his brothers the priests, and they built the Sheep Gate. They consecrated it and set its doors. They consecrated it as far as the Tower of the Hundred, as far as the Tower of Hananel."

Today, let's reflect on Nehemiah 3:1, a seemingly simple verse that holds a powerful message about unity and purpose. In this passage, we see Eliashib, the high priest, taking the lead alongside his fellow priests to rebuild the Sheep Gate. This gate was a crucial entry point into Jerusalem and held significant spiritual meaning.

As we dive into this verse, we can draw valuable lessons for our own lives. Firstly, notice how Eliashib did not undertake this task alone. He recognized the importance of working together with his brothers, the priests, to accomplish their shared goal. Likewise, God encourages us to cultivate unity among fellow believers. When we join forces, we become stronger, more resilient, and can achieve great things for His kingdom.

Furthermore, the priests consecrated the Sheep Gate and set its doors. They understood the significance of dedicating their work to the Lord. In our own lives, it is essential to consecrate our actions, talents, and endeavors to God's glory. By doing so, we invite God's presence and blessing into every aspect of our lives.

Lastly, we notice that the priests extended their consecration beyond the Sheep Gate, going as far as the Tower of the Hundred and the Tower of Hananel. This demonstrates their dedication to completing the task diligently and thoroughly. It serves as a reminder that our commitment to God's work should extend beyond what is expected of us. We should strive to give our best in all that we do, going above and beyond in service to God and others.

Today, let us reflect on the example set by Eliashib and his fellow priests. May we seek unity and purpose in our own lives, working alongside our brothers and sisters in Christ. Let us consecrate our actions and offer them to God, inviting His presence and guidance. And may we approach every task with diligence and wholehearted commitment, always striving to honor God through our efforts.

Prayer: Lord, thank you for the example of unity and purpose we find in Nehemiah 3:1. Help us to cultivate unity among believers and to consecrate our actions to Your glory. Grant us the strength and dedication to serve You wholeheartedly in all that we do. In Jesus' name, we pray, Amen.

TRANSITION. OPPORTUNITY.
DIVINE ENCOUNTER.

_____

_____

_____

_____

_____

_____

_____

_____

_____

_____

WELCOMING GOD'S PRESENCE

DAY 38

Verse: Genesis 18:1 ESV - "And the Lord appeared to him by the oaks of Mamre, as he sat at the door of his tent in the heat of the day."

In the heat of the day, as Abraham sat at the door of his tent, he was about to encounter a remarkable visitation from the Lord. Little did he know that this encounter would not only bring him joy but also reveal the power of hospitality and the blessings that come with welcoming God's presence into our lives.

Abraham, known for his faith and righteousness, was not aware of who his visitors were initially. However, his response to their arrival speaks volumes about his character. He eagerly welcomed them, offering shade, water, and food, displaying an unmatched hospitality that reflects the love and kindness he had for others.

In our daily lives, we often find ourselves preoccupied with various responsibilities, worries, and the busyness of the world. However, like Abraham, we should be mindful of creating moments of stillness and openness to God's presence. Just as the

Lord appeared to Abraham at the door of his tent, God desires to reveal Himself to us in personal and unexpected ways.

Hospitality is not only about providing physical comfort but also about creating an atmosphere of openness and warmth in our hearts. When we open our hearts and lives to God, He enters in and brings His blessings, guidance, and peace. Just as Abraham's hospitality resulted in the promise of a son, our welcoming attitude toward God can lead to the fulfillment of His promises in our own lives.

Take a moment to reflect on your own life. Are you consciously making space for God's presence? Are you inviting Him into the everyday moments, just as Abraham welcomed his visitors? Cultivating a spirit of hospitality towards God allows us to experience His love, wisdom, and guidance in our lives like never before.

Let us strive to be like Abraham, eagerly awaiting the Lord's arrival, and actively seeking opportunities to welcome His presence. As we do so, we will witness the transformative power of divine encounters, the blessings that flow from our hospitality, and the joy that comes from walking closely with our Creator.

Prayer: Father God, thank you for your constant presence in our lives. Help us to be like Abraham, eagerly welcoming you into our hearts and homes. Teach us to be hospitable, creating space for your divine encounters and opening ourselves to your blessings and guidance. May our lives be a reflection of your love and kindness. In Jesus' name, we pray, Amen.

Remember, as you embrace a spirit of hospitality towards God, may you be filled with His presence and experience the abundant blessings He has in store for you. Have a blessed day!

TRANSITION. OPPORTUNITY. DIVINE ENCOUNTER.

_____

_____

_____

_____

_____

_____

_____

_____

_____

DOOR OF IMMORALITY

DAY 39

Welcome to this beautiful day of reflection and growth. Today, let us explore *Proverbs 5:8 from the English Standard Version of the Bible*. This verse reminds us of the importance of guarding ourselves against temptation and negative influences.

Imagine this verse lovingly inscribed on your door, serving as a gentle reminder each time you enter or exit your home. Let it be a powerful symbol of your commitment to living a righteous and purposeful life.

"Keep your way far from her, and do not go near the door of her house."

Within this verse, we find wisdom that encourages us to steer clear of paths that may lead us astray. It serves as a reminder to avoid situations and individuals that could entice us towards actions that contradict our values and beliefs. By keeping a safe distance, we protect our hearts, minds, and spirits from the potential harm that may come our way.

In a broader context, this verse speaks to the importance of making wise choices in various aspects of our lives. It advises us to be mindful of the influences we allow into our homes, relationships, and even our thoughts. By exercising discernment, we actively create an environment that supports our growth, happiness, and spiritual well-being.

As you encounter this verse daily, let it serve as a guiding light, urging you to make deliberate choices aligned with your values and aspirations. May it empower you to resist temptation, cultivate healthy boundaries, and pursue a life filled with integrity, love, and purpose.

Prayer: Lord Jesus, thank you for being a guiding light. Help us to make wise decision throughout our day and our lives. Teach us to be mindful of the the influences that come our way. We pray for discernment and wisdom to avoid situations that don't bring glory to you. In Jesus name, Amen.

Remember, you have the strength and wisdom within you to navigate life's challenges and make choices that honor your true self. May this daily devotional on your door be a constant reminder of the path you have chosen, guiding you towards a life of peace, joy, and fulfillment.

Keep shining bright, my friend, and embrace each day as an opportunity to grow in wisdom and grace.

TRANSITION. OPPORTUNITY.
DIVINE ENCOUNTER.

_____

_____

_____

_____

_____

_____

_____

_____

_____

_____

DOOR OF PROTECTION

DAY 40

Genesis 7:16 (NLT) - A male and female of each kind entered, just as God had commanded Noah. Then the LORD closed the door behind them.

Have you ever experienced a situation where doors seemed to be closing all around you? Maybe it was a missed opportunity, a relationship that ended, or a dream that didn't come to fruition. It can be disheartening and confusing when things don't go as planned or when we face unexpected challenges.

In Genesis 7:16, we read about Noah and the incredible task he was given by God. He was instructed to build an ark to save his family and the animals from the impending flood. Noah diligently followed God's instructions, and when the time came, he entered the ark with his family. Then something remarkable happened, which holds a powerful lesson for us today.

The Bible tells us that "the Lord closed the door." Imagine the moment when the door of the ark was sealed shut. Noah and his family were safe inside, while the world outside was consumed by the floodwaters. In that moment, they experienced both the protection and provision of God.

At times, God may close doors in our lives. It may feel like disappointment or failure, but we must remember that God's ways are higher than ours (Isaiah 55:8-9). When God closes a door, it's not to harm us, but rather to protect us or guide us onto a better path. We may not always understand His reasons at first, but we can trust that He knows what is best for us.

Noah's obedience was crucial in this story. Despite the ridicule and doubt he faced from others, he remained faithful to God's commands. It was his obedience that allowed him to experience the incredible miracle of the closed door. Similarly, when we trust and obey God, even when it seems difficult or unclear, we position ourselves to witness His faithfulness and experience His blessings.

So, if you find yourself facing closed doors today, remember Noah's story. Trust in God's wisdom and timing. Embrace the closed doors as opportunities for growth, redirection, or protection. Keep seeking God's guidance, and He will open the right doors at the right time.

Prayer: Father God, thank You for the reminder that You are the ultimate doorkeeper in our lives. Help us to trust in Your plans even when they differ from our own. Grant us the wisdom to discern Your guidance and the faith to obey, knowing that You have our best interests at heart. May we find peace and assurance in Your closed doors, knowing that You are working all things together for our good. In Jesus' name, Amen.

Remember, God's closed doors are not an end but an invitation to trust Him more and experience His faithfulness. Keep your heart open to His leading, and He will guide you through every season.

Blessings and peace be with you!

TRANSITION. OPPORTUNITY.
DIVINE ENCOUNTER.

_____

_____

_____

_____

_____

_____

_____

_____

_____

EMBRACING GOD'S PERFECT DESIGN

DAY 41

*J*ob 38:10 ESV - "And prescribed limits for it and set bars and doors"

Have you ever marveled at the awe-inspiring power and wisdom of our Creator? Job 38 reminds us of God's sovereignty and His intricate attention to detail in all aspects of life. In this verse, God speaks to Job, reminding him of His divine authority over the sea.

The sea, with its vastness and unpredictability, is a testament to God's divine might. Yet, hidden within it, God has set boundaries, placing limits to its power. He has graciously established bars and doors, ensuring that the sea remains within its designated place.

As we reflect on this verse, we can draw valuable lessons for our own lives. Just as God has set boundaries for the sea, He has also set boundaries for us. These boundaries are not meant to restrict or hinder us, but rather to guide and protect us.

In our journey through life, we may encounter challenges and uncertainties that seem overwhelming. However, we can find comfort in knowing that God, in His infinite wisdom, has placed limits on these trials. He knows our strengths and weaknesses better than anyone else, and He will never allow us to face more than we can bear.

Sometimes, we may feel trapped or confined within the boundaries God has set for us. We may long for more freedom or desire to break free from what seems like limitations. However, it is essential to remember that God's design for our lives is perfect. He knows what is best for us, even when we don't fully understand or appreciate it.

Just as the sea is held back by God's bars and doors, we can trust that He is working in our lives, setting the perfect limits for our growth and protection. In those moments of frustration or doubt, let us surrender our desires to God and embrace His divine plan for us.

Today, let us take comfort in knowing that God is in control. He has set boundaries for our lives, not to hinder us, but to guide us. Trust in His perfect design, even when it may be challenging to comprehend. Embrace His limits and find peace in the knowledge that He is always with us, leading and protecting us every step of the way.

Prayer: Lord, thank you for your sovereignty and wisdom. Help us to trust in your perfect design for our lives, even when it may be difficult to understand. Open our hearts to embrace the boundaries you have set, knowing that they are for our growth and protection. Grant us the strength to surrender our desires to you and find peace in your presence. In Jesus' name, Amen.

TRANSITION. OPPORTUNITY.
DIVINE ENCOUNTER.

GUARD OF THE DOOR

DAY 42

Bible Verse: Esther 6:2 (NLT) - *"In those records he discovered an account of how Mordecai had exposed the plot of Bigthana and Teresh, two of the eunuchs who guarded the door to the king's private quarters. They had plotted to assassinate King Xerxes."*

Have you ever felt like your actions or efforts have gone unnoticed or unappreciated? It can be disheartening when we invest our time and energy into something, only to feel as though it has gone unnoticed. However, the story of Mordecai in the book of Esther reminds us that even when it seems like no one is paying attention, God sees and rewards our faithfulness.

In Esther 6:2, we learn that King Xerxes was reviewing the chronicles, which contained records of significant events and achievements during his reign. As he perused through these accounts, he stumbled upon an entry that detailed how Mordecai, one of his trusted subjects, had uncovered a plot to assassinate him. This revelation came at a crucial time, as the king was about to honor someone for their loyalty.

It is fascinating to consider that this significant entry had remained unnoticed until this very moment. Mordecai's act of bravery and loyalty had seemingly slipped through the cracks, but God's timing is always perfect. Just when it seemed like Mordecai's actions would go unrecognized, the king's attention was directed towards him, setting the stage for a remarkable turn of events.

This story reminds us that no act of goodness or faithfulness goes unseen by our Heavenly Father. We may feel like our efforts are insignificant or forgotten, but God is an ever-watchful guardian of our lives. He sees every act of kindness, every moment of integrity, and every sacrifice we make in His name. He is the ultimate guard of the door, ensuring that our deeds do not go unnoticed or unrewarded.

When we find ourselves in situations where our efforts seem unnoticed or unappreciated, let us remember the story of Mordecai. Let it be a source of encouragement, knowing that God is aware of our faithfulness and will bring forth His divine recognition in due time. We can find solace and motivation in the fact that our Heavenly Father is always watching over us, guarding our actions and ultimately orchestrating His plans for our lives.

So, continue to be faithful, even in the seemingly ordinary moments of life. Trust that God sees and knows your heart, and He will reward your faithfulness at the perfect time. You are never unseen or forgotten; you are watched over by the loving hands of our Heavenly Father, the ultimate guard of the door.

Prayer: Lord Jesus, thank You for Your constant presence in my life. Help me to remain faithful and steadfast, even when it feels like my efforts go unnoticed. Remind me that You are the ultimate guard of the door, watching over me and preparing the way for Your divine recognition. May my actions always bring glory to Your name. In Jesus' name, I pray, Amen.

TRANSITION. OPPORTUNITY. DIVINE ENCOUNTER.

_____

_____

_____

_____

_____

_____

_____

_____

_____

UNLATCH THE DOOR

DAY 43

Song of Solomon 5:4 (NLT) - "My lover tried to unlatch the door, and my heart thrilled within me."

Have you ever experienced the thrill of anticipation when someone you love is about to enter your presence? The mere thought of their arrival fills your heart with joy and excitement. In the Song of Solomon, we find a beautiful metaphorical representation of the intimate relationship between the bride and her lover. Within this poetic imagery lies a profound spiritual truth that we can apply to our daily lives.

In Song of Solomon 5:4, the lover attempts to unlatch the door, symbolizing an invitation to enter into deeper intimacy. This verse invites us to reflect on our relationship with God, who continually seeks to draw us closer to Himself. Just as the bride's heart thrilled within her, our hearts should leap with anticipation at the opportunity to commune with our Creator.

Imagine for a moment the door of your heart being unlatched by God, who longs to dwell within you. He desires to take your hand and guide you into a deeper understanding of His love, grace, and presence. Will you embrace this divine invitation?

Unlatching the door entails several key elements:

1. Openness: To unlatch the door, we must be open and receptive to God's presence in our lives. It requires a willingness to let go of our preconceived notions, doubts, and fears, allowing Him to work in and through us.

2. Intentionality: Just as the lover intentionally tries to unlatch the door, we must be intentional in seeking God's presence. This involves setting aside dedicated time for prayer, reading His Word, and engaging in worship, creating space for Him to enter our lives.

3. Vulnerability: Unlatching the door requires vulnerability. It means exposing our true selves to God, allowing Him to see our struggles, doubts, and weaknesses. In doing so, we invite Him to bring healing, restoration, and transformation into our lives.

4. Trust: Trust is essential in embracing the divine invitation. We must trust that God has our best interests at heart, that He knows us intimately, and that He will lead us into paths of righteousness and abundance.

As we embrace the divine invitation to unlatch the door of our hearts, we can experience the joy, peace, and fulfillment that comes from a deep and intimate relationship with God. Let us be encouraged to open ourselves fully to His presence, allowing Him to unlock the fullness of His love within us.

Today, take a moment to reflect on your relationship with God. Are you willing to unlatch the door of your heart, inviting Him into every aspect of your life? Embrace the divine invitation and experience the profound joy of communing with your Creator.

Prayer: Lord, thank You for continually inviting me into deeper intimacy with You. Help me to be open, intentional, vulnerable, and trusting as I unlatch the door of my heart. May Your presence fill me with joy, peace, and an insatiable hunger for more of You. In Jesus' name, Amen.

TRANSITION. OPPORTUNITY.
DIVINE ENCOUNTER.

_____

_____

_____

_____

_____

_____

_____

_____

_____

THE THREE DOORKEEPERS

DAY 44

Scripture: Jeremiah 52:24 (NLT) - "Then the captain of the guard took as prisoners Seraiah the high priest, Zephaniah the priest of the second rank, and the three doorkeepers."

In Jeremiah 52:24, amidst the account of the fall of Jerusalem, we come across a seemingly insignificant mention of three individuals - Seraiah the high priest, Zephaniah the priest of the second rank, and the three doorkeepers. While their roles may appear minor, there is a valuable lesson to be learned from their presence.

Doorkeepers were responsible for guarding the entrances to the temple. They played a crucial role in ensuring that only those who were authorized and purified could enter and worship God. Though their duty may have seemed mundane, they were entrusted with a vital task of upholding the sanctity and holiness of the temple.

Likewise, in our own lives, we often find ourselves in roles that may seem small or unimportant. We may feel overlooked or undervalued, wondering if our contributions truly matter. However, just like the doorkeepers, every role we play has significance in God's kingdom.

As believers, we are called to be faithful in whatever God has entrusted to us, whether it be in our workplaces, families, or communities. Our faithfulness in the seemingly small tasks can have a ripple effect on those around us. When we approach our roles with a heart of dedication and excellence, we create an atmosphere where God's presence can be felt.

Additionally, the doorkeepers' role involved ensuring that only the authorized and purified could enter the temple. In a spiritual sense, we are called to be doorkeepers of our hearts and minds. We must guard against negative influences, worldly distractions, and impure thoughts that could hinder our relationship with God.

Let us be mindful of the responsibility we have to protect our spiritual well-being, ensuring that we are continually seeking God's presence and walking in His ways. By doing so, we create an environment within ourselves that is open and receptive to God's guidance and blessings.

Today, let us take inspiration from the three doorkeepers in Jeremiah 52:24. No matter how big or small our roles may seem, we can faithfully fulfill them with the knowledge that God sees and values our efforts. May we be diligent in guarding our hearts and minds, allowing God to work through us in all we do.

Prayer: Dear Lord, thank you for the reminder that every role we play in your kingdom has value and significance. Help us to faithfully fulfill our duties, no matter how small they may seem. Give us wisdom and discernment to guard our hearts and minds, so we can create an environment where your presence can dwell. In Jesus' name, we pray, Amen.

Remember, you are a valued and important part of God's plan. Stay faithful and continue to seek His guidance in all that you do. God bless you abundantly!

TRANSITION. OPPORTUNITY.
DIVINE ENCOUNTER.

_____

_____

_____

_____

_____

_____

_____

_____

_____

_____

UNWAVERING PERSISTENCE

DAY 45

"*And he will answer from within, 'Do not bother me; the door is now shut, and my children are with me in bed. I cannot get up and give you anything.'*" - Luke 11:7 ESV

Doors can represent different opportunities, hopes, and dreams that seem out of reach. Sometimes, it feels as if these doors are shut tight, and there's no way to open them. But let me encourage you today, for behind every closed door lies the potential for persistence.

In Luke 11:7, Jesus shares a parable about a man who was persistent in seeking help from his neighbor. The neighbor initially declined, stating that the door was shut, and he couldn't offer assistance. However, due to the man's unwavering persistence, the neighbor eventually relented and provided what was needed.

This parable teaches us a valuable lesson about persistence. Just like the man at the door, we must persevere when faced with closed doors in our lives. It's easy to give up when things don't go our way, but persistence is the key that unlocks new possibilities.

When faced with closed doors, it's important to remember three essential qualities: faith, determination, and patience.
1. Faith: Have faith that behind every closed door, God is working. Trust in His timing and His plans for your life. Even when it seems impossible, remember that God specializes in the impossible.
2. Determination: Be determined to keep knocking on that closed door. Don't let setbacks discourage you. Keep seeking, keep asking, and keep believing. Your persistence will eventually pay off.
3. Patience: Practice patience throughout your journey. Understand that God's timing is perfect, and He knows what's best for you. Sometimes, closed doors are meant to redirect us towards something greater. Trust in His wisdom and be patient as He orchestrates the perfect plan.

Remember, each closed door is an opportunity for growth, learning, and resilience. Embrace the challenges, for they can lead you to unexpected blessings. Keep knocking, keep seeking, and keep persisting. The door may open when you least expect it, revealing a path that will exceed your expectations.

Prayer: Father God, thank you for the reminder that closed doors are not the end of the road. Help me have unwavering faith, determination, and patience when faced with obstacles. Grant me the strength to persist and trust in Your perfect plan for my life. In Jesus's name, I pray, Amen.

May today be a day of renewed persistence, knowing that God is with you every step of the way. Keep your eyes open for the doors He will open, and trust that they will lead you to remarkable places.

TRANSITION. OPPORTUNITY.
DIVINE ENCOUNTER.

_____

_____

_____

_____

_____

_____

_____

_____

DOORS OF AUTHENTICITY

DAY 46

Malachi 1:10 (ESV) - "Oh that there were one among you who would shut the doors, that you might not kindle fire on my altar in vain! I have no pleasure in you, says the Lord of hosts, and I will not accept an offering from your hand."

Welcome to today's devotional reflection! Today, we explore a thought-provoking verse from the book of Malachi. In this passage, God expresses His disappointment in the people of Israel for offering empty, insincere sacrifices upon His altar. He longs for someone to take a stand and close the temple doors, preventing further meaningless worship.

At first glance, it may seem puzzling that God would desire the temple doors to be shut. However, this request represents a call for genuine devotion and worship from His people. It is a plea for them to recognize the true purpose of their offerings and approach Him with sincerity and reverence.

In our own lives, it is essential to reflect upon our motives when we come before God. Are our prayers and acts of worship merely rituals, devoid of heartfelt passion and genuine faith? Are we going through the motions without truly connecting with our Heavenly Father? These questions remind us of the importance of authenticity in our relationship with Him.

Closing the temple doors metaphorically means taking a step back from our religious routines and examining the state of our hearts. It is an invitation to pause and evaluate the sincerity of our worship, ensuring that our actions align with our innermost beliefs. God desires a genuine connection, where our hearts and actions are united in worship and devotion.

Today, let us respond to God's call by examining our motives and intentions. Are we offering our time, talents, and resources to the Lord in a way that truly honors Him? Let us shut the doors on vain and empty worship, and instead open our hearts to a vibrant, authentic relationship with our Heavenly Father.

As we seek to deepen our connection with God, may we remember that He delights in our genuine worship. Let us approach His altar with reverence, sincerity, and love, knowing that our authentic devotion brings joy to His heart.

Prayer: Lord God, forgive us for the times when our worship has become routine or insincere. Help us to examine our hearts and motives, that we may offer ourselves to You with authenticity. May our worship be a pleasing fragrance to You, and may we always seek to honor You in all that we do. In Jesus' name, we pray, Amen.

May this devotional inspire you to reflect upon the authenticity of your worship and draw closer to God in genuine devotion. Have a blessed day!

TRANSITION. OPPORTUNITY.
DIVINE ENCOUNTER.

_____

_____

_____

_____

_____

_____

_____

_____

_____

_____

DOORS MADE OF BRASS

DAY 47

Verse: "Furthermore, he made the court of the priests, and the great court, and doors for the court, and overlaid the doors of them with brass." - 2 Chronicles 4:9 (KJV)

In the book of 2 Chronicles, we encounter a remarkable passage that describes the works of King Solomon as he oversaw the construction of the magnificent temple of God. Among the many incredible details mentioned, one verse stands out, inviting us to reflect upon the significance it holds for our lives today.

The verse speaks of the doors of the temple, overlaid with brass. While this may seem like a simple architectural detail, it carries a profound spiritual message that resonates with us even now. These doors symbolize the access we have to the blessings, grace, and presence of God.

Just as the doors of the temple were adorned with brass, a strong and durable material, so too are the doors of our hearts meant to be firm and secure. Through our faith in Christ, we are invited to open these doors wide, allowing the Lord to enter and transform our lives.

It is through this open door that we receive God's abundant

blessings. His love, mercy, and grace pour into our lives, illuminating our paths and guiding us towards the fullness of His purpose. As we approach each day, let us remember to fling wide the doors of our hearts, eagerly anticipating the wonders that God has in store for us.

Moreover, this verse also reminds us of the importance of the temple itself and its role as a place of worship and encounter with God. Just as Solomon oversaw the construction of a physical temple, we are called to cultivate a spiritual temple within ourselves. Our bodies, hearts, and minds can become a dwelling place for the Holy Spirit, where God's glory resides and His presence is felt.

So, let us dedicate ourselves to the construction of this spiritual temple, ensuring that our thoughts, actions, and words align with God's will. Through prayer, reading the Scriptures, and seeking His guidance, we fortify the doors of this inner sanctuary, making it a holy place where we commune with our Heavenly Father.

As we immerse ourselves in the beauty of 2 Chronicles 4:9, let us hold on to the truth it reveals. Open wide the doors of your heart and allow God to pour His blessings upon you. Cultivate a spiritual temple within you, where His presence dwells and transforms every aspect of your life. May you experience the depths of His love and discover the abundant blessings He has prepared specifically for you.

Prayer: Father God, I thank You for the privilege of being able to approach You and experience Your blessings. Help me to open wide the doors of my heart, so Your presence may fill every corner of my life. Guide me in constructing a spiritual temple within me, where Your glory shines and Your will is done. I long to experience the depths of Your love and discover the blessings You have prepared for me. In Jesus' name, Amen.

TRANSITION. OPPORTUNITY. DIVINE ENCOUNTER.

_____

_____

_____

_____

_____

_____

_____

_____

_____

DOORS OF INVITATION

DAY 48

Verse: Ezekiel 41:23 (KJV) - "And the temple and the sanctuary had two doors."

Today, let's take a moment to reflect on the significance of sacred spaces and the doors that lead us into them. In the book of Ezekiel, we find a description of the temple and sanctuary, highlighting the presence of two doors. While this verse may seem simple at first glance, it holds a deeper spiritual meaning that we can apply to our lives.

1. Doors of Invitation:

The presence of two doors signifies an invitation to enter into the holy presence of God. Just as the doors of the temple beckoned worshippers to come closer, God extends an invitation to each one of us to draw near to Him. He desires an intimate relationship with us, where we can experience His love, grace, and guidance. So, let us respond to His invitation with open hearts, ready to enter into His sacred presence.

2. Doors of Separation:

The presence of doors in the temple also served as a symbol of separation. The sacred spaces were set apart from the ordinary, reminding us that our encounters with God are meant to be distinct and transformative. As we step through the doors, we are called to leave behind the distractions and concerns of the world, allowing God to work in us and through us. Let us embrace these doors of separation as an opportunity to focus our hearts and minds solely on Him.

3. Doors of Access:

Lastly, the two doors represent the accessibility of God's presence. No matter who we are or what we've done, God welcomes us with open arms. The doors remind us that His grace knows no bounds and we can approach Him confidently, knowing He will receive us with love and compassion. Through Jesus Christ, the ultimate door to God's presence, we have unlimited access to the Father.

Today, let us pause and reflect on the doors before us—the doors that invite us, separate us, and grant us access to our Heavenly Father. As we enter into our own sacred spaces, may we remember that God eagerly awaits our arrival, ready to envelop us in His love and guide us along His divine path.

Prayer: Lord, thank You for the invitation to enter into Your presence. Help us to recognize the doors that lead us closer to You. As we step through these doors, may we experience the separation from worldly distractions and find comfort in Your accessible love and grace. Guide us in our daily walk, and may our sacred spaces be a constant reminder of Your ever-present companionship. In Jesus' name, we pray, Amen.

Remember, that sacred spaces are not limited to physical buildings but can be found in the quiet moments of our lives when we intentionally seek God's presence. May your day be blessed as you open the doors of your heart and draw near to Him.

TRANSITION. OPPORTUNITY.
DIVINE ENCOUNTER.

_____

_____

_____

_____

_____

_____

_____

_____

_____

_____

DOORS OF THE SHADOW OF DEATH

DAY 49

Scripture: Job 38:17 (KJV) - "Have the gates of death been opened unto thee? Or hast thou seen the doors of the shadow of death?"

Good morning! Today, let's take a moment to reflect on the beauty and wonder of the morning dew, as we dive into the powerful words found in the book of Job.

In Job 38, we find God responding to Job's questioning of His ways and the trials he had endured. God reminds Job of His sovereignty and eternal wisdom by asking him a series of thought-provoking questions, including the one found in verse 17.

The gates of death and the doors of the shadow of death symbolize the depths of human understanding and the mysteries of life. It is a reminder that there are aspects of this world, of God's creation, that are beyond our comprehension. We may never fully understand why certain things happen or why we experience trials and hardships.

Yet, in the midst of life's uncertainties, God's wisdom and creativity shine through in the simplest of things. Take, for instance, the morning dew. As the sun rises each day, it illuminates the earth, causing tiny droplets of water to form on leaves, flowers, and grass. These glistening droplets are like nature's tears of joy, reflecting the beauty of a new day.

The morning dew teaches us a valuable lesson about God's character. It reveals His attention to detail, His ability to create something exquisite out of something as ordinary as water. It reminds us that even in the midst of difficulties, there is still beauty to be found. God's creative hand is evident everywhere if we take the time to notice.

Just as the morning dew refreshes and nourishes the plants, God's love and grace provide us with strength and renewal each day. When we feel overwhelmed or burdened by the challenges of life, let us remember that God is with us, offering comfort, guidance, and hope.

Today, take a moment to step outside and observe the morning dew. Allow its presence to remind you of God's unfathomable wisdom and creativity. Let it be a gentle nudge to seek His presence in every aspect of your life, trusting that He is working all things together for your good.

Prayer: Lord God, thank You for the beauty of the morning dew, a simple reminder of Your incredible wisdom and creativity. Help us to trust in Your guidance, even when we face challenges that are beyond our understanding. May Your love and grace refresh our souls daily. In Jesus' name, Amen.

May you have a blessed and wonder-filled day, as you continue to seek God's presence and trust in His unfailing love!

TRANSITION. OPPORTUNITY.
DIVINE ENCOUNTER.

_____

_____

_____

_____

_____

_____

_____

_____

_____

_____

EMBRACING THE BLESSING OF BELIEF

DAY 50

Verse: John 20:26 (KJV) - "And after eight days again his disciples were within, and Thomas with them: then came Jesus, the doors being shut, and stood in the midst, and said, Peace be unto you."

Today, let us reflect on a powerful encounter that took place between Jesus and his disciples, specifically focusing on Thomas. As we dive into this passage from John 20:26, we discover invaluable lessons about faith, doubt, and the transformative power of belief.

In this verse, we find the disciples gathered together, including Thomas, who had missed the earlier appearance of Jesus. It is interesting to note that the disciples were locked behind closed doors, possibly still grappling with confusion, fear, and doubt. However, Jesus, in His infinite love and grace, enters transcending all barriers, both physical and emotional.

The first thing that strikes us is Jesus' greeting, "Peace be unto you." These words carry deep meaning and significance. During their uncertainty, Jesus offers them peace, assuring them that He is present and in control. Likewise, in our own lives, in the middle of our doubts and struggles, Jesus extends the same peace to us. He longs to calm our anxious hearts and remind us that He is ever near.

Now, let us focus on Thomas, often referred to as "Doubting Thomas." When Thomas hears of Jesus' appearance, he expresses his skepticism, stating that unless he sees and touches the wounds in Jesus' hands and side, he will not believe. Thomas represents the human tendency to doubt, to seek tangible evidence before embracing faith. Yet, Jesus does not abandon or reject Thomas in his doubt. Instead, He meets Thomas right where he is.

Eight days later, Jesus appears once again, specifically for Thomas. He lovingly invites Thomas to touch His wounds, removing all doubt from his heart. Through this encounter, Jesus teaches us the importance of meeting people where they are in their faith journey. He shows us that doubt is not a barrier to His love, but rather an opportunity for Him to reveal Himself in a deeper, more personal way.

As we reflect on John 20:26, let us remember that doubt does not define us; rather, it is an invitation to seek the truth more earnestly. Jesus desires to meet us in our doubts, uncertainties, and questions, offering us the peace that surpasses understanding. He longs for us to experience the transformative power of belief, knowing that true faith is built upon a personal encounter with Him.

Today, let us embrace the blessing of belief. May we approach Jesus with open hearts, seeking His presence in the middle of our doubts. And may His peace fill our souls, enabling us to walk confidently in the assurance of His love and grace.

Prayer: Lord, thank You for Your unwavering love and understanding. Help us, like Thomas, to seek You even in our doubts. Strengthen our faith, Lord, and grant us the peace that comes from knowing You intimately. May we experience the transformative power of belief and share Your love with others who may be wrestling with doubt. In Jesus' name, we pray. Amen.

Remember, you are never alone in your faith journey. Reach out to fellow believers, seek wise counsel, and continue to grow in your relationship with Jesus. May God bless you abundantly as you walk in the light of His love.

TRANSITION. OPPORTUNITY.
DIVINE ENCOUNTER.

_____

_____

_____

_____

_____

_____

_____

_____

_____

EMBRACING TRUE SACRIFICE

DAY 51

"*Then it shall be, that whatsoever cometh forth of the doors of my house to meet me, when I return in peace from the children of Ammon, shall surely be the Lord's, and I will offer it up for a burnt offering.*" - Judges 11:31 (KJV)

In the ancient biblical story of Jephthah, we witness a solemn vow made in a moment of desperation. Jephthah, a valiant warrior, found himself in a dire situation, facing the daunting enemy of the Ammonites. In his desperation, he made a hasty promise to God that, upon his victorious return, he would offer as a burnt offering whatever first emerged from his house to greet him.

At first glance, this passage may puzzle us and even evoke discomfort. How could Jephthah make such a vow, knowing that it might involve sacrificing something precious to him?

Yet, as we dive deeper into this story, we uncover profound lessons about the nature of sacrifice and the importance of our commitments to God. Jephthah's vow was not a reflection of God's desire for human sacrifice but a testament to Jephthah's devotion and trust in God's faithfulness.

1. Trusting God in Desperate Times:

Jephthah's vow illustrates the depths of his trust in God, even in the middle of trying circumstances. In our own lives, we may face challenging situations and feel pushed to our limits. Yet, like Jephthah, we can place our trust in God, knowing that He is with us in every trial and will guide us through.

2. The Cost of Our Vows:

Jephthah's vow also reminds us to be mindful of the commitments we make to God. While not all vows demand sacrifice, we should consider the weight and implications of our promises before making them. Let us be cautious not to make hasty commitments but instead seek God's guidance and wisdom in all our decisions.

3. Surrendering Our Most Precious:

Though we may not be called to make literal burnt offerings, we are called to surrender our most cherished possessions, desires, and ambitions to God. This act of surrender allows Him to shape and mold us according to His divine plan. As we let go of our own will, we open ourselves to experience the abundant blessings and fulfillment that come from aligning our lives with His purpose.

Prayer: Father God, help us to trust You even in the most challenging circumstances. Grant us the wisdom to make commitments that align with Your will, while surrendering our lives fully to You. May we find comfort in knowing that You are faithful and will guide us on our journey. In Jesus' name, we pray, Amen.

Remember, God's desire is for our hearts and our obedience. Let this story of Jephthah's vow encourage you to trust in God's faithfulness, surrender your life to Him, and walk in His perfect will. May you find peace and blessings as you embrace true sacrifice.

TRANSITION. OPPORTUNITY.
DIVINE ENCOUNTER.

_____

_____

_____

_____

_____

_____

_____

_____

_____

THE BEAUTY OF PURPOSEFUL DESIGN

DAY 52

Verse: "And the snuffers, and the basons, and the spoons, and the censers, of pure gold: and the entry of the house, the inner doors thereof for the most holy place, and the doors of the house of the temple, were of gold." - 2 Chronicles 4:22 (KJV)

Today, let us reflect on the intricate details and purposeful design found within the sacred temple of God, as described in 2 Chronicles 4:22. This verse takes us into the remarkable craftsmanship of the temple's inner doors, the entryways, and the vessels made of pure gold.

In the grandness of the temple, we find a beautiful representation of God's attention to detail and His desire for order and beauty in all things. Every element within the temple was crafted with precision, reflecting the excellence and majesty of the Lord.

Likewise, God's design extends beyond the physical temple into our lives. We are fearfully and wonderfully made, each uniquely crafted by our Creator. Our purpose and design are not accidental, but rather intentional and divine.

Just as the doors of the temple served as entryways to the most holy place, we are called to open the doors of our hearts to

God's presence. Through prayer, worship, and seeking His guidance, we allow Him to dwell within us, transforming us into vessels of His love, grace, and mercy.

Furthermore, like the vessels made of pure gold, we are called to shine with God's glory. We are His ambassadors, reflecting His light and character to the world around us. Each one of us has been gifted with talents, abilities, and unique qualities. When used for His glory, we can bring about a tremendous impact in the lives of others.

As we meditate on 2 Chronicles 4:22, let us remember that just as the temple was a physical representation of God's presence, we too are living temples of the Holy Spirit (1 Corinthians 6:19). Let us embrace our purposeful design and invite God to work through us, so that our lives may reflect His beauty, grace, and love to all those we encounter.

Prayer: Lord Jesus, thank You for the intricate design and purpose You have placed within me. Help me to recognize and embrace the unique qualities and gifts You have given me. May my life be a vessel that reflects Your beauty and glory to those around me. Guide me in opening the doors of my heart to Your presence, and may Your Spirit dwell within me. In Jesus' name, I pray, Amen.

Remember, you are fearfully and wonderfully made with a purpose that only you can fulfill. Embrace the beauty of your design and allow God to work through you to impact the world around you. May you have a blessed day!

TRANSITION. OPPORTUNITY.
DIVINE ENCOUNTER.

THE BEAUTY IN DIVINE CRAFTSMANSHIP

DAY 53

Scripture: 1 Kings 6:31 (KJV) - "And for the entering of the oracle he made doors of olive tree: the lintel and side posts were a fifth part of the wall."

Today, let's dive into the remarkable craftsmanship and symbolism found in the doors of the temple as described in 1 Kings 6:31. This verse offers us a glimpse into the meticulous attention to detail and the divine artistry present in every aspect of God's dwelling place.

The doors of the temple, constructed from olive wood, serve as a powerful reminder of God's provision and peace. The olive tree, renowned for its strength and longevity, signifies the stability and endurance of our faith. Just as olives are pressed to produce oil, our lives are often filled with challenges and trials that refine us, ultimately leading to an outpouring of God's anointing upon us.

The lintel and side posts being a fifth part of the wall is a testament to the proportion and balance in God's design. The precise measurements indicate the importance of harmony and order in our lives as believers. As we align ourselves with God's plan, allowing Him to be the cornerstone of our existence, our lives become a testament to His perfect workmanship.

In the same way, the doors of the temple served as an entryway into the oracle, the holiest place where God's presence dwelled. These doors were not merely physical barriers but a symbolic representation of the invitation to enter into communion with God. They remind us that through Jesus Christ, who declared Himself as the door (John 10:9), we have direct access to the Father.

Today, let us reflect on the beauty and depth of God's craftsmanship in our lives. Just as the doors of the temple were carefully crafted, we are fearfully and wonderfully made by our Heavenly Father (Psalm 139:14). Each one of us possesses unique qualities and talents that can be used to glorify God and bless others.

Embrace the truth that you are a masterpiece in the hands of the Master Craftsman. Allow His divine artistry to shape and mold you, transforming your life into a radiant reflection of His glory. Walk through the doors of opportunity and purpose that God opens for you, knowing that He has designed them with love and intention.

Prayer: God, thank You for the intricate design and craftsmanship evident in all of creation, including our lives. Help us to embrace the unique qualities You have given us and to walk confidently through the doors of opportunity You open. May we always be a testament to Your perfect workmanship. In Jesus' name, Amen.

Take a moment today to appreciate the divine craftsmanship in your life and the doors that God has opened for you. Remember, you are fearfully and wonderfully made, and your purpose in God's plan is significant. Have a blessed day, my friend!

TRANSITION. OPPORTUNITY. DIVINE ENCOUNTER.

_____

_____

_____

_____

_____

_____

_____

_____

THE CALL OF WISDOM

DAY 54

Scripture: Proverbs 8:3 (KJV) "She crieth at the gates, at the entry of the city, at the coming in at the doors."

In the book of Proverbs, wisdom is personified as a wise and discerning woman who stands at the gates, calling out to all who will listen. She eagerly awaits those who seek understanding, knowledge, and guidance on their journey through life.

Just as a city gate is a place of entry and exit, wisdom is always available to us, calling out to us at the doors of our hearts and minds. It is through wisdom that we can make sound decisions, navigate challenges, and embrace a life of purpose and fulfillment.

Today, let us reflect on the significant role wisdom plays in our lives. Wisdom is not just an accumulation of knowledge; it is the application of that knowledge, the ability to discern right from wrong, and the pursuit of a life well-lived.

Wisdom calls to us in various ways throughout our daily experiences. It may come in the form of advice from a trusted friend, an inspiring book, or even a gentle nudge from within our own hearts. It is up to us to recognize and heed its call.

When we listen to wisdom's call, we open ourselves to

growth, understanding, and harmony. It guides us away from hasty decisions, impulsive actions, and words spoken in anger. Wisdom encourages us to seek understanding before passing judgment, and to show kindness and compassion to those around us.

As we journey through life, let us not neglect the call of wisdom. Let us be attentive to her voice, for she desires to lead us towards a life filled with purpose, joy, and peace.

Prayer: Father God, thank you for the gift of wisdom. Help us to recognize wisdom's call in our lives and give us the discernment to listen to it. May we grow in understanding, make choices that honor you, and walk in the path of righteousness. Guide us, Lord, and give us the grace to live wisely each day. In Jesus' name, we pray, Amen.

Remember to stay open to the call of wisdom each day. Embrace the opportunity to grow, learn, and make choices that align with God's will. May your journey be filled with wisdom, blessings, and the joy of walking in the light.

TRANSITION. OPPORTUNITY. DIVINE ENCOUNTER.

_____

_____

_____

_____

_____

_____

_____

_____

_____

DOORS OF INTROSPECTION

DAY 55

Verse: Isaiah 26:20 (KJV) - "Come, my people, enter thou into thy chambers, and shut thy doors about thee: hide thyself as it were for a little moment, until the indignation be overpast."

In times of adversity and uncertainty, God's Word provides us with peace and guidance. Isaiah 26:20 reminds us of the comforting promise of finding shelter in God's presence during challenging seasons. Let us dive deeper into this verse and explore its timeless message for our lives today.

As we navigate the storms of life, we may encounter situations that leave us feeling overwhelmed, anxious, or even fearful. However, God extends an invitation to His people, assuring them of a place of refuge and safety. He tells us to enter our "chambers" and shut the doors, symbolizing a time of introspection and seeking His presence.

The "chambers" mentioned in this verse represent the secret place of communion with God. It is a call to retreat from the chaos around us and find comfort in prayer, meditation, and studying His Word. In these moments, we can shut out the noise that distracts us and focus our hearts and minds on the One who holds us securely in His hands.

The latter part of the verse encourages us to "hide thyself as it were for a little moment, until the indignation be overpast." Here, God assures us that the trials we face are temporary and will pass in due time. Just as a storm eventually gives way to clear skies, so too will our challenges be overcome through God's guidance and strength.

When we seek refuge in God's presence, we find peace that surpasses understanding. It is in these intimate moments of connection with our Heavenly Father that we discover His unwavering love and faithfulness. As we rest in His promises, our fears are replaced with hope, and our worries are transformed into unshakable trust.

Today, let us respond to God's invitation to enter our chambers and seek His presence. Take a moment to close the doors of your heart to the distractions of the world and open them wide to the One who longs to comfort and guide you. Embrace this time of shelter and allow God's peace to wash over you.

Remember, the challenges we face are temporary, but God's love and provision are eternal. Trust in His promises, and rest assured that He will see you through every storm. May you find comfort, strength, and renewed hope as you dwell in the secret place of God's loving presence.

Prayer: Lord, thank You for the invitation to find refuge in Your presence. Help us to shut out the noise of the world and seek peace in our secret place of communion with You. In times of adversity, grant us the strength to trust in Your promises and find peace that surpasses understanding. We surrender our fears and worries to You, knowing that You will guide us through every storm we face. In Jesus' name, Amen.

TRANSITION. OPPORTUNITY.
DIVINE ENCOUNTER.

_____

_____

_____

_____

_____

_____

_____

_____

DOORS OF BETRAYAL AND FORGIVENESS

DAY 56

Verse: Micah 7:5 (KJV) - "Trust ye not in a friend, put ye not confidence in a guide: keep the doors of thy mouth from her that lieth in thy bosom."

In a world where trust can be easily shattered, it can be disheartening to face betrayal from those we hold dear. The words of Micah 7:5 remind us to be cautious with our trust and not to put undue confidence in mere mortal beings. However, this cautionary verse also opens the door for a deeper reflection on the importance of forgiveness and the power of love.

Life is filled with countless relationships, friendships, and companionships. In our interactions, we often find comfort, and support. But what happens when someone we trust disappoints us? It is in these moments that we are faced with a choice - a choice to hold onto bitterness or to embrace forgiveness.

Forgiveness is not an easy road to travel, yet it is a transformative journey that liberates our hearts from the burdensome weight of resentment. When we choose to forgive, we release ourselves from the chains of anger and allow healing to take place within us. Remember, forgiveness does not excuse the wrong, but it frees us from the grip of pain.

Moreover, while human relationships can falter, there is one constant and unwavering love that stands above all else - the love of our Heavenly Father. His love surpasses our understanding, extending grace and mercy even when we fall short. As recipients of such boundless compassion, let us strive to extend that same love to others.

In moments of betrayal, let us not allow bitterness to consume us, but rather let the love of God guide our responses. By choosing to forgive, we reflect the character of our Heavenly Father and open the door for reconciliation and healing.

Today, let us take a moment to reflect on those relationships in our lives that have been strained or broken. If there are wounds that need healing, let us seek the strength to forgive, embracing the transformative power of love. And as we navigate the complexities of trust, may we place our ultimate confidence in the unwavering love of our Heavenly Guide.

Remember, you are never alone. The One who knows your heart, your pain, and your struggles is always with you, ready to extend a hand of comfort and guide you towards a path of forgiveness and love.

Prayer: Father God, in moments of betrayal and hurt, grant us the strength to forgive and the wisdom to extend love. Help us to trust in Your unfailing guidance, knowing that Your love is the truest and most secure foundation for our hearts. In Jesus' name, we pray, Amen.

May your heart be filled with the transformative power of forgiveness and the boundless love of our Heavenly Father. Have a blessed day!

TRANSITION. OPPORTUNITY.
DIVINE ENCOUNTER.

_____

_____

_____

_____

_____

_____

_____

_____

THE DOOR OF DIVINE PROVISION

DAY 57

Verse: "Though he had commanded the clouds from above, and opened the doors of heaven, And had rained down manna upon them to eat, and had given them of the corn of heaven." - Psalm 78:23-24 (KJV)

Today, let us reflect upon the abundant provision of our loving Creator. The passage from Psalm 78:23 reveals a beautiful testament to God's faithfulness and care for His people.

Imagine the scene described in this verse: the clouds parting, doors of heaven opening, and heavenly manna gently descending upon a people in need. This divine act of provision showcases the amazing power and compassion of our Lord. It serves as a reminder that God can supply our needs even in the most unexpected ways.

Just as God rained down manna on the Israelites in the wilderness, He desires to provide for us abundantly. We may not receive literal manna, but we can find comfort in knowing that God's provision is not limited by our circumstances or limited understanding. He has countless ways to meet our needs.

In our daily lives, it's easy to become consumed by worry or anxiety about our needs. Yet, this verse reminds us to trust in God's unwavering ability to provide, just as He did for the Israelites. As we seek His guidance, He promises to open doors and shower us with blessings beyond our own efforts.

Moreover, let us not forget that the ultimate provision from God came in the form of His Son, Jesus Christ. Through Jesus, God poured out His love, grace, and salvation for the entire world. This gift reveals the depth of His desire to provide for our spiritual needs as well.

Today, take a moment to reflect on the abundance of God's provision in your life. Consider the ways He has provided for you in the past, whether big or small. Trust that just as He provided for the Israelites, He will continue to provide for you today and in the days to come.

May you find strength and peace in knowing that our heavenly Father is a faithful provider. Trust in Him, seek His guidance, and open your heart to receive His abundant blessings.

Prayer: Lord, thank You for being our loving provider. Help us to trust in Your provision, both in our physical and spiritual needs. Open our eyes to see the countless ways You have already blessed us. Grant us the wisdom to seek Your guidance and the faith to rely on Your abundant provision. In Jesus' name, we pray, Amen.

Remember, you are never alone on this journey of faith. God is with you every step of the way. May His abundant provision bring you joy and peace today and always.

TRANSITION. OPPORTUNITY.
DIVINE ENCOUNTER.

_____

_____

_____

_____

_____

_____

_____

_____

_____

_____

DOORS OF REFINING FIRE

DAY 58

Verse: "Open thy doors, O Lebanon, that the fire may devour thy cedars." - Zachariah 11:1 (KJV)

Today we dive into a thought-provoking verse from the book of Zachariah. Although it may seem confusing at first glance, there is a beautiful message hidden within these words. Let us explore the significance of Lebanon's doors and the devouring fire spoken of in this passage.

In ancient times, Lebanon was renowned for its majestic and towering cedar trees. These symbolized strength, beauty, and prosperity. Lebanon's doors were an invitation for the world to witness its abundance. However, in this verse, we find an unusual request: "Open thy doors, O Lebanon, that the fire may devour thy cedars."

At first, it may seem contradictory to wish destruction upon something so magnificent. However, when we examine the context, we discover a profound spiritual lesson. Lebanon represents the world, and the cedar trees symbolize the pride, self-sufficiency, and materialism that often dominate our lives.

The devouring fire mentioned here can be seen as a metaphor for the refining work of God's love and grace. Sometimes, in order to truly experience the transformative power of God, our pride and self-sufficiency need to be consumed by the fire of His divine presence. It is in these moments of surrender that we can truly find restoration and renewal.

God, as the True Shepherd, desires to lead us on a path of humility, dependence, and reliance upon Him. He longs to replace our worldly pursuits with spiritual treasures that bring lasting joy and fulfillment. By allowing the fire of His love to consume our pride, we open ourselves up to a deeper relationship with Him and the abundance of His blessings.

Today, let us examine our hearts and willingly open the doors of our lives to God's refining fire. As we release our self-centered desires and ambitions, we create space for His transforming work. In doing so, we invite His grace to shape us into vessels of His love, compassion, and kindness. May we embrace the pruning process that leads to a fruitful and purposeful life in Him.

Prayer: Loving God, I humbly open the doors of my heart to You today. Please help me let go of my pride, self-sufficiency, and worldly pursuits. Consume them with the fire of Your love and grace. Mold me into a vessel that reflects Your character and shares Your love with others. In Jesus' name, I pray, Amen.

Remember, embracing God's refining fire allows us to be transformed into vessels of His love and grace. May we always be open to His leading and allow Him to shape us into the image of Christ. Have a blessed day, filled with the joy and peace that comes from surrendering to His divine will.

TRANSITION. OPPORTUNITY.
DIVINE ENCOUNTER.

_____

_____

_____

_____

_____

_____

_____

_____

_____

_____

DOORS OF SPIRITUAL DISCERNMENT

DAY 59

Scripture: *"So ye in like manner, when ye shall see these things come to pass, know that it is nigh, even at the doors."* - Mark 13:29 (KJV)

Today, let us reflect upon a powerful message found in the book of Mark, where Jesus exhorts us to be watchful and prayerful in light of the signs of His coming. In this verse, Jesus emphasizes the importance of recognizing the signs and understanding that His return is imminent.

In our fast-paced lives, it can be easy to lose sight of the eternal significance of these words. However, as followers of Christ, we are called to be vigilant, aware of the world around us, and attuned to the signs that point to His glorious return. This is not meant to instill fear or anxiety but to ignite a sense of anticipation and preparedness.

To watch and pray involves actively observing the world with spiritual discernment. It means being mindful of the prevailing conditions, both in society and within our own hearts. We are called to pay attention to the signs that align with biblical prophecies, such as moral decay, the rise of false teachings, and an increase in global unrest. These signs urge us to draw closer to God, seeking His wisdom and understanding.

Simultaneously, prayer becomes our refuge and strength. It is through prayer that we align our hearts with God's will, seek His guidance, and find comfort in His presence. As we navigate the challenges of this world, prayer becomes our constant conversation with our Heavenly Father, where we lift up our concerns, joys, and desires, and surrender ourselves to His perfect plan.

Let us remember that watching and praying is not an isolated act but a way of life. It is an ongoing commitment to remain spiritually awake and connected to God. By doing so, we cultivate a deeper relationship with Him, grow in faith, and find strength to navigate the ebb and flow of life's circumstances.

Today, I encourage you to embrace the call to watch and pray. Take a moment to assess your spiritual posture. Are you attentive to the signs around you? Are you spending intentional time in prayer, seeking God's guidance and presence? May we commit ourselves to be faithful watchers and prayer warriors, eagerly awaiting the return of our Savior.

Prayer: Father God, thank You for the reminder to watch and pray. Open our eyes to the signs of Your coming and give us discernment to navigate this world with wisdom and grace. Help us to cultivate a fervent prayer life, seeking Your will above all else. May we be found faithful and prepared when You return. In Jesus' name, we pray, Amen.

Remember, you are never alone in this journey. God is with you every step of the way. Stay watchful, remain prayerful, and embrace the hope of Christ's imminent return.

Blessings and peace be with you!

TRANSITION. OPPORTUNITY.
DIVINE ENCOUNTER.

_____

_____

_____

_____

_____

_____

_____

_____

_____

DOOR OF SORROW AND RESTORATION

DAY 60

Verse: *"Because it shut not up the doors of my mother's womb, nor hid sorrow from mine eyes."* - Job 3:10 (KJV)

In the book of Job, we witness a man who experienced unimaginable pain and sorrow. Job's life took a sudden turn, and he found himself engulfed in darkness. In the middle of his anguish, he cried out, expressing his deep sorrow and longing for the tranquility of the womb that had brought him into the world.

Sometimes, we also find ourselves in seasons of darkness, where it feels as if sorrow has become our constant companion. It is during these times that hope can seem distant, and the weight of our circumstances can be overwhelming. Yet, even in the depths of despair, we can find comfort in knowing that God sees and understands our pain.

Job's lamentation reminds us that God does not hide sorrow from our eyes. He is intimately aware of the hardships we face, and His heart is filled with compassion for His children. In the middle of our darkest moments, we can take comfort in the fact that God is present, even when it may feel like He is silent.

Though Job was unaware of the bigger picture and the

reasons behind his suffering, his story teaches us that God's plans are far greater than our understanding. In the middle of our pain, God is working behind the scenes, orchestrating a masterpiece of redemption and restoration.

When faced with trials, it is natural to question, to cry, and long for relief. But let us not forget that our God is a God of hope. He can transform our darkest nights into mornings filled with joy. In the depths of our sorrow, He offers us a glimmer of hope, assuring us that He is with us every step of the way.

Today, if you find yourself in a season of darkness, hold on to the hope that God sees your pain and understands your heartache. Trust in His faithfulness, even when your circumstances seem overwhelming. Remember that God is not finished writing your story, and He will bring forth beauty from the ashes.

Prayer: Lord, in times of darkness, we turn to You for hope and comfort. Help us to trust in Your promises and to lean on Your unfailing love. When sorrow surrounds us, may we find peace in Your presence and strength. Give us the wisdom to see beyond our circumstances and to cling to the hope that You provide. In Jesus' name, Amen.

Through the darkest nights, remember that God is working behind the scenes, bringing about a dawn of hope and restoration. Hold on to His promises and find strength in His presence. He will lead you through the darkness into a future filled with His abundant grace and joy.

TRANSITION. OPPORTUNITY.
DIVINE ENCOUNTER.

_____

_____

_____

_____

_____

_____

_____

_____

_____

DOOR OF ABUNDANT BLESSINGS

DAY 61

*S*cripture: 1 Kings 7:50 (KJV) "And the bowls, and the snuffers, and the basons, and the spoons, and the censers of pure gold; and the hinges of gold, both for the doors of the inner house, the most holy place, and for the doors of the house, to wit, of the temple."

Today's verse takes us back to the time when King Solomon was building the magnificent temple for the Lord. In this passage, we find a description of the various items made from pure gold that were used in the temple's construction. These included bowls, snuffers, basins, spoons, censers, and even the hinges for the doors.

As we reflect on this verse, we can draw inspiration from the abundance of God's provision. The fact that these intricate and valuable items were crafted from pure gold demonstrates the grandeur and majesty of God's dwelling place. It reminds us that our Heavenly Father delights in providing for His children, not only with basic necessities but also with an abundance of blessings.

Just as God provided for the construction of the temple with the finest materials, He desires to bless us abundantly in our lives. However, it's important to note that God's provision goes beyond material possessions. His provision encompasses all aspects of our lives, including spiritual, emotional, and relational needs.

When we face challenges or feel discouraged, we can find comfort in knowing that God is our ever-present helper. He is creative in His provision, using various means to meet our needs and exceed our expectations. It could be through unexpected opportunities, the kindness of others, or even through personal growth and development.

God's provision is not limited by our circumstances. Even in times when resources may seem scarce, He can multiply what we have and make a way where there seems to be no way. His wisdom and creativity know no bounds, and He can provide for us in ways that we may not even anticipate.

Therefore, let us approach each day with an attitude of gratitude and expectancy, knowing that our Heavenly Father is a provider who loves to bless His children. May we trust in His abundance, seek His guidance, and remain open to His creative solutions in every area of our lives.

Prayer: Lord, thank You for being a generous and loving provider. Help us to trust in Your abundant provision, even in times of uncertainty. Open our eyes to see Your creativity and wisdom at work, and fill our hearts with gratitude for Your blessings. May we always rely on Your guidance and remain open to the ways You choose to provide for us. In Jesus' name, Amen.

Remember, you are loved, cherished, and never alone. God is with you every step of the way, ready to pour out His blessings and provision upon your life. Stay encouraged and keep seeking His presence.

Have a blessed day!

TRANSITION. OPPORTUNITY.
DIVINE ENCOUNTER.

_____

_____

_____

_____

_____

_____

_____

_____

_____

DOOR OF OBEDIENCE

DAY 62

Verse: *"And it shall be, that whosoever shall go out of the doors of thy house into the street, his blood shall be upon his head, and we will be guiltless: and whosoever shall be with thee in the house, his blood shall be on our head, if any hand be upon him."* - Joshua 2:19 (KJV)

In this verse from the book of Joshua, we witness an extraordinary act of faith and obedience displayed by Rahab, the harlot of Jericho. She had sheltered the Israelite spies in her house, risking her own life and the lives of her family members. Rahab's actions not only saved the lives of the spies but also ensured the fulfillment of God's plan to conquer the city of Jericho.

From this passage, we can glean several crucial lessons about obedience and the rewards that come from trusting in God's guidance.

1. The Power of Obedience: Rahab's obedience to the instructions given by the Israelite spies played a pivotal role in her own deliverance and that of her family. She believed in the promise of protection spoken by the spies, and her obedience demonstrated her faith in God's plan. Obedience to God's

commands may not always make sense in the moment, but it aligns us with His will and opens the door to His blessings and divine intervention in our lives.

2. The Principle of Accountability: Rahab understood the principle of accountability. She recognized that by following the spies' guidance and staying within the confines of her house, her family would be safe. She accepted the responsibility for their well-being and trusted in God's provision. Similarly, as believers, we have a responsibility to those around us. Our obedience to God's commands not only impacts our own lives but also has the potential to bring blessings and protection to our loved ones.

3. The Faithfulness of God: Rahab's story vividly illustrates God's faithfulness to His promises. He honored Rahab's obedience by safeguarding her and her family when the Israelites conquered Jericho. This serves as a powerful reminder that God is always faithful to His Word, and He rewards those who put their trust in Him. Even in our own lives, when we choose to obey God's commands and walk in His ways, we can trust that He will guide and protect us through every situation.

Today, let us be inspired by Rahab's unwavering faith and obedience. Let us recognize that our obedience to God's commands and trust in His plan will bring about blessings and protection not only in our lives but also in the lives of those around us. May we always choose to follow God's leading, knowing that His faithfulness will never waver.

TRANSITION. OPPORTUNITY.
DIVINE ENCOUNTER.

_____

_____

_____

_____

_____

_____

_____

_____

_____

THE DOOR TO EMBRACE VULNERABILITIES

DAY 63

Verse: Judges 16:3 (KJV) - "And Samson lay till midnight, and arose at midnight, and took the doors of the gate of the city, and the two posts, and went away with them, bar and all, and put them upon his shoulders, and carried them up to the top of an hill that is before Hebron."

Today's verse from Judges 16:3 shares a remarkable story of Samson's incredible strength and determination. However, beyond the physical feat, there is a deeper lesson for us to uncover—the power of embracing vulnerability.

Samson, known for his extraordinary strength, found himself in a vulnerable situation. He had fallen for Delilah's deceitful charm, revealing the secret of his strength—the source of his power. With this knowledge, Delilah betrayed Samson, leading to his capture.

Despite the challenging circumstances, Samson did not allow vulnerability to defeat him. Instead, he rose from his despair, demonstrating resilience and resourcefulness. In the middle of the night, he took hold of the city gates, the symbol of power and security, and carried them away.

This act symbolizes the strength we can find in embracing

our vulnerabilities. It reminds us that our weaknesses do not define us, but rather offer an opportunity for growth, transformation, and relying on God's strength.

In our own lives, vulnerability may arise through various experiences—heartbreak, failure, loss, or even sharing our deepest fears and insecurities. Yet, it is in these moments that we can draw nearer to God, seeking His guidance and comfort.

When we acknowledge our vulnerabilities, we open ourselves to a greater understanding of our dependence on God's grace. It is through our weaknesses that His strength can shine most brightly. As the Apostle Paul wrote in 2 Corinthians 12:9, "My grace is sufficient for thee: for my strength is made perfect in weakness."

Today, let us reflect on Samson's story and find the courage to face our vulnerabilities head-on. May we recognize that it is through these moments of vulnerability that God can transform us, empower us, and carry us to new heights. Trust that He is with you, ready to strengthen and guide you through every situation.

Prayer: Father God, thank You for the reminder that vulnerability does not make us weak but presents an opportunity for growth and dependence on Your strength. Help us embrace our vulnerabilities and trust that You will carry us through every circumstance. May Your grace be sufficient for us, and may we find comfort in Your unwavering love. In Jesus's name, we pray, Amen.

Remember, you are never alone in your vulnerabilities. God's strength is readily available to uplift and guide you. Embrace the journey of growth and allow His grace to shine through your weaknesses. Stay encouraged, and may God bless you abundantly.

TRANSITION. OPPORTUNITY.
DIVINE ENCOUNTER.

THE DOOR OF UNUSUAL MEANS

DAY 64

Scripture: 1 Samuel 21:13 (KJV) - "And he changed his behaviour before them, and feigned himself mad in their hands, and scrabbled on the doors of the gate, and let his spittle fall down upon his beard."

In our journey of faith, we often encounter challenging situations that leave us feeling vulnerable and weak. We may find ourselves in circumstances where we feel the weight of the world pressing down on us, questioning our abilities and strength. However, as we explore the story of David in 1 Samuel 21:13, we discover an important lesson about finding strength in unexpected places.

David, who would later become a renowned king of Israel, was facing immense adversity. Fleeing from King Saul, who sought to take his life, David found himself seeking refuge in the land of Gath. Fearful for his safety, David devised a plan to protect himself: he pretended to be insane.

Though this may seem like an unusual response, David's actions were driven by a deep trust in God's providence. He turned to unusual means to preserve his life, highlighting his unwavering faith in God's ability to protect him, even in the darkest of times.

Sometimes, God calls us to step outside our comfort zones and embrace unexpected methods to navigate through challenging circumstances. Just as David relied on his creativity, we too can find strength in thinking outside the box. Our Heavenly Father, in His infinite wisdom, often provides us with unique solutions that may not align with our preconceived notions.

During those times when we feel weak and disheartened, let us remember that God is not limited by our human understanding. He can work through unusual means to bring about His purposes in our lives. As we seek His guidance, He will equip us with creative solutions and empower us to overcome any obstacle that stands in our way.

In our own journeys, let us find comfort in knowing that strength is not solely found in our own abilities, but in our unwavering trust in God. When we surrender our perceived limitations to the Almighty, He can transform our weaknesses into strengths, and our challenges into opportunities for growth.

Prayer: Dear Lord, thank You for reminding us that You are the ultimate source of strength in our lives. Help us to trust in Your guidance and to embrace unusual means when faced with adversity. Teach us to rely on Your infinite wisdom and creativity rather than our own understanding. Grant us the courage to step outside our comfort zones and find strength in unexpected places. In Jesus' name, we pray, Amen.

Reflection: Take a moment to reflect on the challenges you are currently facing. Consider how you can rely on God's guidance and embrace unusual methods to navigate through these difficulties. Trust that He will provide you with the strength and creativity needed to overcome any obstacle.

TRANSITION. OPPORTUNITY.
DIVINE ENCOUNTER.

_____

_____

_____

_____

_____

_____

_____

_____

_____

THE DOOR OF TRUSTING IN GOD

DAY 65

Scripture: 2 Kings 18:16 (KJV) - "At that time did Hezekiah cut off the gold from the doors of the temple of the Lord, and from the pillars which Hezekiah king of Judah had overlaid, and gave it to the king of Assyria."

In the face of adversity, it can be easy to lose sight of our faith and succumb to fear. The story of Hezekiah in 2 Kings 18 teaches us a valuable lesson about trusting in God even when circumstances seem dire.

During Hezekiah's reign as king of Judah, the mighty Assyrian army, led by King Sennacherib, launched a campaign to conquer the land. In an attempt to appease the Assyrians, Hezekiah resorted to stripping the gold from the doors of the temple of the Lord and pillars, offering it as tribute to the enemy.

At first glance, this action may seem like a desperate act of compromise. However, upon closer examination, we see that Hezekiah's decision was an act of faith in disguise. Instead of relying solely on his own strength and resources, Hezekiah demonstrated his trust in God's sovereignty.

Hezekiah recognized that the gold and material possessions

were fleeting in the grand scheme of things. By giving up the temple's gold, he displayed a willingness to surrender earthly treasures for the sake of his people and their trust in God. He understood that true victory could only come from the Lord.

In our own lives, we often face challenges that may tempt us to compromise our faith or rely on our own limited abilities. It is during these moments that we must remember Hezekiah's example. Instead of relying on worldly solutions, let us trust in God's omniscience.

When we find ourselves in the middle of opposition, we can turn to prayer, seeking guidance and strength from the One who holds all things in His hands. Just as Hezekiah trusted in God's deliverance, we too can trust that the Lord will provide a way, even when it seems impossible.

Today, let us reflect on Hezekiah's unwavering trust in God. May his story inspire us to remain faithful and steadfast in the face of adversity. Remember, our God is always with us, and He is more than capable of turning our trials into triumphs. Trust in His plan, lean on His wisdom, and experience the peace that surpasses all understanding.

Prayer: Lord God, thank You for the inspiring story of Hezekiah. Help us to trust in You wholeheartedly, even when faced with opposition and challenges. Strengthen our faith and grant us the wisdom to seek Your guidance in all things. May we always remember that You are our ultimate source of strength and victory. In Jesus' name, we pray, Amen.

Remember, you are never alone in your journey of faith. God is with you, guiding, protecting, and providing for you every step of the way. Trust in Him, and He will see you through.

TRANSITION. OPPORTUNITY. DIVINE ENCOUNTER.

_____

_____

_____

_____

_____

_____

_____

_____

_____

THE DOOR OF EXCELLENCE

DAY 66

Verse: 2 Chronicles 3:7 (KJV) - "He overlaid also the house, the beams, the posts, and the walls thereof, and the doors thereof, with gold; and graved cherubims on the walls."

Welcome to today's devotional! Today, let's explore the fascinating details found in 2 Chronicles 3:7 and discover the profound spiritual lessons hidden within.

In this verse, we witness the meticulous attention to detail that went into the construction of the Lord's temple. The skilled craftsmen overlaid the house, beams, posts, walls, and doors with pure gold. Additionally, they carved beautiful cherubims on the walls. This level of precision and creativity demonstrates the immense value they placed upon honoring God's dwelling place.

As we reflect on this verse, we are reminded of the importance of excellence and dedication in our own lives. Just as the temple was adorned with gold and intricate carvings, we too should strive to offer our best to the Lord in everything we do. Our actions, attitudes, and even the smallest details of our lives can become offerings of worship to our Heavenly Father.

Moreover, this verse also emphasizes the significance of

cherubims adorning the walls. Cherubims were angelic beings associated with the presence of God, serving as guardians and messengers. They remind us that God's presence dwells among His people when they seek Him wholeheartedly. As we cultivate our relationship with God, He surrounds us with His love, protection, and guidance, just as the cherubims adorned the temple walls.

Today, let us be inspired by the dedication and creativity displayed in the construction of the temple. May we approach each day with a desire to honor God, offering Him our best in every area of our lives. Let us remember that God's presence is with us, like the cherubims on the walls, guarding and guiding us every step of the way.

Prayer: Lord Jesus, thank you for the beautiful example set by the craftsmen who built Your temple. Help us to offer our best to You, not only in grand gestures but also in the smallest details of our lives. May Your presence surround us like the cherubims, guiding and guarding us on our journey. In Jesus' name, we pray, Amen.

May you be blessed with a day filled with the joy of honoring God in all you do. Remember, you are loved, cherished, and capable of great things!

TRANSITION. OPPORTUNITY.
DIVINE ENCOUNTER.

_____

_____

_____

_____

_____

_____

_____

_____

_____

THE DOOR OF DILIGENCE

DAY 67

Scripture: 2 Chronicles 4:9 (KJV) - "Furthermore he made the court of the priests, and the great court, and doors for the court, and overlaid the doors of them with brass."

In the book of 2 Chronicles, we come across a verse that may seem mundane or easily overlooked. However, when we take a closer look at this verse, we find wisdom and valuable lessons hidden within its words. The verse describes the construction of various courts and doors, specifically mentioning that the doors were overlaid with brass. Though seemingly simple, this verse holds a profound message for our daily lives.

1. Diligence in Our Endeavors:

The construction of the courts and doors by the skilled craftsmen required dedication and diligence. It serves as a reminder that our daily tasks, no matter how seemingly insignificant, deserve our full attention. Whether we are at work, studying, or serving others, let us strive to do so with excellence and diligence, knowing that our efforts can be a reflection of our character and faith.

2. Attention to Detail:

Overlaying the doors with brass showcases the importance of paying attention to the finer details. Just as the craftsmen spared no effort in ensuring the doors were adorned with brass, let us also approach our lives with attentiveness and thoroughness. By giving attention to the small things, we can create a strong foundation for greatness in our endeavors.

3. Beauty in Simplicity:

Though not explicitly stated, we can deduce that the overlaid brass doors were not only functional but also added beauty to the courts. This reminds us that even in the simplest tasks or aspects of our lives, there is an opportunity to bring beauty and joy. Let us not underestimate the impact of small acts of kindness, a word of encouragement, or a simple smile. These seemingly insignificant gestures can make a significant difference in the lives of those around us.

4. Collaborative Efforts:

The construction of the courts and doors required a collective effort by skilled craftsmen. It serves as a reminder that we are not meant to navigate through life alone. Just as the builders worked together, let us seek opportunities to collaborate and support one another. By fostering a sense of unity and cooperation, we can accomplish more and create a harmonious community.

Today, as we reflect on 2 Chronicles 4:9, let us be reminded that even in the seemingly ordinary aspects of life, there are valuable lessons to be learned. May we approach each day with diligence, attention to detail, a desire to bring beauty, and a heart willing to collaborate with others. In doing so, we can create a life that is not only pleasing to ourselves but also honors and glorifies God.

Remember, you are capable of making a positive impact in every aspect of your life. May you shine brightly today and always, reflecting the wisdom found in seeking God in even the most ordinary of tasks.

TRANSITION. OPPORTUNITY.
DIVINE ENCOUNTER.

DOOR OF SUSTENANCE AND RESOURCES

DAY 68

As we dive into the sacred Scriptures, we come across a marvelous chapter in the book of Nehemiah that highlights the Fish Gate. This gate played a significant role during the restoration of Jerusalem's walls, symbolizing a powerful message for our lives today. Let us embark on a journey to uncover the spiritual lessons hidden within the Fish Gate.

The Fish Gate, located on the northern side of Jerusalem, received its name due to its proximity to the fish market. In ancient times, fish represented abundance, provision, and sustenance. Similarly, in our spiritual journey, the Fish Gate can be seen as a gateway to the abundant blessings and provision that God has in store for us.

In Nehemiah 3:3, we read that the Fish Gate was repaired by the sons of Hassenaah.

"But the fish gate did the sons of Hassenaah build, who also laid the beams thereof, and set up the doors thereof, the locks thereof, and the bars thereof."

This gate's restoration signifies the importance of unity and collaboration among God's people. Just as the sons of Hassenaah worked together to rebuild the gate, we, too, are called to work in harmony with our fellow believers, supporting and encouraging one another in our faith.

Furthermore, the Fish Gate carried a deeper symbolic meaning. In the New Testament, Jesus called His disciples to become "fishers of men," urging them to spread the Good News and bring others into His Kingdom. Similarly, the Fish Gate reminds us of our divine calling to share the love of Christ with those around us. It serves as a reminder to cast our nets wide, reaching out to those who are lost, broken, and in need of God's grace.

Just as the Fish Gate played a crucial role in the restoration of Jerusalem's walls, we, too, have a part to play in God's redemptive plan for humanity. Each of us has unique gifts, talents, and opportunities that can be used to impact the lives of others positively. Whether it's through acts of kindness, sharing the Gospel, or extending a helping hand, we are called to be ambassadors of God's love, bringing restoration and hope to a broken world.

Today, let us reflect on the significance of the Fish Gate in Nehemiah's time and draw inspiration from its restoration. May we embrace our divine calling to be fishers of men, spreading God's love and grace to all those we encounter. Let us remember that, just as the Fish Gate was repaired through unity, collaboration, and faith, we too can achieve great things when we work together in the service of our Lord.

Prayer: Lord, thank you for the lessons we learn from the Fish Gate. Help us to embrace our divine calling to be fishers of men, sharing Your love and grace with those around us. Teach us to work in unity and collaboration, supporting one another as we strive to fulfill Your purposes. May our lives bring restoration and hope to a broken world. In Jesus' name, we pray, Amen.

Remember, you are uniquely gifted and have a significant role to play in God's plan. Embrace your divine calling and let your light shine bright!

TRANSITION. OPPORTUNITY. DIVINE ENCOUNTER.

_____

_____

_____

_____

_____

_____

_____

_____

_____

DOOR OF THE VALLEY AND HOPE

DAY 69

*T*oday, we embark on a journey of discovering the spiritual significance of the Valley Gate mentioned in Nehemiah 3:13 NIV - *The Valley Gate was repaired by Hanun and the residents of Zanoah. They rebuilt it and put its doors with their bolts and bars in place. They also repaired a thousand cubits of the wall as far as the Dung Gate.* Like many passages in the Bible, this gate holds a deeper meaning that can guide us in our daily lives. Join me as we explore the treasures hidden within these ancient walls.

The Valley Gate, positioned near the lowest part of Jerusalem, was essential for safeguarding the city from potential threats. Symbolically, it represents the valleys we encounter in our lives—the seasons of struggle, pain, or uncertainty. It's in these valleys that we often find ourselves questioning our purpose, feeling overwhelmed, or even losing hope.

However, just as the Valley Gate was crucial for Jerusalem's protection, these valleys we walk through serve a purpose in our spiritual growth. They provide opportunities for us to seek God's guidance, find strength in His promises, and experience His transformative power.

1. A Gateway of Reflection:

The Valley Gate serves as a reminder to pause and reflect on our journey. It prompts us to examine our hearts and seek God's presence even in the midst of challenging circumstances. Take time each day to reflect on God's faithfulness, His promises, and His never-ending love for you.

2. A Gateway of Dependence:

In the valley, we learn to lean on God like never before. We realize our limitations and surrender our worries, fears, and burdens into His capable hands. Trust in His provision, knowing that He will sustain you and guide you through the darkest moments.

3. A Gateway of Transformation:

Just as the Valley Gate was rebuilt, God desires to restore and transform our lives. In the valleys, He molds our character, strengthens our faith, and equips us for the journey ahead. Embrace the process, knowing that God is working all things together for your good.

4. A Gateway of Hope:

Lastly, the Valley Gate reminds us that no matter how deep the valley may be, hope can always be found. When we feel surrounded by darkness, God's light shines brightest. Hold onto the promises found in His Word and allow hope to anchor your soul.

As we navigate the valleys in life, let us remember that God walks beside us, providing strength, comfort, and guidance. Embrace the Valley Gate as an opportunity for growth and transformation. May it serve as a constant reminder that, no matter the circumstances, we are never alone.

Prayer: Lord God, thank you for the Valley Gate and the lessons it teaches us. Help us to embrace the valleys in our lives, knowing that through them, you are at work within us. Strengthen our faith, grant us hope, and guide us through every challenge we face. In Jesus' name, we pray, Amen.

Takeaway: Throughout our lives, we will encounter valleys

that test our faith. However, by embracing the lessons found within the Valley Gate, we can find hope, transformation, and a deeper connection with God. Trust in His guidance, knowing that He is leading you towards a brighter future.

TRANSITION. OPPORTUNITY.
DIVINE ENCOUNTER.

_____

_____

_____

_____

_____

_____

_____

_____

_____

DOOR OF BROKENNESS AND REPENTANCE

DAY 70

Today, let's embark on a journey of spiritual reflection as we explore the profound significance of the Dung Gate mentioned in Nehemiah 3:14 NIV - *The Dung Gate was repaired by Malkijah son of Rekab, ruler of the district of Beth Hakkerem. He rebuilt it and put its doors with their bolts and bars in place.*

In ancient Jerusalem, the Dung Gate stood as one of the entrances to the city. It was named so because it was the designated gate through which the city's waste was carried out, symbolizing impurity and the need for cleansing. While this gate may seem insignificant at first glance, it holds a powerful spiritual lesson for us today.

1. Acknowledging our brokenness: Just as the Dung Gate represented the disposal of waste, it reminds us of our own spiritual state. We all carry the burden of sin and brokenness, reminding us of our need for a Savior. Recognizing our imperfections and turning to God in repentance is the first step towards divine transformation.

2. Cleansing through God's grace: Despite its unappealing nature, the Dung Gate was essential for the city's cleanliness and hygiene. Similarly, God's grace has the power to cleanse and

purify us from the filth of sin. Through the sacrifice of Jesus Christ, we are offered forgiveness, redemption, and a fresh start. Embracing His grace allows us to experience a transformative journey towards spiritual renewal.

3. Embracing transformation: Just as the Dung Gate served a necessary purpose for the city's well-being, our transformation in Christ is vital for our spiritual growth. God desires to take our brokenness and transform it into something beautiful. When we surrender our lives to Him, He begins a process of renewing our hearts, minds, and attitudes. We become vessels of His love, grace, and mercy, shining His light in a world desperately in need of His transformational power.

As you reflect upon the Dung Gate, consider the areas in your life that need God's transformative touch. Are there patterns of sin, negative habits, or brokenness that you long to be cleansed from? Remember, God's love is greater than any filth or mistake we carry. Approach Him in prayer, seeking His forgiveness and guidance, and trust Him to bring about a divine transformation in your life.

Prayer: Lord God, I humbly come before You, acknowledging my brokenness and the areas in my life that need transformation. Thank You for Your love and grace that cleanse me from all my sins. I surrender myself to You, inviting You to transform me into the person You created me to be. Help me to walk in Your ways and be a vessel of Your love and light in this world. In Jesus' name, I pray, Amen.

Remember, God is always at work in our lives, bringing transformation and renewal. May you find comfort and hope in the knowledge that through Christ, you can experience the beauty of divine transformation. Be blessed!

TRANSITION. OPPORTUNITY.
DIVINE ENCOUNTER.

THE DOOR OF REFRESHMENT

DAY 71

And Shallum the son of Col-hozeh, ruler of the district of Mizpah, repaired the Fountain Gate. He rebuilt it and covered it and set its doors, its bolts, and its bars. And he built the wall of the Pool of Shelah of the king's garden, as far as the stairs that go down from the city of David. -Nehemiah 3:15 (ESV)

Have you ever been thirsty on a scorching hot day, desperately seeking a source of refreshment? In Nehemiah 3:15, we encounter an extraordinary gate among the restored walls of Jerusalem: the Fountain Gate. This gate held great significance, not only for the city's protection but also as a symbol of spiritual nourishment and renewal.

1. A Gateway to Provision:

The Fountain Gate marked the entrance to the city's water supply, emphasizing its importance in sustaining life. Just as physical water quenches our thirst, Jesus offers a spiritual spring of living water that satisfies our deepest longings (John 4:13-14). He is the ultimate source of provision, always ready to supply our needs and refresh our souls.

2. A Symbol of Cleansing:

Water is often associated with purification and renewal. The

Fountain Gate reminds us of the cleansing power of God's Word. Ephesians 5:26 tells us that Christ cleanses us through the washing of water by the Word. As we enter through the gate of God's truth, His Word purifies and transforms us, washing away our sins and making us new.

3. A Place of Spiritual Restoration:

The Fountain Gate served as a gathering point for those seeking spiritual restoration. Likewise, Jesus invites us to come to Him when we are weary and burdened, promising to give us rest (Matthew 11:28). Through prayer, worship, and meditating on His Word, we can find comfort and renewal in His presence.

4. A Call to Share Living Water:

Just as the Fountain Gate provided water for the city, we are called to share the living water of Christ with others. Jesus encourages us to let our hearts overflow with His love and grace, becoming conduits of His life-giving Spirit (John 7:38). By sharing the Good News, we can lead others to the Fountain Gate and offer them the same refreshment we have experienced.

Prayer: Lord, thank you for being the ultimate source of living water, quenching our spiritual thirst and sustaining us each day. Help us to continually seek you, entering through the gate of your Word and finding renewal in your presence. May we become vessels of your love, sharing the living water with those around us. In Jesus' name, we pray, Amen.

Take a moment today to reflect on the significance of the Fountain Gate in Nehemiah's time and how it relates to your own spiritual journey. Allow the Holy Spirit to guide you as you seek the refreshing presence of God and share His living water with others.

TRANSITION. OPPORTUNITY. DIVINE ENCOUNTER.

_____

_____

_____

_____

_____

_____

_____

_____

_____

DOOR OF RECONSTRUCTION

DAY 72

Verse: Nehemiah 3:6 (NLT) - *The Old City Gate was repaired by Joiada son of Paseah and Meshullam son of Besodeiah. They laid the beams, set up its doors, and installed its bolts and bars.*

Good day! Today, let's explore the significance of the Old City Gate mentioned in Nehemiah 3:6. In the book of Nehemiah, we witness a beautiful narrative of restoration and rebuilding after the Israelites returned from exile. The Old City Gate played a vital role in this process, serving as a symbol of hope, strength, and renewed faith.

1. Historical Context:

The Old City Gate, also known as the gate of the old town, was one of the gates surrounding Jerusalem. This gate's reconstruction marked a significant milestone in the city's revival, as it represented the reestablishment of Jerusalem's commerce and trade.

2. Symbol of Unity:

The rebuilding of the Old City Gate was a collective effort. Nehemiah 3 reveals that various groups of people, including priests, goldsmiths, and merchants, joined together to reconstruct it. This unity among the Israelites demonstrates the power of collaboration and agreement in achieving a common goal. It reminds us that we are stronger when we work together in pursuit of God's purposes.

3. A Spiritual Application:

Just as the Old City Gate was restored physically, it also carries spiritual significance for us today. In our lives, we may encounter brokenness, whether it is in relationships, dreams, or faith. But the story of Nehemiah encourages us to trust in God's restoration power. He is the ultimate rebuilder of our lives, mending what is broken and making all things new.

4. Welcoming the Divine Presence:

Gates in ancient cities were more than just physical entrances; they were also symbolic thresholds. The reconstruction of the Old City Gate allowed the Israelites to invite God's presence back into their city. Similarly, as we rebuild areas of brokenness in our lives, we create space for God to enter and transform our hearts. Let's open our hearts to receive His grace, love, and guidance.

5. A Call to Action:

Today, let the Old City Gate serve as a reminder of the reconstruction God desires to bring into your life. Take a moment to reflect on areas that may need His touch, whether it's relationships, dreams, or personal struggles. Trust that He is faithful and able to bring restoration where it is needed most. Seek His guidance, and allow Him to lead you through the process.

Prayer: Father God, thank You for being our ultimate restorer and rebuilder. Help us trust in Your faithfulness and seek Your guidance in every area of our lives. As we rebuild what is broken, may Your divine presence fill our hearts and lead us towards a life of wholeness and purpose. In Jesus' name, we pray, Amen.

Remember, God's restoration power knows no limits. Stay faithful, hopeful, and open to His transforming work in your life. Have a blessed day!

TRANSITION. OPPORTUNITY.
DIVINE ENCOUNTER.

_____

_____

_____

_____

_____

_____

_____

_____

_____

DOOR OF DISTRACTIONS AND DETERMINATION

DAY 73

Nehemiah 6:1 (NIV) - "When word came to Sanballat, Tobiah, Geshem the Arab and the rest of our enemies that I had rebuilt the wall and not a gap was left in it—though up to that time I had not set the doors in the gates—"

Today, let's draw inspiration from Nehemiah 6:1 and reflect on the importance of remaining focused and determined in the face of distractions. As we journey through life, we often encounter various obstacles that seek to divert us from our purpose and hinder our progress. However, Nehemiah's example teaches us valuable lessons on perseverance and staying true to our calling.

In this verse, we find Nehemiah amid great opposition from his enemies. Despite their attempts to discourage him, Nehemiah had successfully led the rebuilding of the wall, closing every gap. However, the doors in the gates were yet to be installed, presenting an opportunity for his adversaries to strike.

In our own lives, distractions often arise when we are on the verge of accomplishing something significant. These distractions can come in the form of doubt, fear, criticism, or even unexpected circumstances. They aim to weaken our determination and derail us from our purpose. However, Nehemiah's response teaches us how to overcome such distractions.

First, Nehemiah recognized the source of the distractions – his enemies. Similarly, we must identify the negative influences or voices that seek to hinder our progress. By acknowledging their presence, we can better prepare ourselves to face the challenges they bring.

Second, Nehemiah refused to compromise his focus and determination. Despite the unfinished gates, he remained steadfast in his commitment to complete the task at hand. Like Nehemiah, we must have unwavering determination, refusing to be swayed by distractions, doubts, or setbacks. By keeping our eyes on the goal, we can press forward with resilience.

Lastly, Nehemiah sought God's guidance and wisdom throughout his journey. By relying on his faith and trusting in the Lord's provision, Nehemiah found the strength to persevere. In our own lives, we should remember to turn to God in prayer, seeking His guidance, comfort, and strength. He will equip us with the necessary tools to overcome distractions and obstacles along the way.

As we reflect on Nehemiah's example, let us be encouraged to stay focused and determined in pursuing our God-given purposes. Though distractions may arise, let us trust in the Lord's guidance, knowing that with His help, we can overcome any obstacles that come our way. Remember, you are capable, creative, and called to great things!

Prayer: Lord, thank You for the example of Nehemiah and his unwavering determination. Help us to identify distractions in our lives and give us the strength to stay focused on the tasks You have entrusted us with. Fill us with Your wisdom and guidance, and empower us to overcome obstacles along the way. In Jesus' name, we pray, Amen.

Takeaway: Today, let's commit to recognizing distractions,

staying focused, and seeking God's guidance in all that we do. With determination and faith, we can overcome any hindrances and fulfill our God-given purposes. Stay encouraged and remember that you have the ability to overcome!

TRANSITION. OPPORTUNITY.
DIVINE ENCOUNTER.

_____

_____

_____

_____

_____

_____

_____

_____

_____

_____

THE DOOR OF VIGILANCE

DAY 74

Verse: Nehemiah 7:3 (KJV) - *"And I said unto them, Let not the gates of Jerusalem be opened until the sun be hot; and while they stand by, let them shut the doors, and bar them: and appoint watches of the inhabitants of Jerusalem, every one in his watch, and every one to be over against his house."*

As we dive into Nehemiah 7:3, we find Nehemiah, a faithful servant of God, providing insightful guidance to the people of Jerusalem regarding the security of their city. Although this verse may seem to focus on physical protection, it carries a powerful spiritual lesson for us today.

Nehemiah understood the importance of diligence and being watchful. He recognized that the doors of Jerusalem should not be opened until the sun was hot, symbolizing the need for caution and discernment. Likewise, in our spiritual lives, we too must exercise vigilance and discernment when it comes to protecting our hearts and minds.

Just as Nehemiah urged the people to appoint watches and stand guard, we should be mindful of the influences and distractions that can lead us away from God's perfect plan for our lives. Whether it be negative thoughts, temptations, or worldly distractions, we must be intentional about guarding our hearts and minds from anything that hinders our spiritual growth.

Furthermore, Nehemiah's call to assign individuals to be responsible for their own houses teaches us the significance of personal accountability. Each person in Jerusalem was entrusted with guarding their household, emphasizing the importance of taking ownership of our spiritual lives. We are responsible for nurturing our relationship with God and ensuring that our homes are filled with His love, peace, and truth.

Let us remember that our daily walk with God requires diligence, watchfulness, and personal accountability. Just as Nehemiah encouraged the people of Jerusalem to protect their city, God calls us to safeguard our hearts, minds, and homes from anything that may hinder our growth and relationship with Him.

Today, let's take a moment to reflect on the gates we allow to enter our lives. Are we diligently guarding our hearts against negative influences? Are we actively seeking God's wisdom and discernment? Let us pray for strength, guidance, and the discernment to shut the doors to anything that may hinder our spiritual journey. May we strive to be faithful stewards of our hearts and minds, knowing that God's protection and love surround us always.

Prayer: Father God, thank you for the example of Nehemiah and his commitment to guarding Jerusalem. Help me to be diligent in protecting my heart and mind from anything that may hinder my relationship with You. Give me discernment to recognize negative influences and the strength to shut the doors to them. Guide me in being a faithful steward of my spiritual life and the atmosphere within my home. In Jesus' name, I pray, Amen.

Remember, you are loved, cherished, and never alone. May God bless you abundantly as you journey with Him each day.

TRANSITION. OPPORTUNITY. DIVINE ENCOUNTER.

_____

_____

_____

_____

_____

_____

_____

_____

_____

DOOR OF REMEMBRANCE

DAY 75

Verse: Ecclesiastes 12:2-4 (NLT) - Remember him before the light of the sun, moon, and stars is dim to your old eyes, and rain clouds continually darken your sky...Remember him before the door to life's opportunities is closed and the sound of work fades. Now you rise at the first chirping of the birds, but then all their sounds will grow faint.

Today, let us reflect upon the beautiful wisdom found in Ecclesiastes 12:4. This verse reminds us to remember our Creator before the inevitable changes and challenges that come with the passing seasons of life.

As we journey through life, we experience various seasons – seasons of joy and laughter, seasons of growth and abundance, but also seasons of struggle and sorrow. Just like the light of the sun, moon, and stars may dim with age, and rain clouds persistently darken our skies, we too encounter circumstances that can cast shadows on our hearts and minds.

In the face of life's trials and uncertainties, it is crucial to remember our Creator, who remains constant and unchanging throughout every season. He is our guiding light, offering comfort, wisdom, and strength to navigate through the darkest of times.

When the skies of life become clouded with doubt, fear, or sorrow, we must intentionally turn our hearts towards God. He invites us to seek His presence, to trust in His unfailing love, and to find comfort in His promises. In doing so, we allow His light to break through the clouds, illuminating our path and providing hope for our weary souls.

In every season, whether we find ourselves in the brightness of summer or the chill of winter, God's love and faithfulness endure. He is with us, offering His unwavering support and guidance, even when life seems overwhelming.

Today, I encourage you to set aside a moment to reflect on the season of life you find yourself in. Are you experiencing the warmth of the sun's rays or the shadows of dark clouds? Regardless of your circumstances, remember that our Creator remains by your side, ready to bring light, comfort, and peace.

Take this opportunity to draw near to God through prayer, meditation, and the study of His Word. Allow Him to speak to your heart and guide you through the changing seasons. Embrace the lessons and growth that come with each chapter of life, knowing that God's love and provision are constant.

Remember, just as the sun rises after a storm, there is always hope and renewal in God's presence. Embrace the seasons of life, trusting in His perfect timing and unwavering love.

Prayer: Father God, thank You for being our constant companion through the changing seasons of life. Help us remember to seek Your presence and find comfort in Your unfailing love. Guide us through both joyful and challenging times, and teach us to embrace the lessons each season brings. In Jesus' name, we pray, Amen.

May you find strength and assurance in the knowledge that God is with you through every season of life. Embrace His presence, and may His light shine brightly upon your path, filling your heart with peace and joy.

TRANSITION. OPPORTUNITY.
DIVINE ENCOUNTER.

_____

_____

_____

_____

_____

_____

_____

_____

_____

_____

DOOR OF PEACE IN UNCERTAIN TIMES

DAY 76

Verse: John 20:19 (ESV) - "*On the evening of that day, the first day of the week, the doors being locked where the disciples were for fear of the Jews, Jesus came and stood among them and said to them, 'Peace be with you.'*"

In the midst of fear and uncertainty, Jesus appeared to His disciples, offering them a powerful message of peace. Locked away behind closed doors, the disciples were consumed by fear, unsure of what the future held. But Jesus, in His loving and compassionate nature, came to them, breaking through their fears and offering them the gift of His peace.

Today, we find ourselves living in a world that is often filled with anxiety, worry, and doubt. We face various challenges, whether personal or global, that can shake our sense of security and leave us feeling overwhelmed. But just as Jesus brought peace to His disciples, He longs to do the same for us.

It is important to remember that peace is not the absence of trouble or difficulty, but rather a powerful presence that surpasses our circumstances. The peace Jesus offers is not dependent on the world around us, but on the unwavering love and grace of our Savior. He is our source of peace, and His presence is always available to us, even in the darkest of times.

When we find ourselves locked away in fear, like the disciples, let us remember that Jesus is with us. He stands among us, ready to calm our troubled hearts and speak words of peace into our lives. We can find comfort in knowing that He understands our fears and anxieties, and He longs to offer us His peace.

In order to experience the peace of Jesus, we need to open the doors of our hearts and invite Him in. We can do this through prayer, seeking His guidance, and surrendering our worries to Him. As we trust in His faithfulness, we can begin to let go of our fears and embrace the peace that only He can provide.

May today be a reminder that Jesus is standing among us, offering His peace. Let us choose to release our fears, open our hearts to Him, and allow His peace to fill every corner of our lives. In doing so, we can face each day with confidence, knowing that we are not alone, and that His peace will guide us through any storm.

Prayer: Dear Lord, thank You for the peace that You offer us, even in the midst of uncertainty. Help us to release our fears and anxieties, and to open our hearts to Your presence. Fill us with Your peace that surpasses all understanding, and help us to trust in Your faithfulness. In Jesus' name, we pray, Amen.

Remember, you are loved, and you are not alone. May the peace of Jesus be with you always.

TRANSITION. OPPORTUNITY.
DIVINE ENCOUNTER.

_____

_____

_____

_____

_____

_____

_____

_____

_____

DOOR OF INTENTION

DAY 77

*I*n Ezekiel 42:12, we come across a profound verse that speaks to the importance of being intentional in our pursuit of God's presence. It reads, "According to the way of the chambers that were facing south, into them the entrance was through the door at the end of the passage that was parallel to the wall, corresponding to the structure of the chambers on the south."

This verse may seem cryptic at first glance, but it holds a beautiful message for us today. Just as the chambers faced south, we are called to orient our hearts towards God, seeking His presence with intention and dedication.

Imagine these chambers as a metaphor for our lives. Each room represents a different aspect, our relationships, work, or personal growth. As we navigate through these chambers, it is crucial that we ensure our entrance into each one is aligned with the structure of the chambers on the south. In other words, we must enter each area of our lives with a desire to follow God's ways and live in accordance with His will.

When we choose to dwell in the presence of God, our lives are transformed. We begin to see His guidance and blessings in every area, bringing a divine order and peace that transcends our understanding. It is in His presence that we find wisdom, strength, and the assurance of His unfailing love.

However, dwelling in God's presence is not a one-time event, but a daily commitment. It requires us to intentionally seek Him through prayer, reading His Word, and cultivating a heart of worship. Just as the chambers had an entrance, we too must actively choose to enter into God's presence each day, engaging in a personal and intimate relationship with Him.

Today, let us reflect upon our lives and consider the chambers we are dwelling in. Are they aligned with God's ways? Are we intentionally seeking His presence in each area? May we make a conscious effort to orient our hearts towards God, entering each room of our lives with a desire to honor Him and invite His presence to guide us.

As we journey through life with the intention of dwelling in God's presence, may we experience the fullness of His blessings and find peace, joy, and fulfillment in His loving embrace.

Prayer: Dear Lord, thank You for the privilege of dwelling in Your presence. Help us to align every area of our lives with Your ways and seek You with intentionality. May Your divine order and peace reign in our hearts as we commit to living in Your presence each day. In Jesus' name, we pray, Amen.

TRANSITION. OPPORTUNITY. DIVINE ENCOUNTER.

_____

_____

_____

_____

_____

_____

_____

_____

_____

_____

DOOR OF DIVINE ENCOUNTERS

DAY 78

Verse: *"And the way before them was like the appearance of the chambers which were toward the north, as long as they, and as broad as they: and all their goings out were both according to their fashions, and according to their doors."* - *Ezekiel 42:11 (KJV)*

Today, let's explore the significance of sacred spaces and what they can teach us about our spiritual journey. In the book of Ezekiel, we come across a description of chambers in the temple, each with its own unique characteristics and purpose. These chambers were carefully designed, not only in their physical appearance but also in the way they functioned. They were places of divine encounter, where people could draw near to God and seek His presence.

As we dive into this verse, we are reminded that God's dwelling place is not confined to a physical structure but resides within the hearts of those who believe in Him. Our bodies become temples, and it is our responsibility to create sacred spaces within ourselves, where we can connect with God on a deeper level.

In our daily lives, we often find ourselves caught up in the hustle and bustle of the world, leaving little room for solitude and reflection. However, by intentionally setting aside time and creating a sacred space, we invite God to work in us and through us.

Just as the chambers in the temple had their unique features, we too possess distinct qualities that make us who we are. Our individuality allows us to experience God's presence in different ways. Some may find comfort in nature, others in art or music, and some in the stillness of prayer. Discover what brings you closer to God and incorporate it into your sacred space.

Remember, creating a sacred space isn't limited to a specific location; it can be as simple as a quiet corner in your home, a serene spot in nature, or even a mental retreat during a busy day. Find a place where you can be fully present with God, away from distractions and noise, and allow His peace to surround you.

In this sacred space, let your creativity flow. Engage in prayer, meditation, studying scripture, journaling, or any other practice that helps you draw near to God. Embrace the freedom to express your thoughts, dreams, and desires, knowing that God eagerly listens and guides your steps.

As you embrace the concept of sacred spaces, may you discover a deeper connection with God and a renewed sense of purpose in your spiritual journey. Allow your sacred space to be a refuge for your soul, a place where you can encounter God's love, wisdom, and grace.

Prayer: Lord God, thank You for the gift of sacred spaces. Help me to create an environment where Your presence can be felt and experienced. Open my heart and mind to discover the unique ways in which I connect with You. May my sacred space be a refuge where I can draw near to You, find comfort, and receive guidance. In Jesus' name, I pray, Amen.

Take a moment today to reflect on the importance of sacred spaces in your spiritual life. May your journey be blessed as you seek to cultivate a deeper relationship with God.

TRANSITION. OPPORTUNITY.
DIVINE ENCOUNTER.

_____

_____

_____

_____

_____

_____

_____

_____

_____

DOORS OF GOD'S DWELLING PLACE

DAY 79

Verse: Ezekiel 41:25 (KJV) - "And there were made on them, on the doors of the temple, cherubims and palm trees, like as were made upon the walls; and there were thick planks upon the face of the porch without."

Today, let's dive into the captivating imagery presented in Ezekiel 41:25. This verse describes the intricate details of the doors of the temple, adorned with cherubim and palm trees, resembling the artwork found on the temple walls. Additionally, thick planks graced the porch, enhancing the beauty of God's dwelling place.

One thing we can discern from this passage is the importance of attention to detail when it comes to worshiping God. The meticulous craftsmanship of the doors, cherubim, palm trees, and planks reminds us that we should offer our best to God. Whatever we do, whether it's in our daily lives or in service to Him, we should strive for excellence.

As believers, our lives can be seen as a temple where God resides. Just as the temple in Ezekiel's vision was adorned with intricate details, we too should cultivate our hearts and minds, making them pleasing and welcoming to God. Let us seek to cultivate qualities such as love, compassion, forgiveness, and faithfulness, building a beautiful dwelling place for our Heavenly Father within us.

Furthermore, the presence of cherubim and palm trees on the doors symbolizes the heavenly realm and abundant life. It reminds us that when we open the doors of our hearts to God, we invite His presence and experience His blessings in our lives. These spiritual blessings bring richness, joy, and peace beyond measure.

Lastly, the thick planks on the porch serve as a reminder of the solid foundation we need to build our lives upon. Just as a sturdy porch supports the entrance to a home, our faith and trust in God provide a firm foundation for our lives. When we stand on the unshakable truth of God's Word, we can confidently face any challenge that comes our way.

Today, let's reflect on the beauty of God's dwelling place and consider how we can offer our best to Him. May we strive for excellence in all that we do, cultivate a heart that welcomes God's presence, and build our lives on the solid foundation of His Word. As we do so, we will witness the beauty and blessings that flow from a life centered on Him.

Prayer: Dear Lord, thank You for inviting us into Your presence and making our lives a dwelling place for You. Help us to offer our best to You in all that we do and to cultivate a heart that is pleasing to You. May our lives be built on the solid foundation of Your Word, and may Your blessings and beauty flow abundantly in and through us. In Jesus' name, we pray, Amen.

Remember, you are loved, valued, and cherished by God. May His presence dwell richly within you today and always.

TRANSITION. OPPORTUNITY.
DIVINE ENCOUNTER.

_____

_____

_____

_____

_____

_____

_____

_____

_____

DOORS OF TRANSFORMATION

DAY 80

Scripture: Ezekiel 41:24 (KJV) "And the doors had two leaves apiece, two turning leaves; two leaves for the one door, and two leaves for the other door."

In the book of Ezekiel, the prophet gives us a detailed description of the temple's construction. Although some may find it challenging to engage with such intricate details, every aspect of God's dwelling place carries profound spiritual significance. Today, let us focus on the symbolism found within the doors of the temple.

The doors mentioned in Ezekiel 41:24 are described as having two leaves, two turning leaves, and a total of four leaves in all. These doors were not ordinary doors but rather unique entrances into God's presence. They were designed with great intentionality, reflecting the divine nature and purpose of the temple.

The twofold nature of the doors symbolizes the invitation extended to all of humanity. God's dwelling place is not limited to a select few; it is open to all who seek Him. Just as these doors swing wide open, so does God's invitation to enter into a relationship with Him. He desires for everyone to draw near and experience His love, grace, and transforming power.

Furthermore, the turning leaves signify the importance of seeking God with a heart that is willing to change and yield. To enter through these doors, we must be ready to let go of our old ways and embrace the transformation that comes through encountering the living God. As the leaves pivot, granting access to the sacred space, God invites us to turn away from our sin, our doubts, and our self-reliance, and turn towards Him in humble surrender.

Lastly, the four leaves remind us of the completeness and fullness found in God's presence. They represent the wholeness of our being and the holistic nature of our relationship with Him. As we enter through these doors, we are invited to bring every aspect of our lives before the Lord—our joys, our fears, our hopes, and our struggles. God desires to encompass every part of us, offering His love, healing, and direction.

Today, let us reflect on the doors of the temple and the profound symbolism they hold. Remember that God's invitation is extended to all, without exception. Approach His dwelling place with a heart willing to turn and yield, allowing Him to transform you from the inside out. Embrace the fullness of His love and grace, knowing that within His presence lies the abundant life we were created to experience.

Prayer: Lord God, thank You for the invitation to enter into Your presence. Help me approach Your dwelling place with a humble and willing heart. Teach me to surrender my old ways and embrace the transformation You offer. Fill me with Your love, grace, and wholeness as I seek to draw near to You each day. In Jesus' name, I pray, Amen.

Remember, God's dwelling place is not confined to a physical temple. Our hearts can become His dwelling place when we invite Him in. May you experience the beauty and intimacy of His presence today and always. Stay blessed!

TRANSITION. OPPORTUNITY.
DIVINE ENCOUNTER.

_____

_____

_____

_____

_____

_____

_____

_____

_____

DOORS OF CONNECTION

DAY 81

Verse: "Also, thou son of man, the children of thy people still are talking against thee by the walls and in the doors of the houses, and speak one to another, every one to his brother, saying, Come, I pray you, and hear what is the word that cometh forth from the Lord." - Ezekiel 33:30 (KJV)

In the book of Ezekiel, we find the prophet speaking on behalf of God to His people. In this verse, Ezekiel is confronted with the reality that some of the people were talking against him, questioning his authority as a messenger of God. Despite the opposition, Ezekiel remained steadfast in his role, faithfully delivering the word of the Lord.

This verse provides us with a valuable lesson about the power of connection, particularly in the context of worship. Just as the people gathered by the walls and doors of their houses, eagerly awaiting the word from the Lord, we too are called to come together in unity to seek and hear His voice.

Worship is not merely a solitary experience; it is a collaborative act. When believers come together, it creates a combined effort that improves our spiritual journey. We are encouraged to share, discuss, and learn from one another, just as the people did in this verse. Through this exchange, we deepen our understanding of God's Word and grow in our faith.

In the present day, technology enables us to connect with fellow believers from all around the world. We can engage in online forums, join virtual worship services, or participate in group studies, all of which create meaningful connections with like-minded individuals. These interactions provide opportunities for us to encourage, support, and challenge one another in our spiritual walk.

As we reflect on Ezekiel 33:30, let us remember the importance of community in our worship. Let us actively seek out connections with other believers, both in person and through digital platforms. By coming together, we can create a space where the word of God is shared, discussed, and lived out, building each other up in faith.

Prayer: Father God, thank you for the gift of community. Help us to actively seek connections with fellow believers, that we may grow together in our faith and support one another. We pray for meaningful encounters with others who can inspire and challenge us on our spiritual journey. May our worship be a reflection of the unity and love we share as children of God. In Jesus' name, Amen.

Remember, as you engage with others in worship and seek connections, you are not alone. Together, we can encourage and inspire one another as we seek to live out our faith. May your journey be filled with blessings, growth, and an ever-deepening connection with God and His people.

TRANSITION. OPPORTUNITY. DIVINE ENCOUNTER.

_____

_____

_____

_____

_____

_____

_____

_____

_____

_____

YOUR CHOICE OF DOORS

DAY 82

Welcome to today's devotional centered around Matthew 7:13-14:-"*Enter by the narrow gate. For the gate is wide and the way is easy that leads to destruction, and those who enter by it are many. For the gate is narrow and the way is hard that leads to life, and those who find it are few.*"

In these verses, Jesus uses a metaphorical gate to describe the two contrasting paths that lie before us: the broad way and the narrow way. The broad way represents the path of least resistance, the way that appears easy and enticing, but ultimately leads to destruction. On the other hand, the narrow way signifies the path that is often challenging, requiring determination and sacrifice, but leads to eternal life.

As we journey through life, it is essential to understand the significance of this teaching. The broad way is filled with distractions, temptations, and worldly desires that pull us away from God's purpose. It promises instant gratification, but it fails to deliver lasting joy and fulfillment. It may seem appealing, as it aligns with the norms of society and requires little effort, but it ultimately leads to emptiness and separation from God.

In contrast, the narrow way, though challenging, provides us with a deeper connection to our Creator. It calls us to surrender our own desires and ambitions, seeking instead to align our lives with God's will. This path requires self-discipline, perseverance, and a willingness to go against the crowd. Yet, it is on this narrow path that we discover true joy, peace, and the fullness of life that comes from walking with God.

Let us reflect on which path we are currently traveling. Are we following the crowd, allowing the world's values and temptations to shape our decisions? Or are we choosing the narrow way, embracing the challenges and sacrifices that come with following Christ?

Remember, the narrow gate may be difficult to find, and it may seem lonely at times, but it leads to eternal life in the presence of our heavenly Father. God invites us to walk with Him on this path, offering His guidance, strength, and unwavering love.

Let us pray: Father God, help us to choose the narrow way, even when it seems tough or unpopular. Grant us the wisdom to discern the influences that lead us away from You, and guide us towards a life that reflects Your will. May we find joy and fulfillment in walking closely with You.. In Jesus' name, Amen.

Take a moment today to reflect on the path you are currently traveling. May you find courage and strength to choose the narrow way that leads to eternal life. God bless you abundantly!

TRANSITION. OPPORTUNITY. DIVINE ENCOUNTER.

_____

_____

_____

_____

_____

_____

_____

_____

_____

THE SHEPHERD'S DOOR

DAY 83

Scripture: John 10:2 ESV - *"But he who enters by the door is the shepherd of the sheep."*

Today, let us reflect upon the profound imagery of Jesus as the Good Shepherd and ourselves as His beloved sheep. In John 10:2, Jesus presents a powerful metaphor to help us understand His role in our lives. He compares Himself to the shepherd, and we are the sheep under His loving care.

Shepherds in biblical times were responsible for the welfare and protection of their flock. They would lead their sheep to green pastures, provide them with nourishment, and guide them away from danger. As our Good Shepherd, Jesus fulfills this role perfectly, tending to our needs, protecting us, and leading us into abundant life.

When Jesus speaks of entering through the door, He is referring to the proper way the shepherd approaches his sheepfold. The shepherd would enter through the gate, which was the designated entrance, ensuring the safety and security of the sheep. In our lives, Jesus is the only true way to find peace, safety, and fulfillment.

As sheep, we can find great comfort in knowing that Jesus,

our Shepherd, has entered through the proper door. He has come in the way that leads to our eternal security and abundant life. By accepting Him as our Savior and Lord, we invite Him to care for us, guide us, and lead us into the fullness of His purpose for us.

Just as sheep depend on their shepherd for everything, we too can rely on Jesus for all our needs. He provides us with spiritual nourishment through His word, the Bible, and His Holy Spirit, guiding us in wisdom and understanding. He knows each one of us intimately, calling us by name and leading us along the right path.

Today, let us take a moment to reflect on the incredible love and care Jesus extends to us as our Good Shepherd. May we trust Him more deeply, surrendering our lives entirely to His loving guidance. Let us rejoice in His presence, knowing that through Him, we have found eternal safety and abundant life.

Prayer: Lord, thank You for being our Good Shepherd. We are grateful for Your love, guidance, and protection. Help us to trust You more and surrender our lives completely to Your care. Lead us in the way of righteousness and grant us the wisdom to follow Your voice. In Jesus' name, we pray, Amen.

Takeaway: Today, let us remember that as sheep under the care of our Good Shepherd, we can find peace, protection, and purpose. Let us trust in His guidance and rely on His love, knowing that He will lead us to green pastures and still waters. May we embrace the abundant life He offers and follow Him faithfully each day.

TRANSITION. OPPORTUNITY.
DIVINE ENCOUNTER.

DOORS OF ADORNMENT

DAY 84

Scripture: 1 Kings 6:34 (ESV) - ...and two doors of cypress wood. The two leaves of the one door were folding, and the two leaves of the other door were folding.

Today, let's marvel at the beauty and significance of the temple described in 1 Kings 6:34. This verse captures a moment of completion, as King Solomon ensured that every inch of God's house was adorned with the finest gold. The temple, a place of worship and divine dwelling, was a testament to God's presence among His people.

In the Old Testament, God chose to establish His presence within the temple, a physical structure built by human hands. The lavish use of gold symbolized the glory and majesty of God. It reflected the reverence and honor the people had for their Creator. Every detail, from the walls to the altar, was meticulously crafted and adorned, reminding the people of God's greatness and their commitment to Him.

Today, as believers, we are the temple of the living God (1 Corinthians 3:16). Though no longer made of bricks and mortar, our bodies have become the dwelling place of the Holy Spirit. Just as Solomon adorned the temple with gold, we are called to adorn our lives with qualities that reflect God's character: love, joy, peace, patience, kindness, goodness, faithfulness, gentleness, and self-control (Galatians 5:22-23).

Consider the beauty of a life adorned with God's presence. Our actions, words, and attitudes can become a reflection of His glory. When we make room for the Holy Spirit to dwell within us, we show love, peace, and compassion to those around us. Our lives become a living testimony of God's grace and transforming power.

Today, let us purposefully invite the Holy Spirit to dwell within us. Let us seek God's guidance and wisdom as we interact with others and face the challenges of each day. Just as the gold-covered temple attracted the attention of all who saw it, may our lives draw others closer to God.

Prayer: Lord, thank You for choosing to dwell within us, making us Your living temples. Help us to embrace the responsibility of adorning our lives with Your character. May our words, actions, and attitudes reflect Your glory and lead others to You. Guide us each day, Holy Spirit, so that we may be a testament of Your love and grace. In Jesus' name, Amen.

Take a moment today to reflect on how you can further adorn your life with the character of God. May your day be filled with the joy of being a dwelling place for the Holy Spirit. Remember, you are a chosen vessel through which God can shine His light into the world. Have a blessed day!

TRANSITION. OPPORTUNITY.
DIVINE ENCOUNTER.

_____

_____

_____

_____

_____

_____

_____

_____

_____

DOOR OF TRANSITION

DAY 85

Verse: Genesis 6:16 ESV - "Make a roof for the ark, and finish it to a cubit above, and set the door of the ark in its side. Make it with lower, second, and third decks."

Today, let us reflect on the incredible story of Noah and the ark. In Genesis 6:16, God instructs Noah to build an ark as a means of protection for him, his family, and various animals during the great flood. Although the dimensions and construction details may seem specific and technical, they hold a powerful message for our lives today.

1. Preparation: Just as Noah was given detailed instructions on constructing the ark, we are also called to prepare ourselves for the challenges we may face. God's guidance encourages us to seek His wisdom, study His Word, and build a strong foundation of faith. By doing so, we equip ourselves to weather the storms of life.

2. God's Provision: Notice how God provided specific measurements and instructions for the ark's construction. This reveals His attention to detail and His desire to protect His people. In our lives, too, we can trust that God is intimately aware of our needs and will provide for us in ways that are

perfect for our unique situations. We can find peace in knowing that He is our ultimate shelter.

3. Trusting God's Timing: Building the ark took time and dedication from Noah and his family. It was not a simple or quick task. Similarly, in our lives, we must learn to trust God's timing. There may be times when we feel like we are waiting for answers, but rest assured that God is working behind the scenes to bring about His perfect plan. Patience and trust are essential as we wait for God's timing to unfold.

4. God's Promises: Ultimately, the ark served as a tangible reminder of God's promise to protect Noah and his family. In the same way, God has made promises to us in His Word. He promises His unfailing love, His presence in our lives, and eternal salvation through Jesus Christ. As we face daily challenges, we can hold onto these promises, finding comfort and strength in knowing that God is faithful to His Word.

Let's pray: Lord Jesus, thank you for the story of Noah and the ark, reminding us of Your faithfulness and protection. Help us to diligently prepare ourselves for the challenges we may face, trusting in Your provision and perfect timing. May we find comfort in Your promises, knowing You are always with us. In Jesus' name, we pray, Amen.

May you be blessed as you find shelter in God's unwavering love and protection. Remember, you are never alone, and God is always there to guide you through life's storms.

TRANSITION. OPPORTUNITY.
DIVINE ENCOUNTER.

_____

_____

_____

_____

_____

_____

_____

_____

_____

THE DOOR OF CONTENTMENT

DAY 86

*W*elcome to this beautiful day! Today, let's explore the inspiring words from Psalm 84:10, which says, "Better is one day in your courts than a thousand elsewhere; I would rather be a doorkeeper in the house of my God than dwell in the tents of the wicked" (NIV).

This verse speaks to the deep longing in our hearts to be in the presence of God. It reminds us that our fellowship with Him is far more precious and fulfilling than any worldly desire or pursuit. Let's reflect on three key insights we can draw from this verse:

1. The Value of God's Presence: The psalmist beautifully expresses the incomparable worth of spending just one day in the courts of the Lord. In His presence, we find solace, joy, and peace that surpasses all understanding. It is a place where our souls are truly satisfied. Today, let's prioritize seeking God's presence above all else, cherishing our moments with Him and finding delight in His company.

2. The Heart of Contentment: The psalmist compares being a mere doorkeeper in the house of God to dwelling in the tents of the wicked. This comparison teaches us the importance of

contentment. Even the humblest position in God's house is far more desirable than the seemingly glamorous but empty pursuits of the world. Let's cultivate a heart of contentment, recognizing that being close to God is the ultimate treasure we can possess.

3. The Power of Choice: The psalmist's declaration reveals a deliberate choice to prioritize God above all else. We, too, have the power to choose daily where we invest our time, energy, and affections. When we intentionally choose to dwell in God's presence, we open ourselves up to experience His abundant blessings and guidance. Today, let's purposefully choose God and His ways, aligning our hearts with His desires.

As we meditate on Psalm 84:10, let it remind us of the immeasurable value of being in God's presence. May it inspire us to seek Him wholeheartedly, finding contentment and joy in our relationship with Him. Remember, the Lord's strength and love are always available to guide and sustain you throughout each day. Walk with Him, dwell in His presence, and experience the abundant life He offers.

Prayer: Father God, thank You for the gift of Your presence. Help us to value and prioritize spending time with You above all else. Fill our hearts with contentment, knowing that being close to You is the greatest treasure we can possess. Guide us in making daily choices that align with Your will and bring us closer to You. In Jesus' name, we pray, Amen.

Stay blessed as you journey through this day, rooted in the strength and love of our wonderful Creator.

TRANSITION. OPPORTUNITY.
DIVINE ENCOUNTER.

_____

_____

_____

_____

_____

_____

_____

_____

_____

DOOR OF MULTIPLE VOICES

DAY 87

Scripture: John 10:1 (NLT) - "I tell you the truth, anyone who sneaks over the wall of a sheepfold, rather than going through the gate, must surely be a thief and a robber."

In this passage from the Gospel of John, Jesus uses the analogy of a shepherd and his sheep to reveal a profound truth about our relationship with Him. He presents Himself as the Good Shepherd, and we are His precious flock.

Notice how Jesus emphasizes the importance of entering through the gate. He warns that anyone who sneaks over the wall is a thief and a robber. This gate represents Jesus Himself, the only authorized and rightful way to access the abundant life and eternal security that He offers.

Just as a shepherd cares for his sheep, Jesus cares for us. He knows each of us intimately, recognizing our individual needs, fears, and desires. He desires to lead us to green pastures and protect us from harm. But to fully experience His loving guidance, we must willingly enter through the gate, acknowledging Jesus as our Savior and Lord.

In today's world, we encounter various voices and influences vying for our attention. These voices can easily distract us from following God. False teachings, temptations, and worldly desires often entice us to deviate from the path of righteousness. However, Jesus urges us to discern and recognize His voice above all others.

To discern the voice of God, we need to nurture a close relationship with Him. This involves spending time in prayer, reading His Word, and seeking His will for our lives. As we immerse ourselves in the truth of Scripture, the Holy Spirit will guide and remind us of Jesus' teachings, helping us to distinguish His voice from the noise of the world.

Let us remember that the voice of our Good Shepherd is one of love, compassion, and wisdom. His voice brings comfort, peace, and reassurance, even in the midst of life's storms. By faithfully following Him, we can rest securely in His care, knowing that He will lead us to the abundant life He has promised.

So, today and every day, let us choose to listen to the voice of God. May we enter through the gate, trusting in Him alone for our salvation, guidance, and provision. As we do, we will experience the joy and fulfillment that only comes from walking closely with our loving Shepherd.

Prayer: Dear Lord, thank You for being our Good Shepherd. Help us to discern Your voice among the noise of the world. Guide us, protect us, and lead us on the path of righteousness. Give us the wisdom to recognize and follow You faithfully. In Jesus' name, we pray, Amen.

Remember, the voice of our Good Shepherd is always there, ready to lead and guide us. Trust in Him, and find comfort in His loving care.

TRANSITION. OPPORTUNITY.
DIVINE ENCOUNTER.

DOORS OF IDOLATRY

DAY 88

Verse: Isaiah 57:8 (NLT) - "Behind closed doors, idols are set up for worship of foreign gods. Loud shouts of idolatrous joy are heard from the streets in which they live."

Today, let's reflect on Isaiah 57:8 and explore the timeless message it holds for us. In this verse, the prophet Isaiah paints a picture of a society consumed by idolatry. As we dive into its meaning, we can gain valuable insights into our own lives and discover the profound comfort that comes from seeking God's presence.

In ancient times, people erected idols and gave them the greatest attention and devotion. These idols represented false gods, offering temporary pleasures and empty promises. The streets echoed with the sounds of extreme celebrations, as people sought joy and fulfillment in the wrong places.

However, as believers, we are called to a different way of life. We are invited to turn away from false idols and instead embrace the loving presence of our one true God. In His presence, we find comfort, wisdom, and true joy that surpasses any earthly pleasure.

It is all too easy to get caught up in the distractions of this world, seeking fulfillment in material possessions, success, or even the approval of others. But God's desire is for us to find our ultimate satisfaction in Him alone. When we place our trust in the Creator of the universe, we discover an unshakeable foundation for our lives.

In times of uncertainty or when we feel overwhelmed by the demands of life, we can find comfort in God's presence. He offers us guidance, comfort, and the reassurance that we are never alone. When we turn to Him, we open ourselves to experience His peace that surpasses all understanding.

Let us make a conscious effort to examine our lives and identify any false idols that may be competing for our attention. It could be the pursuit of success, excessive worry, or even unhealthy relationships. By surrendering these idols to God, we create space for His presence to fill our hearts and minds.

As we embark on this journey of seeking God's presence, we discover that His love and grace are always available to us. He longs for a deep, personal relationship with each one of us, where we can find rest, purpose, and true fulfillment.

Today, let us be intentional about redirecting our focus towards God, letting go of the distractions that hinder our growth in Him. May we find comfort and joy in His loving arms, knowing that in His presence, we have everything we need.

Prayer: Lord, thank You for Your constant presence in our lives. Help us to identify and let go of any false idols that distract us from experiencing Your love and peace. Teach us to seek You above all else, finding comfort and fulfillment in Your presence alone. In Jesus' name, we pray, Amen.

Takeaway: Take a moment to reflect on the idols that may be competing for your attention. Consider how you can intentionally redirect your focus towards God and find comfort in His presence. Remember, true fulfillment and joy are found in seeking Him above all else.

TRANSITION. OPPORTUNITY.
DIVINE ENCOUNTER.

_____

_____

_____

_____

_____

_____

_____

_____

_____

EMBRACING THE ROLE OF DOORKEEPERS

DAY 89

Verse: Berekiah and Elkanah were to be doorkeepers for the ark. Shebaniah, Joshaphat, Nethanel, Amasai, Zechariah, Benaiah and Eliezer the priests were to blow trumpets before the ark of God. Obed-Edom and Jehiah were also to be doorkeepers for the ark.

(1 Chronicles 15:23-24 NIV)

In the account of David's endeavor to bring the ark of God back to Jerusalem, we encounter an often-overlooked group of individuals—the doorkeepers. These individuals played a crucial role in safeguarding the ark and ensuring its safe passage. Today, we can draw inspiration from their dedication and faithfulness as we consider our own role as doorkeepers of God's presence.

Just as David and the Israelites set up a tent to house the ark, we are called to create a space within our lives to welcome the presence of God. We become doorkeepers when we intentionally set aside time for prayer, meditation, and studying His Word. These practices allow us to draw near to God, inviting His presence to fill our hearts and minds.

As doorkeepers, we are entrusted with guarding the purity and reverence of our personal relationship with God. Our role is to protect and prioritize our connection with Him, ensuring that nothing hinders our communion with the Almighty. Just as the doorkeepers were vigilant in their responsibility, we too must be watchful over our hearts, thoughts, and actions, so that they align with God's will.

Furthermore, the doorkeepers had the honor of witnessing and participating in the offerings and blessings that accompanied the ark's arrival. Similarly, as we embrace our role as doorkeepers, we have the privilege of experiencing the blessings and spiritual growth that come from cultivating a relationship with God.

Our offerings to God may not be physical sacrifices anymore, but we can present our lives as living sacrifices (Romans 12:1). Our acts of obedience, our praise, and our surrender of self all become offerings before the Lord. As we offer ourselves to Him, He will bless us abundantly, pouring His grace, love, and guidance into our lives.

Let us remember that being a doorkeeper is not a burdensome duty, but a position of honor and privilege. It is an opportunity to encounter God's presence and to draw nearer to Him each day. Through our faithful devotion and stewardship, we can experience the transformative power of His love and share it with others.

Prayer: Lord Jesus, thank You for calling me to be a doorkeeper of Your presence. Help me to create a sacred space within my life where You can dwell. Give me the strength to guard my heart and mind, and to prioritize my relationship with You above all else. May my offerings of praise, obedience, and surrender be pleasing to You. In Jesus' name, I pray, Amen.

As you embrace your role as a doorkeeper, may you experience the joy and fulfillment that comes from nurturing a deep and intimate relationship with God. May you find strength and inspiration in His presence, and may your life be a testimony of His love and grace.

TRANSITION. OPPORTUNITY.
DIVINE ENCOUNTER.

DOOR TO ETERNAL BLESSINGS

DAY 90

Verse: John 10:7 KJV - "Then said Jesus unto them again, Verily, verily, I say unto you, I am the door of the sheep."

Today, let us dive into the words spoken by Jesus and re-examine this scripture in the book of John: "I am the door of the sheep." This simple yet powerful statement carries deep spiritual significance and holds a message of hope and salvation for all who hear it.

Imagine a shepherd diligently caring for his flock of sheep. He leads them to green pastures, provides nourishment, and protects them from harm. At nightfall, he guides them into the safety and warmth of the sheepfold, ensuring their well-being. In this context, Jesus describes Himself as the door, the entrance to the sheepfold.

In ancient times, the sheepfold was an enclosed area, safeguarding the sheep from predators and providing a place of rest. Likewise, Jesus is the door, the access point, to eternal blessings and abundant life. Through Him, we find security, salvation, and the rich promises of God.

Let us explore the blessings that Jesus, as the door, offers us:

1. Security: Just as the sheep find refuge within the sheep-

fold, Jesus provides us with a sense of security. In a world filled with uncertainties and trials, He offers us His unwavering presence and protection. When we walk through Him, we find shelter from the storms of life, knowing that we are held in His loving arms.

2. Salvation: Jesus is the only way to eternal life with God. Through His sacrificial death on the cross, He opened the door for us to be reconciled with our Heavenly Father. By accepting Him as our Lord and Savior, we receive the gift of salvation and the assurance of spending eternity in His loving presence.

3. Abundant Life: As we enter through Jesus, we step into a life of abundance. This abundant life is not solely defined by material possessions, but rather by spiritual blessings, joy, peace, and purpose. Through Him, we experience a deep connection with God, His love, and the fulfillment that comes from living according to His teachings.

Today, let us remember that Jesus is the door to eternal blessings. As we walk through Him, we find security, salvation, and the fulfillment of our deepest longings. May we approach Him with gratitude and faith, knowing that He is our shepherd, guiding us every step of the way.

Prayer: Lord Jesus, thank you for being the door to eternal blessings and abundant life. Help us to trust in your loving care and find our security in you. Guide us along the path of salvation and help us experience the richness of life that comes from abiding in you. In your precious name, we pray, Amen.

Remember, Jesus is always there for you as the gate to eternal blessings. May you find comfort and peace as you walk through Him. Have a blessed day!

TRANSITION. OPPORTUNITY.
DIVINE ENCOUNTER.

_____

_____

_____

_____

_____

_____

_____

_____

_____

_____

AFTERWORD

Thank you for embarking on this transformative journey with "The Door: 90 Day Devotional Embracing Transitions, Opportunities, and Divine Encounters." As you have experienced the power of its words, I encourage you to take the next step and share your thoughts with others. Your honest review on platforms like Amazon or wherever you made your purchase can make a significant impact, helping more people discover and benefit from this inspiring devotional. By sharing your feedback, you become part of a community that uplifts and inspires others. **So, go ahead and leave your review today.** Together, let's spread the light of transformation and divine encounters to all who want it.

To learn more about Stephenie Brown, visit:
www.stepheniebrown.com

Made in the USA
Coppell, TX
28 January 2026

70255345R00203

ABOUT PROVERBS 31 MINISTRIES

*She is clothed with strength and dignity;
she can laugh at the days to come.*

PROVERBS 31:25

Proverbs 31 Ministries is a nondenominational, nonprofit Christian ministry that seeks to lead women into a personal relationship with Christ. With Proverbs 31:10-31 as a guide, Proverbs 31 Ministries reaches women in the middle of their busy days through free devotions, podcast episodes, speaking events, conferences, resources, and training in the call to write, speak and lead others.

We are real women offering real-life solutions to those striving to maintain life's balance, in spite of today's hectic pace and cultural pull away from godly principles.

Wherever a woman may be on her spiritual journey, Proverbs 31 Ministries exists to be a trusted friend who understands the challenges she faces and walks by her side, encouraging her as she walks toward the heart of God.

Visit us online today at proverbs31.org!

3. Helm, David C. *1-2 Peter and Jude: Sharing Christ's Sufferings.* Wheaton, IL: Crossway, 2008, p. 32.

DAY 39
1. Grudem, Wayne. *Systematic Theology.* Grand Rapids, MI: Zondervan, 1994, p. 1164.

DAY 40
1. Um, Stephen. *1 Corinthians: The Word of the Cross.* New York, NY. HarperCollins p. 296.
2. Westminster Assembly, "Question 1," The Westminster Shorter Catechism. 1647.

THE RESURRECTED BODY
1. Grudem, Wayne. *Systematic Theology.* Grand Rapids, MI: Zondervan, 1994, p. 832.
2. Grudem, Wayne. *Systematic Theology.* Grand Rapids, MI: Zondervan, 1994, p. 832.

4. Guthrie, Donald. *Hebrews: An Introduction and Commentary,* vol. 15, Tyndale New Testament Commentaries. Downers Grove, IL: InterVarsity Press, 1983, p. 219.

DAY 35
1. Davids, Peter H. *The Letters of 2 Peter and Jude: The Pillar New Testament Commentary.* Grand Rapids, MI: William B. Eerdmans Pub. Co., 2006, p. 111.

THE OLDEST COPIES OF ANCIENT SCRIPTURE IN EXISTENCE TODAY

1. "Discovery Sites," The Leon Levy Dead Sea Scrolls Digital Library. Israel Antiquities Authority. https://www.deadseascrolls.org.il/learn-about-the-scrolls/discovery-sites?locale=en_US.
2. "Dead Sea Scrolls: West Semitic Research Project." University of Southern California School of Religion. https://dornsife.usc.edu/wsrp/biblical-manuscripts/.
3. "Genesis," The Leon Levy Dead Sea Scrolls Digital Library. Israel Antiquities Authority. https://www.deadseascrolls.org.il/featured-scrolls.
4. "Preface to the English Standard Version." English Standard Version Study Bible. Wheaton, IL: Crossway, 2008. https://www.esv.org/preface/.
5. "Plate 275/1, Frag 1," photographed by Shai Halevi, The Leon Levy Dead Sea Scrolls Digital Library. Israel Antiquities Authority. https://www.deadseascrolls.org.il/explore-the-archive/image/B-295662.
6. Leviant, Curt. "Jewish Holy Scriptures: The Leningrad Codex." Jewish Virtual Library. https://www.jewishvirtuallibrary.org/the-leningrad-codex.
7. "Biblical Manuscripts: Leningrad Codex Firkovitch B19A." University of Southern California School of Religion. https://dornsife.usc.edu/wsrp/biblical-manuscripts-2/.
8. "Leningrad Codex: Introduction." University of Southern California School of Religion. https://dornsife.usc.edu/wsrp/cylinder-seals-and-the-west-semitic-research-project/.
9. "Introduction." The Leon Levy Dead Sea Scrolls Digital Library. Israel Antiquities Authority. https://www.deadseascrolls.org.il/learn-about-the-scrolls/introduction
10. *Codex Sinaiticus.* https://www.codexsinaiticus.org/en/codex/name.aspx.

DAY 37
1. Willard, Dallas. *The Allure of Gentleness: Defending the Faith in the Manner of Jesus.* New York, NY: HarperCollins, 2016, p. 31.

DAY 38
1. Helm, David C. *1-2 Peter and Jude: Sharing Christ's Sufferings.* Wheaton, IL: Crossway, 2008, p. 32.
2. Ortlund, Raymond C. Jr. *Isaiah: God Saves Sinners.* Wheaton, IL: Crossway, 2005, p. 20.

DAY 24
1. "Faith," *Merriam-Webster Dictionary*. https://www.merriam-webster.com/dictionary/faith?src=search-dict-box.
2. Ellicott, Charles John. "Galatians 2," *Ellicott's Commentary for English Readers*, 1905. https://biblehub.com/commentaries/ellicott/galatians/2.htm.

DAY 25
1. Spurgeon, Charles H. "Joy, a Duty: Sermon No. 2405." Metropolitan Tabernacle, Newington, CT. March 20, 1887.

DAY 27
1. Hoehner, Harold W. *The Bible Knowledge Commentary: An Exposition of the Scriptures,* 1985, p. 614.

DAY 28
1. Lewis, C.S. *The Weight of Glory, and Other Addresses*. New York, NY: HarperOne, 2001, p. 189.

DAY 29
1. Trench, Richard C. *Synonyms of the New Testament*. Grand Rapids, MI: Eerdmans, 1880, p. 206.

DAY 30
1. Towner, Philip H. *The Letters to Timothy and Titus*. Grand Rapids, MI: Eerdmans, 2006, p. 578.
2. Spurgeon, Charles. *Commenting and Commentaries*. London: Passmore & Alabaster, 1876, p. 1.

DAY 32
1. Moo, Douglas J. *The Letters to the Colossians and to Philemon: The Pillar New Testament Commentary*. Grand Rapids, MI: William B. Eerdmans Pub. Co., 2008, p. 389.
2. Moo, Douglas J. *The Letters to the Colossians and to Philemon: The Pillar New Testament Commentary*. Grand Rapids, MI: William B. Eerdmans Pub. Co., 2008, p. 394.

DAY 34
1. Vincent, Marvin Richardson. *Word Studies in the New Testament, vol. 4*. New York, NY: Charles Scribner's Sons, 1887, p. 502.
2. Guthrie, Donald. *Hebrews: An Introduction and Commentary,* vol. 15, Tyndale New Testament Commentaries. Downers Grove, IL: InterVarsity Press, 1983, p. 218.
3. Jamieson, Robert, A. R. Fausset, and David Brown. *Commentary Critical and Explanatory on the Whole Bible*, vol. 2. Oak Harbor, WA: Faithlife, 1997, p. 468.

3. Bray, Gerald. *Ancient Christian Commentary on Scripture: James, 1-2 Peter, 1-3 John, Jude.* Downers Grove, IL: InterVarsity Press, 2000, p. 172.
4. Neste, Ray Van. *Expository Commentary: Hebrews-Revelation.* Wheaton, IL: Crossway, 2018, p. 424.

DAY 14

1. Naselli, Andrew David. "Why Romans is the Greatest Letter Ever Written." Crossway, August 16, 2022. https://www.crossway.org/articles/why-romans-is-the-greatest-letter-ever-written/
2. *English Standard Version Study Bible.* Wheaton, IL: Crossway, 2008, p. 2151.
3. Mackie, Tim. "Romans 1-4." Bible Project, https://bibleproject.com/videos/romans-1-4/
4. Hughes, R. Kent. *Preaching the Word: Romans, Righteousness from Heaven.* Wheaton, IL: Crossway, 1991, p. 26.
5. Bray, Gerald. *Ancient Christian Commentary on Scripture: Romans.* Downers Grove, IL: InterVarsity Press, 2005, p. 28.
6. Hughes, R. Kent. *Preaching the Word: Romans, Righteousness from Heaven.* Wheaton, IL: Crossway, 1991, p. 27.

DAY 15

1. Merida, Tony. *Christ-Centered Exposition Commentary: Exalting Jesus in Acts.* Nashville, TN: B&H Publishing Group, pp. 31-32.
2. Piper, John. "Why Is Baptism Important?" Desiring God, February 15, 2021. https://www.desiringgod.org/interviews/why-is-baptism-important.

DAY 17

1. Garnsey, Peter, and Richard Saller. *The Roman Empire: Economy, Society and Culture.* University of California Press, 1987, pp. 118-120.

DAY 19

1. "Corinth," *HarperCollins Bible Dictionary: Abridged Edition.* Edited by Mark Allan Powell, San Francisco, CA: HarperOne, 2009.

DAY 22

1. Hughes, R. Kent. *Ephesians: The Mystery of the Body of Christ.* Wheaton, IL: Crossway Books, 2013.

DAY 23

1. *"eleos," Strong's Lexicon.* https://biblehub.com/greek/eleos_1656.htm
2. Hughes, R. Kent and Bryan Chapell. *1-2 Timothy and Titus: To Guard the Deposit.* Wheaton, IL: Crossway, 2012.

DAY 10

1. Baugh, S. M. *Ephesians: Evangelical Exegetical Commentary.* Bellingham, WA: Lexham Press, 2015, pp. 123-124.
2. Schreiner, Patrick. *The Ascension of Christ: Recovering a Neglected Doctrine.* Bellingham, WA: Lexham, 2020, p. 93.

DAY 11

1. Vickers, Brian J. *Expository Commentary: John-Acts.* Wheaton, IL: Crossway, 2019, p. 503.
2. Hughes, R. Kent. *Preaching the Word: Acts, The Church Afire.* Wheaton, IL: Crossway, 1996, p. 235.
3. Schreiner, Patrick. *Acts: Christian Standard Commentary.* Holman Reference, 2022. p. 487.
4. Staton, Tyler. *Praying Like Monks, Living Like Fools: An Invitation to the Wonder and Mystery of Prayer.* Nashville, TN: Nelson Books, 2022.
5. Hughes, R. Kent. *Preaching the Word: Acts, The Church Afire.* Wheaton, IL: Crossway, 1996, p. 235.
6. Schreiner, Patrick. *Acts: Christian Standard Commentary.* Holman Reference, 2022. p. 491.

WHO WAS THE APOSTLE PAUL?

1. Lanier, Greg. "No, 'Saul the Persecutor' Did Not Become 'Paul the Apostle.'" The Gospel Coalition, May 3, 2017. https://www.thegospelcoalition.org/article/no-saul-the-persecutor-did-not-become-paul-thepostle/.
2. The Editors of *Encyclopaedia Britannica.* "How Did St. Paul the Apostle Die?" Encyclopedia Britannica. https://www.britannica.com/question/How-did-St-Paul-the-Apostle-die.

DAY 12

1. Mackie, Tim. "Book of 2 Corinthians Summary: A Complete Animated Overview." Bible Project, https://bibleproject.com/videos/2-corinthians/.
2. Garland, David E. *Christian Standard Commentary: 2 Corinthians.* Holman Bible Publishers, 2021, p. 475.
3. *"Ktisis." Strong's Concordance,* https://www.blueletterbible.org/lexicon/g2937/csb/mgnt/0-1/.
4. Bray, Gerald. *Ancient Christian Commentary on Scripture: 1-2 Corinthians.* Downers Grove, IL: InterVarsity Press, 1999.

DAY 13

1. *English Standard Version Study Bible.* Wheaton, IL: Crossway, 2008, p. 2428.
2. Neste, Ray Van. *Expository Commentary: Hebrews-Revelation.* Wheaton, IL: Crossway, 2018, p. 423.

TWO KEY TRUTHS ABOUT JESUS: GOD INCARNATE, GOD RESURRECTED

1. Pelikan, Jaroslav Jan and E.P. Sanders. "Jesus," *Encyclopedia Britannica*. https://www.britannica.com/biography/Jesus.
2. Alcorn, Randy. *It's All About Jesus: A Treasury of Insights on Our Savior, Lord, and Friend*. Harvest House Publishers, 2020, p. 151.
3. O'Connor, Flannery. *Wise Blood*. Farrar, Straus and Giroux, 1962.
4. Isaacson, Walter. "Einstein and Faith," *Time*. April 5, 2007, p. 47.
5. Henry, Matthew. "1 Corinthians 15." *Matthew Henry's Complete Bible Commentary*. www.christianity.com/bible/commentary/matthew-henry-complete/1-corinthians/15.

DAY 2

1. "What Do Americans Believe About Jesus? 5 Popular Beliefs." Barna Group, April 1, 2015. https://www.barna.com/research/what-do-americans-believe-about-jesus-5-popular-beliefs/.
2. Cooper, Barry. "Messiah / Christ," *Simply Put*. Podcast, Ligioner, https://learn.ligonier.org/podcasts/simply-put/messiah-christ.

DAY 3

1. *"apollumi." Strong's Lexicon,* https://biblehub.com/greek/622.htm.

DAY 4

1. Kuniholm, Peter Ian. "The Donkey in Human History: An Archaeological Perspective," *Bryn Mawr Classical Review*. October 20, 2019. https://bmcr.brynmawr.edu/2019/2019.10.20/#:~:text=Seneb%20may%20have%20owned%20as,Assur%20in%20exchange%20for%20textiles.

WEEK ONE WEEKEND REFLECTION AND PRAYER

1. Hanegraaff, Hank. *Resurrection*. Nashville, TN: Word Publishing, 2000, p. 128.

DAY 6

1. Strauss, Mark L. *Mark: Zondervan Exegetical Commentary on the New Testament*. Edited by Clinton E. Arnold, Grand Rapids, MI: Zondervan, 2014, p. 82.
2. "שוב," *Theological Dictionary of the Old Testament*. Edited by G. Johannes Botterweck and Helmer Ringgren, translated by Douglas W. Stott, Grand Rapids, MI; Cambridge, U.K.: William B. Eerdmans Publishing Company, 2004, p. 475.

DAY 8

1. O'Collins, Gerald G. "Crucifixion," *The Anchor Yale Bible Dictionary*. Edited by David Noel Freedman, New York, NY: Doubleday, 1992, p. 1208.

DAY 9

1. Tan, Paul Lee. *Encyclopedia of 7700 Illustrations: Signs of the Times*. Garland, TX: Bible Communications, Inc., 1996, p. 669.

8. Metzger, Bruce M. and Bart D. Ehrman. *The Text of the New Testament: Its Transmission, Corruption, and Restoration,* 4th edition. New York, NY: Oxford University Press, 2005. (Note: For the sake of clarity, we should affirm that many of these are fragmentary, especially the papyri. Roughly 60 manuscripts contain the entire New Testament, of which Codex Sinaiticus is the only majuscule manuscript.)
9. *Revisiting the Corruption of the New Testament: Manuscript, Patristic, and Apocryphal Evidence (Text and Canon of the New Testament),* edited by Daniel B. Wallace. Grand Rapids, MI: Kregel Academic & Professional, 2011, pp. 28-29.

WHY DO WE TRUST THE BIBLE? INSPIRATION AND INTERNAL EVIDENCE
1. "Biblical Manuscripts." Houston Christian University. https://hc.edu/museums/dunham-bible-museum/tour-of-the-museum/past-exhibits/biblical-manuscripts/.
2. "Homer in Print: The Transmission and Reception of Homer's Works." The University of Chicago Library, 2014. https://www.lib.uchicago.edu/collex/exhibits/homer-print-transmission-and-reception-homers-works/homer-print/.
3. Barrett, Matthew. "The Authority and Inerrancy of Scripture." The Gospel Coalition. https://www.thegospelcoalition.org/essay/authority-inerrancy-scripture/.
4. Brower, Adam. "Can I be Convicted on Witness Testimony Alone?" Banks & Brower, April 5, 2024. https://banksbrower.com/2024/04/05/can-i-be-convicted-on-witness-testimony-alone/.

STEP INTO THE WORLD OF THE NEW TESTAMENT
1. Köstenberger, Andreas J., L. Scott Kellum, and Charles L. Quarles. *The Cradle, the Cross, and the Crown,* second edition. B&H Publishing Group, 2016, pp. 103-104.
2. "New Testament History," *Encyclopaedia Britannica.* https://www.britannica.com/topic/biblical-literature/New-Testament-history.
3. Kölawole, O. P. "An Exploration of Tools for Modern Critical Studies of the New Testament," *International Journal of Research in Humanities and Social Studies,* vol. 9, no. 1. 2022, pp. 23-35. https://doi.org/10.22259/2694-6296.0901004.
4. Chancey, Mark A. *Greco-Roman Culture and the Galilee of Jesus.* Cambridge, MA: Cambridge University Press, 2005.
5. Johnson, L. T. "The New Testament and History." Oxford Academic, 2013. https://doi.org/10.1093/actrade/9780199735709.003.0002.
6. "Historical Methodology and New Testament Study." The Gospel Coalition. https://www.thegospelcoalition.org/themelios/article/historical-methodology-and-new-testament-study/.
7. Chancey, Mark A. *Greco-Roman Culture and the Galilee of Jesus.* Cambridge, MA: Cambridge University Press, 2005.
8. "Historical Methodology and New Testament Study." The Gospel Coalition. https://www.thegospelcoalition.org/themelios/article/historical-methodology-and-new-testament-study/.

ENDNOTES

WHAT YOU HAVE TO LOOK FORWARD TO IN THIS STUDY
1. Bullinger, Ethelbert William. *Figures of Speech Used in the Bible.* London; New York: Eyre & Spottiswoode; E. & J. B. Young & Co., 1898, p. 944.

FOR FURTHER READING, SEE ALSO:
- "How Many Pages Are There in the Bible?" WordCounter, February 21, 2026. https://wordcounter.net/blog/2016/02/21/101241_how-many-pages-are-there-in-the-bible.html.
- Knopp, David. "Word Count and Reading Stats for the Old Testament." David Knopp Blog, January 6, 2015. https://www.davidknoppblog.com/reading-stats-for-the-old-testament/.
- "Facts About the Bible." *King James Bible Dictionary.* https://kingjamesbibledictionary.com/BibleFacts.
- Jenkins, Dan. "How Many Words in the English Bible?" Palm Beach Lakes Church of Christ, July 18, 2021. https://www.pblcoc.org/bulletin-articles/how-many-words-in-the-english-bible/.
- Dexter, Allison. "How Many Words are in the Bible?" WordCounter. https://wordcounter.io/blog/how-many-words-are-in-the-bible.

DIGGING DEEPER: THE ORIGIN AND RELIABILITY OF THE NEW TESTAMENT
1. Meade, John D. and Peter J. Gurry. *Scribes and Scripture: The Amazing Story of How We Got the Bible.* Wheaton, IL: Crossway, 2022, p. 153.
2. Meade, John D., and Peter J. Gurry. *Scribes and Scripture: The Amazing Story of How We Got the Bible.* Wheaton, IL: Crossway, 2022, p. 149.
3. Unger, Merrill Frederick et al. *The New Unger's Bible Dictionary.* Chicago, IL: Moody Press, 1988
4. Hagner, Donald A. *The New Testament: A Historical and Theological Introduction.* Grand Rapids, MI: Baker Academic, 2012, p. 803.
5. Burge, Gary M. and Gene L. Green. *The New Testament in Antiquity: A Survey of the New Testament within Its Cultural Contexts,* 2nd edition. Grand Rapids, MI: Zondervan Academic, 2020, pp. 578-579.
6. Augustine of Hippo. "On Christian Doctrine," *St. Augustine's City of God and Christian Doctrine (A Select Library of the Nicene and Post-Nicene Fathers of the Christian Church, First Series),* edited by Philip Schaff, translated by J.F. Shaw, vol. 2. Buffalo, NY: Christian Literature Company, 1887, p. 538.
7. Beyer, Hermann Wolfgang. *"Κανών," Theological Dictionary of the New Testament,* edited by Gerhard Kittel, Geoffrey W. Bromiley, and Gerhard Friedrich. Grand Rapids, MI: Eerdmans, 1964, p. 596.

NOTES

NOTES

NOTES

NOTES

NOTES

NOTES

PRAYER

Holy Spirit, teach my heart to live with eternity in mind. When I face trials of many kinds, help me to face them in a way that produces joy. When I experience injustice and betrayal, help me to hope in Your coming Kingdom. When I am tempted to find satisfaction in earthly things, remind me of the eternal promises to come. Jesus, You came once for Your people, and I am certain You will come again. Prepare my heart for that day. Lord, come quickly. In Jesus' name, amen.

WEEK 8
WEEKEND REFLECTION AND PRAYER

Have you ever heard somebody say, "It's about the journey, not the destination"? That may be true when you're on a road trip full of misadventure and quirky pit stops. But for the believer, the destination really does matter as much as how we get there. We aren't wandering aimlessly through life, soaking up whatever temporal beauty we can find along the way. We are pilgrims on a journey with our eyes fixed on a clear and certain destination. We are headed toward a reality in which all things will be made new.

Our world is desperate for renewal. Trends, products, or ideologies offer us a chance to "turn over a new leaf" and "have a clean slate." People even quit their jobs, leave their marriages, and move to new cities hoping *this* will be the thing that offers something different and fresh. But God's Word holds out a glorious vision of renewal in Christ Himself. With eyes fixed on this vision, we can endure the trials, pain, and even monotony of this life because in the new heavens and new earth, we will experience pure and unending life with God.

We will see His face.
There will be an end to all suffering and fear.
Death itself, which has been at work in us from the beginning, will finally and fully be crushed.

Not only will physical death end, but relational suffering will end as well. In a world where relationships deteriorate and our own souls turn on themselves in bitterness and selfishness, we have eternal hope. One day God will make it so that we relate to each other in a way motivated by love for Him and each other. We will be set free from all disturbing memories and horrific experiences. In some way we can't even imagine right now, we will look upon the trials of our lives and be able to say with confidence that they were light and momentary, given the glory of eternity (2 Corinthians 4:17).

So why is it so important that we are certain about our destination? Because when you know where you're headed, it changes how you live today.

Let your faith be renewed as you lift your eyes toward eternity. May the glory of that day shine on you and light your way until you arrive safely home.

IMPERISHABLE

1 Corinthians 15:42 says *"what is raised is imperishable"* (ESV). Theologian Wayne Grudem writes: "The fact that our new bodies will be 'imperishable' means that they will never grow old or ever be subject to any kind of sickness or disease. They will be completely healthy and strong forever."[2]

SPIRITUAL

1 Corinthians 15:44 says we will be *"raised a spiritual body."* The word *pneumatikos*, translated as "spiritual," does not imply "nonphysical" but rather "consistent with the character and activity of the Holy Spirit." Our resurrected bodies *will* be physical, just like Jesus' resurrected body when He appeared to His disciples; He ate food with them (Luke 24:41-43; John 21:12-14) and invited them to touch His hands (Luke 24:39). But our bodies will also be completely spiritually aligned with and submitted to the will of God.

RECOGNIZABLE

Several scriptures suggest we will recognize one another in the new heavens and new earth, like Jesus' disciples recognized Moses and Elijah on the mount of Transfiguration in Matthew 17:1-3. Most notably, our bodies are likened to that of Jesus after His resurrection: *"We will be like him because we will see him as he is"* (1 John 3:2). We know from the Gospels that while Jesus' glorified body was not immediately recognized by all His disciples, there was enough continuity that recognition came quickly (Luke 24:30-31).

THE RESURRECTED BODY

A lot of mystery surrounds the exact nature of our resurrected bodies. How old will we be in eternity? Will our bodies be recognizable? Will we have superhuman strength? There's a lot we won't know until we're actually in Jesus' presence, but Scripture does speak to a lot of our questions about the resurrected body.

Based off of the New Testament, we know our bodies will be:

GLORIFIED

Our bodies will be *"raised in glory"* (1 Corinthians 15:43). This term *"glory"* is associated with the radiance surrounding the presence of God (Isaiah 60:1-2), so scriptures like this one imply that the glorified human body may even shine or have some kind of brightness around it.

POWERFUL

Right now, our bodies are characterized by weakness, but one day our bodies will be *"raised in power"* (1 Corinthians 15:43). This does not necessarily mean we will have super strength or other abilities, but it does mean we will have "strength sufficient to do all that we desire to do in conformity to the will of God."[1]

Just as today's key verses assure us that we *"will rise ... and so we will always be with the Lord"* (1 Thessalonians 4:16-17), Romans 6:5 assures us that if we are united to Christ in His death, we will be united to Him in His resurrection. In part, we experience this reality the moment we place our trust in Him and our hearts go from dead to alive. But we will experience the *fullness* of this union when Christ returns and we physically rise from the dead. Resurrection hope is the reason why believers can face even death without fear.

> For you personally, how does the hope of resurrection help combat the fear of death?

In 1 Thessalonians 4:16-17, we read that we will *"meet the Lord."* This description draws heavily on ancient imagery of a dignitary approaching a city, with the city's inhabitants rushing outside the city's walls to greet him and walk alongside him as he enters the gates.[1] There are many differing views about what our meeting with Jesus in the clouds will actually look like, but one thing we do know is that Jesus came for His people once, and He will come for us again.

Verse 17 also promises we *"will be caught up"* by our Savior, using a Greek verb that means "to seize or take for oneself." Jesus will never let go or lose His grip on anyone who belongs to Him. God will be our God, and we will be His people.

> Read Matthew 24:42-44. What does it mean to *"be alert"* as you wait for the second coming of Christ?

> Where in your life do you need reminding that Jesus will never let go of you?

This world is not our home. For now, we all live with a sort of homesickness because we have been created to spend eternity with God. Every human spends their life searching for the answer to one question: Why are we alive? Or in other words: *What is the chief end of man?* This is the first question in the Westminster Catechism, a summary of biblical doctrine in question-and-answer form, created in the 1640s to help teach the Christian faith.

The world has countless answers to this question, but God's Word provides us with the Truth: *We live to glorify God and enjoy Him forever.*[2]

DAY 40

1 THESSALONIANS 4:16-17

PAUL WROTE THAT THE DEAD IN CHRIST WILL RISE FIRST AND THAT LIVING BELIEVERS WILL MEET THE LORD IN THE AIR.

In today's reading, Paul described the day all of our hearts long for — the day when Christ returns as the ultimate victor over sin and death. According to 1 Thessalonians 4:16, His entrance will be triumphant, marked by a chorus of shouts, angelic voices, and trumpets. While His return will be unexpected, it will not be unnoticed.

This moment will be the culmination of where God has been leading us all along, as Jesus will fully usher in His eternal Kingdom so we can experience His glory and friendship forever. On that day, *"the dead in Christ will rise first,"* and believers *"who are still alive ... will be caught up together with them in the clouds to meet the Lord in the air"* (1 Thessalonians 4:16-17).

> In what ways do you long for this day when Jesus returns? How does it encourage you to know that Jesus will show up for us in a way we can't possibly miss?

In 1 Corinthians 15:20, Paul described how *"Christ has been raised from the dead, the firstfruits of those who have fallen asleep."* This term *"firstfruits"* is agricultural: When a tree bears its first fruit, it is evidence that the tree is productive and that a harvest is coming. The resurrection of Christ is evidence that while the full fruit of His Kingdom has not yet been revealed, we, too, will one day rise from the dead.

> In what ways does the concept of "firstfruits" give you confidence in your own future resurrection?

Read Revelation 21. In what ways do these descriptions of the new heavens and new earth excite you?

The new heavens and new earth has implications for our physical bodies as well. When God created us in His image, He created us as embodied creatures. God's design for human embodiment continues on into eternity: At Christ's return, we will physically rise from the dead, and Christ will transform our bodies into a glorified state (Romans 6:5; 1 John 3:2). All of this is a part of our inheritance, promised to us and secured by Christ.

Revelation 22:5 even says we will *"reign forever and ever."* We will have a job in eternity! God's original design in Genesis 1:27-28 was for people to exercise dominion over creation and to rule with righteousness and honor. Sin now compromises our ability to fulfill this calling, but in the new heavens and new earth, *"where righteousness dwells"* (2 Peter 3:13), we will reign over the earth under the Kingship of Jesus and in line with His great purposes.

Is the idea of reigning with Christ forever a new concept for you? How is this idea *"based on his promise,"* as 2 Peter 3:13 says? Consider God's promises in the following scriptures:

- Hebrews 12:28:

- Matthew 5:19:

- 2 Timothy 2:12:

Beyond the beauty of the redeemed physical world we will live in, we will be fully in the presence of God and will worship Him forever. We get small glimpses of this coming day when we gather as God's people to worship Him now, but in the new heavens and new earth, the joy of worship "will be multiplied many times over and we will know the fulfillment of that which we were created for."[1]

Reflect back on Revelation 21. What words or phrases stick out to you about how we will relate to God in eternity?

DAY 39

2 PETER 3:13

PETER SAID BELIEVERS ARE WAITING FOR NEW HEAVENS AND A NEW EARTH.

If you were to ask a random person on the street what they think heaven will be like, they would likely paint a picture of ethereal spirits floating around in white clothes — and maybe a cloud here and there. An angel with a harp, perhaps?

If that image of eternity feels lackluster or not particularly exciting, that's because it falls woefully flat in comparison to what God's Word actually says about our future reality. For example, today's key verse describes our eternal dwelling place not just as "heaven" but as *"new heavens and a new earth"* (2 Peter 3:13). This is not only a **spiritual** reality but a **physical** reality we can look forward to.

Romans 8:19-22 also describes how all of creation (the earth) is currently waiting for the day when it will be freed from the *"bondage to decay"* and be eternally transformed. We will live forever in a physical new heavens and new earth, a place with mountains, buildings, streets we will walk on, and even food we will eat with our redeemed bodies (Revelation 21:9-27; Revelation 19:9).

> Have you thought about eternity as a physical reality before? What feelings does that evoke, or how is it different from the way you've imagined heaven in the past?

Our future dwelling place will be one of abundance, joy, and beauty. Revelation 21-22 describes the city of God as having streets of clear gold and a river running through it. There will be no sun and no need for lamp posts, for the glory of the Lord will be all the light we need. All of this illustrates a physical place God is preparing for us (John 14:2-3).

Read Matthew 6:19-21. What does it look like for you to anchor your hope and treasure in eternity?

1 Peter 1:3-5 describes our inheritance as imperishable, undefiled, and unfading. Which of those three attributes most excites you?

Perhaps the best news is that our inheritance in Christ is different from earthly inheritances that can be squandered or even taken away based on relational breakdown, like falling out of favor with our parents. Since God's Word explains that every believer will bear the fruit of repentance and obedience during their lives, we know believers will never squander away God's riches (Romans 6:22; Philippians 1:6). It's as good as impossible. If you are truly in Christ, there is nothing you can do to lose this gift from God.

True faith always bears fruit in a holy life — so we can't just live however we want. At the same time, believers can be certain that our eternal inheritance is already being secured by God's power and will be ready for us to receive when Christ returns.

How do we navigate this harsh reality? We remember that our living hope in the Kingdom of God is not like that! 1 Peter 1:3 grounds our hope in *"the resurrection of Jesus Christ."* Through Christ's defeat of death, He has secured for us an **imperishable** future in which death is finally and fully crushed.

> What does Romans 6:9 say about the possibility that Jesus will *"die again"*? How does this guarantee an imperishable inheritance in Him?

Not only is our inheritance imperishable, but it's **undefiled** — untouched by sin. We now live in a world where sin mars everything both in us and around us. Even when we do good, our motives are mixed (Proverbs 16:2; Matthew 6:1), and we have to wage spiritual war against sin every day (Ephesians 6:12). But where we are headed, this war will end in our victory through Christ. We can anticipate a glorious eternity where "every woman sleeps safely, every man is honorable, and every child is cherished."[3] Sin and its effects will no longer be the mode through which the world operates.

> Even today, in a world full of sin, how can you actively reflect the purity and holiness of your future eternal reality?

Lastly, our inheritance is **unfading**. Everything in our current world fades. Our bodies, once youthful and resilient, wear out with age. Gifts that were once shiny and new end up in the thrift shop. But our heavenly inheritance will never decay. Eternal life with God will never grow less sweet over time. In fact, 1 Peter 1:5 says salvation will be *"revealed in the last time"* — the day Jesus returns — and then in heaven, our time with Him will never end. Our trillionth day with Jesus will be every bit as wonderful as the first moment we meet Him face to face.

DAY 38

1 PETER 1:3-5

PETER PRAISED GOD FOR GIVING BELIEVERS NEW BIRTH INTO
A LIVING HOPE KEPT IN HEAVEN FOR US.

Usually an inheritance is based on two things: 1) death and 2) relationship. A person designates heirs to receive their earthly assets after they die, and they make those choices based on the relationships they have while they're still alive. An heir is usually not a stranger — it's someone we know and love.

Today's key verses remind us this is also true in God's Kingdom: Because Jesus died on the cross out of love for us, we have an inheritance in heaven that includes eternal life with God and all the blessings that come with salvation. This reality is so great that it seems the Apostle Peter found it hard to fully define what it is — instead, he contrasted what it's not.[1] Our inheritance is *"**imperishable**, **undefiled**, and **unfading**"* (1 Peter 1:4, emphases added).

1 Peter 1:3 also says we have *"a living hope"* because we are heading toward an inheritance that cannot be destroyed. This can be hard for us to comprehend — because everything we see around us on earth right now will someday die, break down, wear out, or be used up.

> Take a moment to sit with your present circumstances. What in your life could be characterized as perishing, defiled, or fading?

It can seem discouraging to think about, but in order for the hope and glory of eternity to take root in our hearts, it's actually helpful to contrast it with the darkness of our present day. From the moment we are born, we begin a daily trek toward our final breath. We plant gardens in the summer, yet without fail, the cold and dark of winter ushers in death once more. As theologian Ray Ortlund puts it, "Death watches us, stalks us, takes aim, and shoots straight."[2]

Our trials are doing something good. God has promised life and enjoyment with Him forever when we have *"stood the test"* (James 1:12). Today we may be in the middle of the testing, but the ultimate goal for those who trust in Jesus is not freedom from pain and suffering in this life — it's the crown of life with our Savior and King in eternity.

One day, not only will *your* trials cease, but *all* trials will cease when Christ returns and makes everything new.

Why do you think it's significant that James and Paul both say we will be **crowned** in God's eternal Kingdom? Consider what it means for someone to wear a crown (as opposed to, for example, a really nice hat). What does it indicate about their status, authority, power, and identity?

The wisdom of the world says that to win at life, we must make an impact, leave a legacy, or build a life of comfort and meaning. The wisdom of God says that to win at life, we endure trials and suffering as people who love Him. This instills all of us believers with profound hope. **Our trials are not keeping us from experiencing life with God.** The very trials we are experiencing today will one day be exchanged for a crown of glory from the King of the universe.

What specific trials are you enduring right now that will one day be exchanged for a crown of glory? How does this future crowning reframe the way you experience your trials?

Just a few verses earlier in James, we are instructed to consider it joy when we face trials of many kinds (James 1:2). Our trials aren't just pain to endure but a conduit through which we ultimately experience joy in God. Theologian Dallas Willard describes joy as a "pervasive sense of well-being infused with hope and rooted in the goodness of God."[1] We can experience this joy *even in trials* because we know Jesus is good and faithful until the end, and a crown is coming.

How does James' teaching on trials shift your perspective toward joy today?

DAY 37

JAMES 1:12

JAMES WROTE THAT BELIEVERS WHO ENDURE WILL RECEIVE THE CROWN OF LIFE.

The New Testament describes the Kingdom of God in a way that runs counterintuitive to human wisdom. Perhaps most notably, Jesus' Sermon on the Mount paints a picture of a Kingdom where the persecuted, reviled, and poor in spirit inherit blessings and an eternal reward. In God's economy, flourishing is not found through human strength, status, or achievement but through weakness, humility, and dependence on Him.

> Read Matthew 5:3-11 (part of the Sermon on the Mount). How does Jesus' definition of blessing differ from what the world would say?

In today's key verse, James — who was actually Jesus' earthly brother as well as His eventual disciple and apostle (Mark 6:3; Galatians 1:19; 1 Corinthians 15:4-7) — picked up on this counterintuitive language. In James 1:12, he described the blessing that awaits the person who endures trials: *"Because when he has stood the test he will receive the crown of life that God has promised to those who love him."*

This is the same crown Paul referred to in 1 Corinthians 9:25 when he spoke of athletes receiving a *"perishable"* wreath after finishing a race, whereas believers receive the reward of an *"imperishable crown"* when our race of life is done. We who endure and keep running in faith, even under the weight of trials, will receive life with God forever in perfect joy and holiness.

This is where God is leading us — an eternal home where there will be resolution for all conflict, comfort for all afflictions, and healing for all brokenness. When we know where we're going, it changes how we live our lives today. This vision of eternity in Revelation 21:4 allows us to endure suffering, injustice, and pain with a hope-filled confidence that one day the curse of sin really *will* be reversed and we *will* live in the presence and comfort of God forever.

> How does knowing where you are headed change how you endure suffering, disappointment, and loss today?

Since the fall of humanity in Genesis 3, all of us live under the curse of sin and its penalties, including death. Our bodies break down, and we feel the effects of the curse deep in our bones. We witness tragedy firsthand, hear tales of atrocity afar, and are keenly aware that we live in a world where death always seems to win.

The Old Testament prophet Isaiah once described this curse as a shroud that enfolds all people, yet he also promised that one day the sovereign Lord *"will swallow up the burial shroud"* forever (Isaiah 25:7). This is a promise Jesus kept on the cross (1 Corinthians 15:54), and it will also be **completely** fulfilled in eternity when *"death will be no more"* (Revelation 21:4). Not only will death be no more, but the *effects* of death will be no more. Mourning. Crying. Pain. All of it will be gone forever when Christ returns and the curse is finally and fully reversed.

> Read Isaiah 25:6-8. How did Isaiah describe sin and death? Yet how do these verses also give you hope for your specific pain and sorrow?

Finally, there is another interesting nuance to how the Bible describes eternity. It's not that we will look back on the pain and suffering of our earthly lives and won't feel sad about it anymore — it seems we won't remember it. We won't even think about remembering it (Isaiah 65:17).

> Read and reflect on 2 Corinthians 4:17-18. How does this relate to Revelation 21:4?

> Where else in Scripture do you see the promise of death's defeat?

DAY 36

REVELATION 21:4

JOHN WROTE THAT GOD WILL WIPE AWAY EVERY TEAR.

When was the last time you cried? Has it been a few years? A few minutes? Either way, we've all been brought to tears by the brokenness of this world. In fact, most people reportedly cry about three times a month — it's hard to make it through even a couple weeks without sorrow.

A reality without any death, pain, or tears may seem impossible. It's hard to even imagine. Yet that is exactly what today's key verse promises to us as believers in Jesus. Not only will these *"previous things"* pass away in eternity (Revelation 21:4), but they won't even be remembered or come to mind.

This verse comes from Revelation, which is a book of prophecy about God's plan for eternity and gives us a glimpse into the place God is preparing for His people: a place where all death, pain, and sadness will be no more. In the phrase *"He will wipe away every tear"* (Revelation 21:4), the verb *"wipe away"* comes from the Greek word *exaleipho*, which also means "to erase or smear away." This same word is used in Revelation 3:5 — where God promises never to *"erase"* the names of His people from the *"book of life"* — as well as in Colossians 2:14, which says Jesus has *"erased the certificate of debt"* we owed because of our sin.

As certainly as God erases our record of sin and secures our eternal salvation in Christ, He will one day wipe away every tear from our eyes. In Christ, our eternal comfort is secured.

> How can you rest in the surety of God's comfort today (knowing that He promises even more comfort in the future)?

WEEK 8
SURE OF WHERE WE'RE GOING

ELLEN ADKINS

NOTES

NOTES

Codex Sinaiticus (A.D. 400)
MANUSCRIPTS OF THE NEW TESTAMENT

In addition to Old Testament manuscripts, the Codex Sinaiticus is a powerful witness to the reliability of the New Testament. Again, while we have many older *fragments* of scrolls, this document contains the oldest *complete copy* of the New Testament known to exist. Found in the Sinai Peninsula, it is now preserved in the British Library.[10] Codex Sinaiticus provides a crucial link between our modern New Testament translations and the original writings.

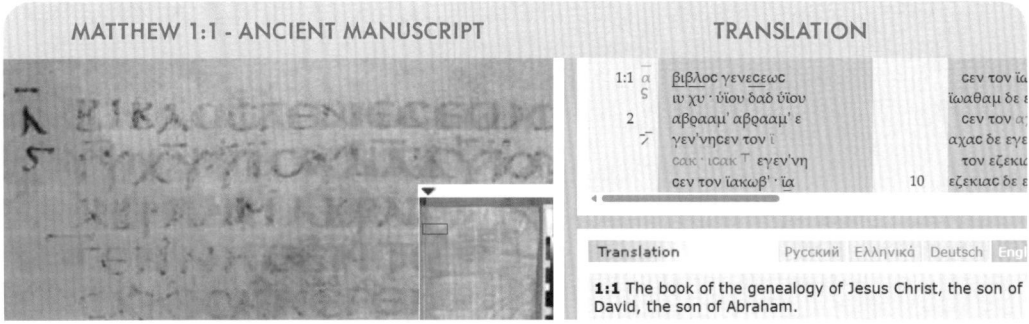

Here is a scan of one of these ancient scrolls of Matthew 1:1. This is over 1600 years old! See if you can see the first word for "book" — βίβλος or biblos *(the foundation for our word "Bible").*

The Dead Sea Scrolls, the Leningrad Codex, and Codex Sinaiticus are only three of thousands of ancient manuscripts that demonstrate consistent transmission of the biblical text over thousands of years. Despite the challenges of hand-copying texts and potential scribal errors, these discoveries confirm that God Himself has preserved the core message of His Scriptures with remarkable fidelity. For Christians and scholars alike, this wealth of manuscript evidence strengthens confidence in the Bible's reliability and trustworthiness.

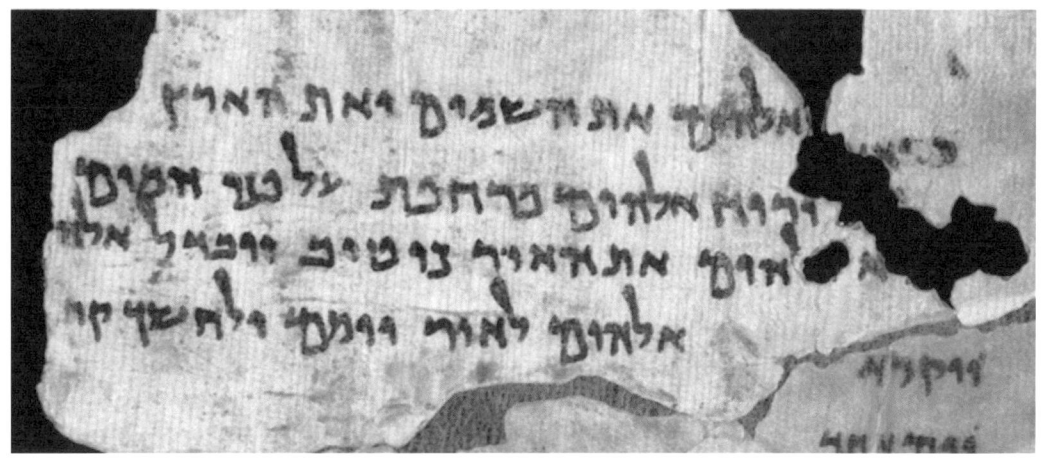

Early copies of scrolls and fragments like this one of Genesis 1:1-5 (catalogued as "Plate 275/1, Frag 1 B-295662," dated around 100 B.C.) demonstrate that core teachings central to Christianity have remained intact across millennia.[5]

The Leningrad Codex (A.D. 1010)
MANUSCRIPTS OF THE OLD TESTAMENT

The Dead Sea Scrolls provided a significant point of comparison for other ancient manuscripts, such as the Leningrad Codex. "Codex" is an old word for "book," and this text is part of a collection at the Russian National Library in St. Petersburg (formerly Leningrad), where it has been for more than 130 years.[6] While there are many older *partial* copies of Scripture, the Leningrad Codex is the oldest *complete manuscript* of the Hebrew Bible.[7] It follows the Masoretic Text, a tradition of meticulously copied Hebrew Scriptures developed by the Masoretes. These scribes introduced a system of vowel markings, punctuation, and accent notes to safeguard the text's meaning and proper recitation, ensuring Hebrew pronunciation would not be lost. The Leningrad Codex reflects this precise system and has become the text used for modern Hebrew translations.[8]

The Dead Sea Scrolls (despite being over a thousand years older!) are strikingly consistent with both the Leningrad Codex and the Masoretic Text, confirming that the Scriptures were transmitted with remarkable care.[9]

THE OLDEST COPIES OF ANCIENT SCRIPTURE IN EXISTENCE TODAY

The preservation of ancient biblical manuscripts plays a crucial role in affirming the reliability of the Bible as we have it today. Through discoveries such as the **Dead Sea Scrolls** and the **Leningrad Codex**, as well as key texts like **Codex Sinaiticus**, we have access to ancient copies of both the Old and New Testament that demonstrate the faithful transmission of Scripture through the centuries.

Below is a photo of the entrance of Qumran Cave 11, where part of the Dead Sea Scrolls were found. Photo by Alexander Schick.[1]

Dead Sea Scrolls (300 B.C.)
MANUSCRIPTS OF THE OLD TESTAMENT

One of the most significant finds in biblical archaeology is the Dead Sea Scrolls. From 1947-1956, Bedouin treasure hunters and archaeologists uncovered thousands of fragments of biblical and early Jewish documents in caves near Khirbet Qumran by the Dead Sea.[2] These scrolls date from the third century B.C. to the first century A.D. and include fragments from every book of the Hebrew Bible except Esther.[3] Many of these texts closely resemble the Masoretic Text, another collection of Hebrew manuscripts that is the basis for the Old Testament in our modern Bibles.[4] This remarkable alignment highlights the extraordinary accuracy with which the Scriptures were copied and preserved over a multitude of years. Before our very eyes, we see proof that the prophecies of Jesus, which all came true, were written hundreds of years before He was ever born.

PRAYER

Heavenly Father, You have already given us so much to enjoy here on earth. Thank You for the additional hope of the blessings we will experience in heaven. Please help us to think on these things more than we already do. Help us to be bold and share our faith. Help us to provoke or stir up one another with kindness. Forgive us our sin, and protect us from all evil. In Jesus' name, amen.

WEEK 7

WEEKEND REFLECTION AND PRAYER

While it's possible to "be so heavenly minded that we're of no earthly good" — a saying you may have heard before — it's also possible to be so earthly minded that we lose our heavenly hope. It does our souls good to think about heaven. So these have been hope-filled study days.

Out of thankfulness for the grace we have received in Christ, believers around the globe, by the power of the Holy Spirit who dwells in us, are doing our best to walk in the truth (3 John 4). We long to walk with God like Adam and Eve did in the garden before sin entered the world, without the knowledge of evil and with pure hearts and minds. And one day that longing will be fulfilled. In eternity, we will know every good thing (Philemon 6), which means knowing God Himself as fully as possible.

God will not only reward us with eternal life, but He also promises to reward us uniquely and personally, above and beyond eternal life, for every little battle won here on earth (2 John 8). We will meet together to celebrate at a gathering more fun than the best football game we've ever been to (Hebrews 10:24-25)! And like newborn babies, we will be presented to our Father God, who sees us as holy because of the love of Jesus (Jude 24-25). We will never entertain another intrusive sinful thought or perform another sinful action, and we will trust every one of our brothers and sisters in Christ because we will all be remade. We will have no reason to doubt God or His people.

It was possible for Adam and Eve to sin in Eden. Our experience in heaven will be even better because it will be *impossible for anyone to do evil ever again*. We will freely do good and enjoy God and His wisdom forever. As surely as God has kept our heart beating until this moment, we can be sure that He is leading us to this blessed future.

This verse is so similar to other scriptures that some scholars think it was a first-century liturgy, or a common saying used to bless church members. Look at Ephesians 1:4, Ephesians 5:27, Colossians 1:22, and 1 Thessalonians 3:13. Why do you think it's important that God presenting us blameless is a consistent idea across the New Testament?

If anyone stands before God *"without blemish,"* it is because God Himself *"is able to protect"* and *"make [us] stand"* in that moment (Jude 24). The ESV translation says He will *"present [us] blameless."*

As an analogy, consider a new mom who has just delivered a baby. The baby passes through blood and other bodily fluids, and then comes a most special moment: The baby is presented to the mother. To her, the baby is perfect in every way.

One day, unless Jesus returns first, all of us will die — but through faith, we are *"born again"* (John 3:3). Those who have turned from a life of sin and trusted in Christ's goodness alone for salvation will stand before the throne of God. At that point, we will have passed through the sinfulness of this world, passed through the waters of baptism if we've been baptized, and spiritually passed through the blood of Jesus, which covers us. This is the only way we can stand before God's holy presence and live forever.

> Not only will we live, but what else does Jude 24 say about the emotions we will experience in eternity? (What will be *"great"*?)

Let this promise encourage you: **The God who protects you today is also the One who will fill you with joy in His presence forever.**

Look up Exodus 33:20, John 1:18, and 1 Timothy 6:16. What do these verses teach us about God?

Now look up Hebrews 1:3, Colossians 1:15, and John 12:44-45. Who reveals God to us?

Outside of Jesus, God is invisible. In the Old Testament, He gave prophets great dreams or visions of His glory (Isaiah 6:1-4). God also manifested His presence with fire and cloud (Exodus 13:21), through angels (Genesis 16:7; Genesis 22:11), or in appearances like a figure passing by Moses (Exodus 33:18-20). But Jesus has taught us that when we get to heaven — when we *"stand in the presence of his glory"* (Jude 24) — the face we will be looking at is Jesus' face.

This is how the invisible God has made Himself visible to us. Jesus is His exact image! Christ rose from the dead with a glorious eternal body, and He sits on the throne of God today. God has no other face or hands or body than the body of Jesus.

The question is: How can *we* possibly stand before that throne and *approach* God's otherwise unapproachable light?

We're told how in Jude 24. Look at the verbs — what does God promise to do?

DAY 35

JUDE 24-25

JUDE PRAISED THE GOD WHO IS ABLE TO PRESENT US
BLAMELESS IN HIS GLORIOUS PRESENCE.

A sporting event with your favorite team or a concert in a stadium filled with thousands of people can be an exciting experience. The ones we came to see make us gasp, cheer, sing, clap, and stomp our feet in unison.

This happy sound of so many people coming together is a small glimpse of the celebrations believers will experience in heaven. Jude 24-25 is an eschatological passage that directs our attention to this reality. The word "eschatology" is a big word that comes from Greek and just means the study of "last things" or "end times" — in other words, when the world as we know it will end.

> Before we continue today's lesson, carefully read the key verses and write down your observations here. What stands out to you? What encourages or convicts you or raises a question in your mind?

While there is so much we could focus on in Jude 24-25, let's explore the idea of *"stand[ing] in the presence of his glory."* Here is a quote from Bible scholar Peter H. Davids regarding this verse:

> "Naturally, the hope of standing before God is the eschatological hope of the followers of Jesus. Moses could not see God's glory and live (Exod 33:18–23), but followers of Jesus are destined to stand in his very presence. They will stand there unblemished because they have kept themselves and God has kept them. And they will stand there in public celebration. The picture is that of a festival in the presence of God, a sea of people singing, praising, and dancing in joyous celebration in the very presence of the God they had served on earth."[1]

Robert Jamieson says, "The assembling or gathering of ourselves for Christian communion in private and public, is an earnest [a deposit] of our being gathered together to Him at His appearing."[3] In other words, the church gathering is a kind of down payment, like we might place when buying a home. How can we buy a home without showing some proof we can afford it? Similarly, how can we look forward to gathering with all Christians in heaven if we aren't gathering in churches now?

Again, there are certainly some exceptions, but it's still wise to reflect and ask ourselves if we are making our best efforts to gather — *episunagoge* — as a regular "*habit*" of worshipping and serving together (v. 25). For every one who can't gather, there are more who can. When we neglect to gather, not only do we miss out on others, but others miss out on us!

> The end of Hebrews 10:25 reminds us to love and encourage each other with increasing intensity — *"all the more"* every day. What do you think this has to do with gathering together and awaiting Jesus' return?

The great Day is surely coming. Guthrie observes, "The possible imminence of the day still supplies a powerful motivation towards high moral standards for many believers."[4] Until Christ returns, may we gather faithfully, speak the truth in love, and think of more ways we can do good in this broken world. God is coming, God sees, and nothing we do will be lost or wasted.

What is one way you could do this for someone else (as opposed to being spiritually passive, disengaging from community, or having a "let it go" attitude toward sin)?

With spurring in mind, we can think of the rest of this teaching as an example of *paroxusmos*. The author of Hebrews reminds us that the great Day of the Lord is coming. If the Day was "*approaching*" when this was originally written, it is now nearer than ever. So what does this have to do with *"not neglecting to gather together"* (v. 25)? Let's look.

At least four times, Hebrews 10:24-25 uses words that make it clear the Christian life is not to be lived alone. Can you find them? (Hint: Look for the *opposite* of words like "me," "my," and "alone.")

At the time Hebrews was written, churches did gather in homes, but the most well-known, regular gathering place of worship for Jewish Christians was the synagogue. When the author of Hebrews said to "*gather*" in verse 25, he even used the verb *episunagoge* (see a form of the word "synagogue" in there?). Donald Guthrie writes that this suggests "official assembly."[2] The author of Hebrews was spurring fellow believers not just to get together with some Christian friends during the week but also to participate in the main gathering of all believers in their community. It's a gentle nudge many of us could use today too.

While there are special circumstances where a Christian cannot attend a local church, this is usually the exception to the rule. Most followers of Jesus around the globe are able to attend some form of a weekly church gathering. How do we know? Because God's Word says *"not neglecting to gather together"* (v. 25), and God doesn't ask us to do anything without giving us power to obey.

DAY 34

HEBREWS 10:24-25

THE AUTHOR OF HEBREWS URGED BELIEVERS TO ENCOURAGE
ONE ANOTHER AS THE GREAT DAY APPROACHES.

Horse riding today is much more humane than in ages past. To get a horse to run, modern riders often use techniques like squeezing the horse with their legs or giving vocal cues. While some riders may give a gentle kick, even this is very different from the cowboy in the 1800s digging his boots' spurs into a horse's side. Still, one might argue that a motivating kick may sometimes be needed — if the horse is refusing to run.

In today's key verses, we find motivation of our own *"as [we] see the day approaching"* (Hebrews 10:25). In other words, we are all about to meet our Maker. As believers, this motivates us *"to provoke love and good works"* (v. 24) — and the word translated into English as *"provoke"* even gives us a picture of spurs.

For some simple proof of this, in your own Bible, look up Acts 15:39. If you have access to a resource like stepbible.org, look up Acts 15:39 and click on the words *"sharp disagreement."* You'll see it is translated from one Greek word: *paroxusmos*. This is the same word for *"provoke"* in our key verse today!

Bible scholar Marvin Richardson Vincent writes that this word in Hebrews 10:24 is also related to incitement, stirring up, or irritation. In Greek translations of the Old Testament, it often means contention, anger, wrath, and altercation.[1] The Bible is clear that we are to be kind, gentle, and gracious rather than angry people (James 1:20). But it's also clear in Hebrews 10:24-25 that we're called to be *provocative* in our encouragement of one another!

> How have you benefited from others provoking or stirring up love and good works in your life?

Heaven will be much better than anything we can imagine. In fact, taking time to try to imagine it can show us where our imagination ends and the blessings of heaven begin. *"For God is not unjust; he will not forget your work and the love you demonstrated for his name by serving the saints—and by continuing to serve them"* (Hebrews 6:10).

For further study, consider looking up these passages and taking some notes below:

- Luke 19:11-27 illustrates greater authority for those who prove faithful.

- Matthew 5:12 describes a heavenly reward that is "*great*," suggesting a scale.

- Matthew 25:14-30, Jesus' parable of the talents, demonstrates varying degrees of rewards.

- Daniel 12:2-3 portrays degrees of glory, especially for those who lead many others to God.

To be clear, the fire in these scriptures doesn't mean some Christians go to hell for eternity (or hell first and then heaven later). But these passages do warn that sin has real consequences for everyone, including Christians. There is *"no condemnation for those in Christ"* (Romans 8:1), but it seems ongoing sin can cause believers to lose rewards of some kind. *"For we must all appear before the judgment seat of Christ, so that each may be repaid for what he has done in the body, whether good or evil"* (2 Corinthians 5:10).

As such, we're wise to diligently guard our hearts and conduct — or as John wrote, *"Watch yourselves"* (2 John 8).

We can really only speculate about individual rewards we might receive in heaven, as Scripture does not explicitly state what these will be. But God has told us everything we *need* to know. And while our primary motivation to do good is simple thankfulness for the grace we have received in Christ, God obviously desires to motivate us by including promises of rewards in His Scriptures!

> What rewards (unearned gifts of grace) are you currently asking God for even here on earth? It could be a bold prayer — or one you've given up praying for.

> What rewards (unearned gifts of grace) do you pray God will grant you in heaven someday?

While we may all share rewards in heaven, it seems there will be personal gifts also. Considering what a *"full reward"* (2 John 8) would mean for *you* can be an inspiration for carefully watching your life this week and doing good to all. This may be as simple as thinking about something you'd enjoy, like vacationing with family, finally learning that instrument, journeying somewhere beautiful, or taking a walk with Jesus ...

Imagine your kids participate in a running club. At the end of every race, each runner receives a medal for finishing. Unlike a paycheck, the medal isn't a **payment** — it's a **reward** for participation. On top of that, you might take your kids out for ice cream as an additional reward for their effort, but this wouldn't be an obligation, and no one would have grounds to complain if you just went home. The ice cream would still be based on their effort, yet it wouldn't be owed. Further, if one son won first place and you gave him extra rewards, like a family trip to the trampoline park, his sisters might also benefit from his win. These layers of rewards illustrate a key biblical truth: **Some rewards are shared, some are personal and particular, and none are payments owed.**

Heaven is similar. All Christ followers are to "*run in such a way to win the prize*" (1 Corinthians 9:24), but Jesus is the only first-place winner. Eternal life is like our "medal," a reward graciously given to all who trust in Christ. Without Jesus' victory, no one would receive eternal life. Yet there will also be additional rewards — some shared and some personal — for those who faithfully obey Him.

> Read Matthew 20:1-16, where Jesus illustrated God's generosity in a parable about workers in a vineyard who all received the same wage despite different efforts. What did the master of the house say about his generosity in verses 15-16?

Scripture also reveals varying eternal rewards in 1 Corinthians 3:13-15, where Paul wrote that believers build on the foundation of Jesus Christ: "*Each one's work will become obvious. For the day will disclose it, because it will be revealed by fire; the fire will test the quality of each one's work. If anyone's work that he has built survives, he will receive a reward. If anyone's work is burned up …*"

> Read the rest of verse 15 to find out what God says about Christians whose works are "*burned up*." Will they still be saved and receive eternal life? What do you think this means?

DAY 33

2 JOHN 8

JOHN WARNED BELIEVERS TO WATCH OURSELVES SO WE CAN RECEIVE A FULL REWARD.

When we finish a job, we naturally expect payment for our work. Sometimes we also mistakenly apply this thinking to eternal life, believing good behavior earns salvation; however, Scripture teaches that eternal life is *given* by grace through faith in Jesus. As we've seen throughout our Bible study, no human goodness can earn salvation.

With this in mind, read 2 John 8 slowly a few times. Note your observations about what this verse calls us to do. What are we promised if we do it? In particular, what kind of reward will we receive?

Now write Ephesians 2:8-9 below. (Even if you know this passage well, writing it out helps us meditate on the meaning and memorize the scriptures!)

Ephesians 2:8 makes it clear that eternal life is not a payment for our good works — yet verses like 2 John 8 speak of a "*full reward*" for "*what we have worked for*." To understand this, let's first distinguish between a **payment** and a **reward**.

According to the Bible, a complete knowledge of everything good for us is both *fueled by* and *beneficial to* a loving community. If we think of it like a sandwich, fully *"knowing every good thing"* in Christ is like the meat or filling, and community is the bread (Philemon 6).

> In what ways have you gained a deeper knowledge of God through your church or Christian community? How has *"knowing every good thing"* made you effective in *doing good*?

As we study Scripture, one thing becomes clear: God has revealed His Truth to us as believers, but our current knowledge is still far from complete or full. Actually, the more we know, the more we see that we have more to learn. Yet as we discussed in yesterday's study of *"walking in truth"* (3 John 4), full knowledge is also part of the bull's-eye we aim for as we follow Christ — and one day, these prayers of ours will be fully answered.

We will never be omniscient, or all-knowing, but we can be sure God is leading us toward *"knowing every good thing that is in us"* (Philemon 6). And let's consider: **God Himself is the good in us!** So we will know God as fully as we possibly can!

> What does 1 Corinthians 13:12 teach us about knowing and being known by God?

As for today's key verse, if you have access to multiple versions of the Bible, try comparing multiple translations or paraphrases of Philemon 6. Pay special attention to what it says about **knowledge** or **understanding**. Jot down your observations here:

While the translations are diverse, we can see some shared patterns. Scholars point out that in Greek, Paul used a compound form of the word for *"full knowledge"* (ESV), *"understanding"* (NIV), or *"knowing every good thing"* (CSB), which means he was referring to a deep, full, or complete kind of knowledge rather than just general understanding.

According to verse 6, what do believers participate in to receive this full knowledge? Since Paul was writing to a church, how might *"participation"* be related to community?

What did Paul pray Philemon would have full knowledge **about**?

Below is a helpful paraphrase of this verse from Douglas Moo. It may be beneficial to read this a couple of times to really process it. We've bolded words important to today's lesson:

"Philemon, I am praying that the **mutual participation** that arises from your faith in Christ might become effective in leading you to **understand and put into practice all the good** that God wills for **us** and that is found in our **community**; and do all this for the sake of Christ" (emphases added).[2]

DAY 32

PHILEMON 6

PAUL PRAYED FOR EFFECTIVE FAITH RESULTING IN THE FULL KNOWLEDGE OF EVERY GOOD THING IN CHRIST.

The Rubik's Cube is a familiar toy to many. It's a multicolored cube with nine squares on each side, and once the squares are mixed up, the object is to sort them back out so each face of the cube is one solid color. Some people memorize patterns to solve Rubik's Cubes in seconds — it's possible. And it's delightfully fascinating to watch, even if you have no idea how to do it yourself. Sometimes we cherish what we still don't quite understand.

Similarly, while today's key verse may be dear and familiar to many of us, here is what Bible scholar Douglas Moo has to say about it: "This verse is universally recognized as the most difficult in Philemon."[1]

Like all of Scripture, there is more to Philemon 6 than initially meets the eye: *"I pray that your participation in the faith may become effective through knowing every good thing that is in us for the glory of Christ."*

This verse is part of a letter the Apostle Paul wrote to a man named Philemon and his house church. Among other things, Paul asked the people of this church to take good care of Onesimus, a believer who had served in ministry with Paul. Philemon 16 describes Onesimus as a "*slave*," using an ancient Greek word (*doulos*) that often described someone selling their labor to pay a large debt. While it's possible Onesimus had previously escaped from servitude under Philemon, Paul did not state this explicitly. In any case, Paul *did* emphasize Onesimus's new identity as a "*dearly loved brother*" in Christ and urged Philemon to welcome him back with love and forgiveness (Philemon 15-16).

Our aim is to be like Jesus, who was without sin. We fail in many ways every day — and God is gracious — but when we draw our bow and arrow, so to speak, we still aim for the bull's-eye. For believers, when we sin, we are grieved by it, and our lives are marked by continually turning from sin and turning to God. As we do this, we become sure of where God is leading us: to be with Him and His people in eternal paradise, where we will *always* walk in the truth.

Just as our hearts flood with joy to see our children doing right, living lives of faith in God, so our heavenly Father looks upon His children with rejoicing — far "*greater joy*" than John's rejoicing with Gaius (3 John 4).

> If you didn't know this before (or even if you did), what does it mean to you that God rejoices in you as His child walking in truth?

> How can you bring Him joy through faithfully obeying Him today?

Compare this to verse 4. What else did John say gave him joy? What does this imply about his relationship to Gaius?

The letter of 2 John is written *"to the elect lady and her children"* (v. 1), which likely refers to a church, but 3 John is the only biblical letter John wrote to a specific individual. In modern cultures, we are often quick to think individualistically — we need help seeing ourselves as part of a community where we depend on others and they depend on us. But ancient people had a more communal mindset, emphasizing that no one lives in a vacuum. What one person does affects the whole. Still, it's also possible to become so corporate-minded that we forget communities are made of individuals ... but John didn't forget to write personally to Gaius.

Most importantly, God knows us personally by name. As you read His Word today, you can trust that God had you in mind when He inspired it. God even inspired John to end his letter asking Gaius to greet his friends *"by name"* (3 John 15).

Who might you pray for or greet today by name, in a personal way?

Through John's letter, God Himself was praising Gaius and his *"fellow believers"* for *"walking in truth"* (vv. 3-4) — so it is wise for us to consider how we can emulate their behavior.

It may sound simple at first, but what does **walking in truth** really mean? Surely it means obeying God. But does anyone walk in truth every minute of every day? All of us sin from time to time, and no one *always* does what is right (1 John 1:8; Ecclesiastes 7:20). Yet we still strive for obedience! We are called to *"be perfect, therefore, as [our] heavenly Father is perfect"* (Matthew 5:48), to be holy as God is holy (1 Peter 1:15-16), and to pursue *"holiness—without it no one will see the Lord"* (Hebrews 12:14).

DAY 31

3 JOHN 4

JOHN HAD NO GREATER JOY THAN TO HEAR THAT BELIEVERS WERE WALKING IN THE TRUTH.

The first time you drive to a new friend's house, you might need to use your GPS. The trip is full of turns onto unfamiliar streets, and you may rely entirely on the navigation system, trusting it to guide you. But eventually, if you make the drive enough times, something unexpected happens: You realize you don't need the GPS anymore. Like removing training wheels from a bike, you can shut it off. Thanks to the repeated guidance of the map, you become more and more confident about your journey.

While every analogy has its limits, we might say this is a small picture of our journey to heaven. God has shown us the way in His Word, and as we journey with Him and grow more familiar with His Word, our faith becomes more and more sure.

Today marks the beginning of Week 7 of our New Testament study, and we're looking at 3 John. This is one of only five books in the Bible that are so short they don't have chapters, only verses. (The others are Obadiah, Philemon, 2 John, and Jude.) This epistle is also the third in a series of short letters most likely written by John the disciple of Jesus, who also wrote the Gospel of John and Revelation. John was writing to a friend and fellow believer named Gaius — let's look at what he said.

> Read 3 John 1-4. In verse 3, why did John rejoice?

WEEK 7
SURE OF WHERE WE'RE GOING

ERIC GAGNON

NOTES

NOTES

PRAYER

Heavenly Father, thank You for walking with me through this week. You've reminded me that my purpose isn't something I have to figure out on my own — it's something You've already prepared for me. I don't have to chase after meaning or strive for approval. My purpose is found in You.

Help me to keep doing good, even when I feel tired or discouraged. Give me the strength to be a peacemaker, to love others well, and to live in a way that reflects Your kindness and grace. Let my words, actions, and faith set an example that draws people closer to You.

Most of all, remind me that Your Word is my guide. When I feel unsure or lost, bring me back to Your Truth. Keep shaping me, teaching me, and equipping me so I can step into each day with confidence, knowing I am exactly where You want me to be. I trust You, Lord. Thank You for being my foundation, my strength, and the One who gives my life meaning. In Jesus' name, amen.

WEEK 6
WEEKEND REFLECTION AND PRAYER

This week we continued exploring what it means to be sure of our purpose, or what we're doing on earth as believers. We spent our time in five letters the Apostle Paul wrote: three to churches he had visited and two to Timothy, his "*son in the faith*" (1 Timothy 1:2). Each letter we've studied confirms God's purpose for us as believers and equips us to live out that purpose with confidence, integrity, and perseverance.

- 2 Thessalonians 3 reminds us of the need for faithfulness in doing good and the importance of maintaining our spiritual stamina.

- Ephesians 4 emphasizes the value of maintaining unity through peace with each other.

- Colossians 3 outlines virtues we can wear every day like clothing as we live out our purpose, reminding us that what's on the inside should match what's on the outside.

- 1 and 2 Timothy further explain our purpose in setting an example for others and the importance of God's Word as our foundation for it all.

Now, as we come to the end of the week, the message is clear: We can be sure of our purpose in Christ because it is rooted in God's Truth, expressed in our obedience, strengthened through our perseverance, and demonstrated in our daily actions.

We can do all this because of the One who calls us, the One who assigns us our purpose, and the One who equips us to walk it out — in love.

As an exercise, we've included four passages below for you to read and then interpret and apply using the framework of 2 Timothy 3:16-17. We've offered one example of how you might respond.

SCRIPTURE	FUNCTION	MEANING	EXAMPLE
Verses	Does the passage: **Teach** (instruct in truth)? **Rebuke** (expose sin)? **Correct** (help us change)? **Train** (shape us for a godly life)?	What does it teach, rebuke, or correct me about? How does it encourage me to grow?	How will I respond?
Revelation 3:15-16	Rebuke	God rebukes lukewarm faith.	I can be more intentional to apply spiritual disciplines that will keep my faith "hot."
James 1:22-25			
Philippians 2:3-4			
Proverbs 6:16-19			
Hebrews 12:11			

We've been given so many gifts from God, and His Word is a precious one. We aren't just supposed to read it and put it back on the shelf. Charles Spurgeon says, "Visit many good books, but live in the Bible."[2] In doing so, as our key verse today says, we will "*be complete, equipped for every good work*" (2 Timothy 3:17).

That's why today's key verses are so important: *"All Scripture is inspired by God and is profitable for teaching, for rebuking, for correcting, for training in righteousness, so that the man of God may be complete, equipped for every good work"* (2 Timothy 3:16-17). Paul wasn't just saying the Bible is a book of good advice — he was saying the Scriptures are directly from God. The phrase *"inspired by God"* is unique to this passage, not appearing anywhere else in the Bible. It could also be translated as "breathed out by God," signifying that Scripture originates from God Himself. It is not merely human wisdom but divine revelation.[1]

> Why is it important for us to believe the Bible is breathed out by God rather than simply written by wise humans? Try to think of at least three different reasons.

The Bible carries divine authority. It's not just ancient text written for people much different from us. Though it was certainly written to people living in different time periods and cultures, the truths are timeless. We can trust that Scripture is "*profitable*" or "*useful*" (v. 16, NIV) today like it was back then.

> List the four functions of Scripture that Paul specifically mentioned in 2 Timothy 3:16:

Despite many challenges, Christians throughout history have dedicated their lives to translating and distributing Bibles across the world so more people can have the immense blessing of direct access to God's Word. God Himself has given us His Word to teach, rebuke, correct, and train us in righteousness. And while God has also given us pastors and teachers to help equip us for the work of ministry and build up the body of Christ, we can read and understand the Bible for ourselves. Similarly, we don't *need* anything other than Scripture to rebuke us — although fellow believers can (and do!) help guide us.

So instead of just reading a passage and moving on, let's practice reading Scripture and looking for how it fulfills the functions mentioned in 2 Timothy 3:16-17.

DAY 30

2 TIMOTHY 3:16-17

PAUL WROTE THAT ALL SCRIPTURE IS INSPIRED BY GOD TO EQUIP US FOR EVERY GOOD WORK.

When you think of your favorite book, you likely think of the author as well. How can we separate *Pride and Prejudice* from Jane Austen? Or *The Lion, the Witch and the Wardrobe* from C.S. Lewis? They are linked together in our minds — because the author matters.

When you think of the Bible, what author comes to mind? Moses? David? Matthew? Paul? You wouldn't be wrong if so, but today's verses tell us an even deeper truth about the Bible: Though there were human hands writing every word, God was and is the true Author.

> How have you experienced God speaking directly into your life and changing your perspective through His Word? You could think of one big moment that stands out or consider how Scripture has changed you subtly over time. Summarize your experience here:

We'll come back to this idea, but first, let's back up and take a look at the context of our key verses. Paul likely wrote 2 Timothy as his final letter before his death, and he encouraged Timothy to stand confident in his faith and hold firmly to the holy Scriptures. As we learned yesterday, Timothy was leading the church at Ephesus and was still growing as a leader. Paul's first letter tells us one of Timothy's roles was to combat false teaching (1 Timothy 1:3). And in order to know what is false, he would have to know what is true.

LOVE
ROMANS 12:10; MATTHEW 5:43-47

- I can live this out by ...

FAITH
HEBREWS 11:6; 2 CORINTHIANS 5:7

- I can live this out by ...

PURITY
PSALM 119:9; 1 THESSALONIANS 4:7

- I can live this out by ...

Paul's charge to Timothy reminds us that we preach the Good News not only with our mouths but with our lives. This is the beauty of the gospel: God uses ordinary people to spread His message. Although Timothy was in church leadership, the call to *"set an example"* is for all of us (1 Timothy 4:12). We all have a measure of influence in whatever roles we have and whatever phases of life we are in. And through the power of the Holy Spirit, we can rise up and lead by example.

When we feel overlooked, rather than retreating in hurt, we can remember people are watching us. They will see how we react. The question is: What kind of example do we want to be?

Instead of staying stuck in rejection, Paul encouraged Timothy to "*set an example.*" The word "*example*" in 1 Timothy 4:12 comes from the Greek term *tupos,* which means a model or pattern.[1] This word conveys intentionally behaving in a way we want others to follow. It also reminds us that being an example isn't passive. We are called to deliberately shape our lives after Jesus so that when others see us, they see a pattern worth imitating.

> Think of a Christian you respect. What behavior of theirs have you admired? Have you ever changed your behavior to follow their example? Why or why not?

Paul didn't leave Timothy guessing about how to be an example. Instead, Paul listed five key ways to actively pursue and practice Christlike character.

For each of the five areas of behavior, look up the related Bible verses below, and write a few specific ways *you* can be an example in this area.

SPEECH
EPHESIANS 4:29; COLOSSIANS 4:6

- I can live this out by ...

CONDUCT
MATTHEW 5:16; PHILIPPIANS 1:27

- I can live this out by ...

DAY 29

1 TIMOTHY 4:12

PAUL WROTE TO TIMOTHY TO SET AN EXAMPLE IN SPEECH, CONDUCT, LOVE, FAITH, AND PURITY.

Have you ever felt overlooked or underestimated? Maybe your opinion was ignored because of your youth. Or if you are older, maybe your advice was considered "out of touch."

It hurts to be underestimated. And when it happens, we can easily assume an "I'll show them" attitude. But the Apostle Paul had other advice for a young pastor named Timothy. Instead of a defiant attitude, Paul encouraged a disciple-like attitude. He wrote to Timothy, *"Don't let anyone despise your youth, but set an example for the believers in speech, in conduct, in love, in faith, and in purity"* (1 Timothy 4:12).

> Think of a time when you were overlooked or underestimated. How did you feel? How might that situation and today's key verse prompt you to act in a different way the next time you feel underestimated?

Timothy had visited the city of Ephesus with Paul, who planted a church there in Acts 18-19, and then Paul continued on his journey, leaving Timothy in a leadership position (1 Timothy 1:3). Any church is hard to lead, but it must have been particularly difficult for Timothy after having Paul as his mentor, then being left on his own.

Timothy was still learning, and Paul's first letter to his young protege was filled with sound doctrine and advice on teaching the Truth, living the Christian life, and leading others. Timothy had a big task, and Paul encouraged him to *"fight the good fight"* (1 Timothy 1:18).

As we get to 1 Timothy 4, Paul paused to encourage Timothy again. We can imagine a fatherly tone as Paul said gently, *"Don't let anyone despise your youth"* (v. 12). Then he provided practical advice that we can also apply to our own lives at any age.

In Colossians 3:13, Paul highlighted two ways Jesus' followers can actively practice these five virtues: *"bearing with one another and forgiving one another."* As we all know, Christians aren't perfect, and the newer someone is in their faith, the earlier they are in the process of taking off their "old self." So Paul's reminder to the Colossians is a good reminder for us about how to treat each other. This passage doesn't tell us to try to *change each other* but to be as gracious as possible and forgive offenses as *God changes us.*

Forgiveness is more than a response to behavior; it can be a choice we predecide before we are ever offended. As C.S. Lewis famously observes, "To be a Christian means to forgive the inexcusable because God has forgiven the inexcusable in you."[1]

> Why is forgiveness necessary for spiritual maturity? What happens within us, and between us and others, when we *don't* intentionally forgive offenses?

Paul ended this section of his letter with the invitation to *"put on love, which is the perfect bond of unity"* (Colossians 3:14). We can consider love to be the final piece of spiritual attire that ties everything together. Without love, the godly virtues we put on can be quickly removed when it's inconvenient to be kind or gentle.

> Read the following verses, and write down what each says about the importance of loving each other. How can you live out these truths today?
>
> John 13:35:
>
>
> 1 Corinthians 13:1-3:
>
>
> 1 John 3:10-14:

How might embracing these three truths about your God-given identity impact your daily attitude and choices?

Paul then went on to tell the believers to "*put on*" a list of virtues. Some translations say "*clothe yourselves*" (v. 12, NIV), which is another helpful description of how we can intentionally choose to model the qualities of Jesus.

Using the columns below, list the virtues we are called to live out in Colossians 3:12. Then, on a scale of 1-5, identify how easy or hard it feels for you to "*put on*" each virtue. Once you've identified an area of growth, spend some time praying and asking God to help you in this area.

Virtues To Put On	Rating on a Scale of 1-5 (1 being "very hard" and 5 being "very easy")				
	1	2	3	4	5
_____	○	○	○	○	○
_____	○	○	○	○	○
_____	○	○	○	○	○
_____	○	○	○	○	○
_____	○	○	○	○	○

DAY 28

COLOSSIANS 3:12-14

PAUL WROTE THAT BELIEVERS SHOULD FORGIVE ONE ANOTHER AS THE LORD FORGIVES US.

Consider the last time you were invited to a special event, like a wedding or a festival. Did you spend time thinking about what to wear? Did you order a special outfit to match the colors or theme of the event?

Sometimes picking the right outfit takes intention. Just as we consider what to wear on the outside, the Apostle Paul invites us to consider even more the spiritual garments we *"put on"* as believers: *"Put on compassion, kindness, humility, gentleness, and patience ... put on love, which is the perfect bond of unity"* (Colossians 3:12-14).

These key verses come from a letter Paul wrote to believers at Colossae. His intent was first to address heresy that was arising in the church, so he outlined the supremacy of Christ. These new believers needed to be equipped with Truth so as not to be deceived by arguments that *sounded* true but weren't.

Then Paul shifted to the idea of spiritual maturity. Colossians 3 opens with strong admonitions for believers to think differently now that our lives are in Jesus Christ. To move forward in faith, we put away old practices of anger, slander, and lying to each other. We take off the old self, and we put on the new self.

> This new self is who we are in Christ. Read the first half of Colossians 3:12, and list the three ways it describes believers in relation to God (before listing what we *"put on"*).
>
> 1.
>
> 2.
>
> 3.

Read Acts 2:1-7. Describe what happened. Who was filled with the Holy Spirit that day?

Read Acts 2:38 (or flip back to Day 15 of this study!). How do believers receive the Holy Spirit today?

All those who declare faith in Jesus Christ share the same Holy Spirit who lives in us. This unites us as a family. It's important to note that unity is a work of God. It was and is a gift from our good Father. But according to Paul, we also play a part in *keeping* the body of believers unified.

Now let's return to our reading for today. Paul wrote to the Ephesians approximately 20 years after Pentecost. The unity in the Spirit that happened that day was already at risk of being broken; just decades after a miracle that united all believers, some of Jesus' followers were ready to pursue their own ways.

In Ephesians 4:3, how did Paul advise believers to keep the unity of the Spirit? Why might it be important to remember that unity requires "*effort*"?

How can we live in *"the bond of peace"* (v. 3) in a world where it sometimes seems Christians are more and more divided? List some practical ways you can pursue the bond of peace with other believers. What might need to change in your own heart in order for this to happen?

Now, in the chart below, list the four characteristics of *"walk[ing] worthy"* that Paul mentioned in Ephesians 4:2. For each one, write your own definition and an example of how you could practice this in the next month in your interactions with other Christians.

CHARACTERISTIC	DEFINITION	EXAMPLE

Ephesians 4:3 says to *"mak[e] every effort to keep the unity of the Spirit through the bond of peace."* In order to *"keep"* something, we must have received it at some point in the past. For early Christians, this *"unity of the Spirit"* first happened at Pentecost in Acts 2. Jesus promised His Father would send the Holy Spirit (John 14:26), and after Jesus' death and resurrection, God kept that promise.

DAY 27

EPHESIANS 4:1-3

PAUL URGED BELIEVERS TO BE EAGER TO MAINTAIN UNITY.

Why is it that people who love each other can sometimes act in unkind ways? Especially when those people also love Jesus, this is a hard question to wrestle with. Yet today's verses show that even 2,000 years ago, believers needed encouragement to show each other humility and gentleness and to pursue unity.

Sadly, even with the Church, we can sometimes act with pride and harshness ... and rather than pursue unity and peace, we can too easily stand on our assumed self-righteousness, seeing division in Christ's body of believers as the unavoidable consequence.

But it matters to God how we treat each other. In fact, in his letter to the Ephesian church, Paul linked our very calling as believers with how we pursue restoration in our relationships. Ideally, belief and conduct will balance one another in our lives: As much as we pursue our love of God and His Word, we are called to pursue unity with other believers.

This unity isn't merely a formal contract but a decision made in love. Love is an important focus in Ephesians, where Paul used forms of the word "love" 19 times — including once in today's passage about *"bearing with one another in love"* (Ephesians 4:2). According to the *Bible Knowledge Commentary*, "More than one-sixth of [Paul's] references to 'love' appear in this small epistle to the Ephesians. This letter begins with love ... and ends with love."[1]

> In Ephesians 4:1, Paul also encouraged believers to *"walk worthy of the calling you have received."* Here "*walk*" is a metaphor for how we live or conduct ourselves. List some areas of your life that may need adjusting to align fully with the calling you have received from Christ:

A. ROME
- Rome's population was close to 1 million when Paul wrote to the church there.
- The church was likely started by Jewish believers who'd been in Jerusalem for Pentecost (Acts 2).
- Paul wrote to the believers before he visited them. When he did visit, he was jailed, but he continued his productive mission work (Acts 28).

B. CORINTH
- Paul planted the Corinthian church on his second missionary journey and lived in Corinth for 18 months.
- He teamed up with Priscilla, Aquila and Apollos here and earned a living making tents (Acts 18:1-11).

C. GALATIA
- Galatia was a region located in what is now Turkey.
- The area was Romanized in Paul's day but was originally settled by Celtic tribes.
- Paul was stoned here in Lystra and left for dead. But he got up and continued to witness for Jesus (Acts 14:8-20).

D. PHILIPPI
- The Philippian church was the first church in Europe, planted by Paul on his second missionary journey.
- Lydia, a wealthy businesswoman selling purple cloth, was the first convert we know of in Philippi.
- Paul and Silas were beaten and jailed here, but they led worship in chains and were freed by an earthquake. They led the jailer and his family to Jesus (Acts 16).

E. EPHESUS
- Ephesus was a large city of 250,000 when Paul visited on his third missionary journey.
- Paul lived here for three years and installed Timothy here as pastor.
- The gospel was received so powerfully that it threatened the city's pagan culture, leading people to burn their magic scrolls in repentance (Acts 19).

F. THESSOLONICA
- Thessalonica was a bustling port city and capital of Macedonia.
- Paul planted the church here on his second missionary journey, but he had to leave quickly due to persecution (Acts 17:1-10).
- Despite trials, the Thessalonians became known for their faith and hope in Christ's return, which Paul encouraged in his letters (1 Thessalonians 1:6-10).

G. COLOSSAE
- Colossae was a smaller city in Asia Minor, overshadowed by its neighbors Laodicea and Hierapolis.
- Paul never visited the Colossian church personally; it was likely planted by Epaphras, one of Paul's co-workers (Colossians 1:7).
- Paul wrote to strengthen them in Christ and warn against false teachings that mixed Jewish law, pagan philosophy, and mystical practices (Colossians 2).

H. CRETE
- Crete was a large island in the Mediterranean, known for its many cities and its reputation for dishonesty and laziness (Titus 1:12).
- Paul left Titus on Crete to organize and strengthen the young churches there, appointing elders in every town (Titus 1:5).
- Paul's letter to Titus emphasized sound teaching, good works flowing from faith, and the transforming power of God's grace (Titus 2:11-14).

CHURCHES THAT RECEIVED LETTERS FROM PAUL

Throughout this week of our study, we'll read scriptures from Paul's epistles (letters) to a variety of churches across the Roman Empire. You can locate several of them on this map, which also provides some interesting facts about each one.

The Greek word for "*weary*" (*enkakeo*) can also mean "to be discouraged or lose heart." Given what we read in 2 Thessalonians 3:6-12, why might faithful believers grow weary of doing good?

What situations tempt you to grow weary of doing good, and what helps you resist that temptation?

The first Christians lived amid many pagan beliefs, including Roman emperor worship and Greek polytheism. And not only did believers face challenges from pagans, but the Jews who didn't believe in Jesus and considered Christianity a new religion opposed them as well.

So it wasn't just the believers at Thessalonica who needed encouragement to press on in doing good. Paul also addressed this idea in his letter to the Galatians: "*Let us not get tired of doing good, for we will reap at the proper time if we don't give up*" (Galatians 6:9). What a reminder that *all* followers of Jesus, no matter where we are, frequently need this encouragement and can offer it to one another.

To wrap up our time today, read Galatians 6:7-9 alongside today's key verses. In your own words, write what it means to you to be "*one who sows to the Spirit.*"

With this in mind, the Apostle Paul was equally concerned with right belief and right behavior in today's key verses. His passion for evangelism and discipleship led him to start churches throughout the Mediterranean on three missionary journeys recorded in Scripture. It was on his second journey (around A.D. 49-52) that Paul visited Thessalonica and established a church there (Acts 17). After his visit, Paul wrote a letter to the believers at Thessalonica. Today's lesson focuses on a passage in Paul's follow-up letter to these same believers.

We can surmise the church was thriving despite persecution (2 Thessalonians 1:3-5), but there were some theological issues. Plus, Paul needed to address some actions that weren't lining up with their new faith.

Paul used the first part of his letter to remind the believers that Jesus would return and bring justice for all they were suffering. He also told what will happen before Christ returns. As Paul wrapped up the letter, he shifted from prophetic warnings to encouragement on how to live — specifically, how to live hardworking, productive lives. Paul contrasted believers who were "*idle*" with those who labored to "*provide for themselves*" and avoid burdening others (2 Thessalonians 3:11-12).

> Read 2 Thessalonians 3:6-12. According to verse 7, what kind of example did Paul and his companions set for the Thessalonians?

> How did Paul describe the behavior of idle people in verse 11? What is the difference between "*busy*" and "*busybodies*"?

Paul sternly warned those who weren't carrying their weight or working hard. But that wasn't everyone. To those who were being productive, he gave a different instruction: "*But as for you, brothers and sisters, do not grow weary in doing good*" (v. 13).

DAY 26

2 THESSALONIANS 3:11-13

PAUL WROTE TO ENCOURAGE BELIEVERS NOT TO GROW
WEARY IN DOING GOOD.

Last week, we focused on being sure of our purpose as believers in Jesus, including our call to disciple others, be humble, accept God's mercy, live by faith, and rejoice in the Lord. This week, we'll continue with the idea of being sure of our purpose, turning our attention to how we live out our beliefs and what they mean for us every day.

Our actions — and our attitude about those actions — matter.

When speaking of those who deceive, Jesus once said: "*You'll recognize them by their fruit*" (Matthew 7:16a). Not by their knowledge or education or eloquent words. Not by position or experience or reputation. This is a general principle we can apply: Actions speak louder than words.

> Before we get to today's key verses, think about some ways you display your faith and also identify fellow Christians. What "fruit" do you expect to see?

It's interesting, and a bit terrifying, that when it comes to faith, we can know all the facts of Scripture, but if our actions don't reflect our beliefs, that kind of faith is dead (James 2:26). True believers desire to do good works, not simply have good theology. It's also possible to do a lot of *seemingly good* things for God but with a heart that lacks genuine faith. For those, there will come a day when Jesus says, "*I never knew you*" (Matthew 7:23). A true heart of faith matters just as much as the fruit of true worship.

WEEK 6
SURE OF WHAT WE'RE DOING

GLYNNIS WHITWER

NOTES

NOTES

PRAYER

Lord, I am so thankful to be part of the body of Christ — Your body. May I live with conviction, boldness, kindness, grace, and humility as I obey Your Word. With Your Spirit alive in me, I know my life will make a difference in this world among my fellow believers and those who are far from You and not yet saved.

The gospel has changed me and saved me. You have given me direction and made it clear that my mission is to know You and to make You known. As I obey, go, teach, disciple, love, give, serve, and reflect You, reveal Yourself to me and those around me. I want to live a life of faith, not an attempt at producing good works to impress others or to atone for my sins — because I could never do enough to deserve Your goodness or earn my salvation.

Help me live by faith that is vibrant and active, serving Your people and Kingdom. Teach me to savor the beauty of every day, to learn from the difficulties and trials, and never to lose sight of the gift of living each moment I have been given for a higher purpose than my own. You are my greatest joy, and I will live each day to worship You.

May my life be the pages upon which You write a symphony. May my soul be the canvas upon which You paint Your masterpiece. May every moment and every breath reveal Your defining mark — that I am Yours, You are mine, and You have my heart. In Jesus' name, amen.

WEEK 5
WEEKEND REFLECTION AND PRAYER

Being certain of our calling and purpose is what gives the Christian life meaning. This week, we've learned about how we are powerfully commissioned by God as His ambassadors of reconciliation. And in light of God's mercy, we can live with bold faith as well as humble rejoicing in the blessings we've been given as sons and daughters of the King.

Just as Paul pointed out in many of his letters, there is a battle between the old self living under the law and the new self living by faith in Christ (Romans 8:13; Galatians 5:24). But as we stay surrendered to the One who has saved us and who empowers us daily, we develop resilience and courage to keep fighting the good fight. Because of Jesus, we lack nothing and have the authority and power to live according to the Spirit.

The beautiful truth is that we are not in this alone. Our communal purpose as the body of Christ drives us. Our complete dependence on God compels us, and our love for Christ guides us. As students of the Word who are Spirit-led, we can be confident that we are equipped for every good work God calls us to do (2 Timothy 3:17).

As we consider what we're doing in this world as followers of Jesus, we can be certain of this: God chose us and sent His Son, who hung on the cross to bear our sins, rising from the grave in victory and giving us His Spirit to dwell within us. Christ is our foundation and endless supply of joy. And He can never be taken away from us. Joy in the Lord cannot be overcome and will always be ours. It is not elusive or unattainable; it's ours for the receiving and declaring!

In this same Romans passage, Paul identified three qualities or effects of choosing joy even when we face difficulties in this life:

Rejoicing in affliction produces _____.

Endurance produces _____.

Proven character produces _____.

If our joy depends on things or people, then when those things and people are gone, our excitement wears off. When others fail us, we find ourselves feeling empty. That's when we need Paul's reminder to *"say it again: Rejoice!"* (Philippians 4:4). To rejoice in this way does not mean we will avoid trials, disappointments, or suffering. In fact, we should *expect* trials — but we do so with confidence that we share in Christ's sufferings, so even trials will lead to joy and hope (1 Peter 4:12-13).

Paul explained how he was able to choose joy when he gave this qualifier: *"Rejoice **in the Lord**"* (Philippians 4:4, emphasis added). Pastor Charles Spurgeon says it this way:

> "God is to be the great object of your joy ... Rejoice in the Father, your Father who is in heaven, your loving, tender, unchangeable God. Rejoice, too, in the Son, your Redeemer, your Brother, the Husband of your soul, your Prophet, Priest, and King. Rejoice also in the Holy Ghost, your Quickener, your Comforter, in him who shall abide with you forever."[1]

According to Luke 10:20, what is another reason we can rejoice? What's one thing you can do today to choose joy in light of this promise?

DAY 25

PHILIPPIANS 4:4

PAUL REMINDED BELIEVERS TO REJOICE IN THE LORD.

When we consider the conditions in which he penned these words, we witness a depth of faith and commitment in Paul that is both astounding and inspiring. Paul was likely writing his letter to Philippi from a dark Roman prison, where he was incarcerated in the A.D. 60s for the "crime" of sharing the gospel and was facing possible execution — yet he found a reason to praise in the face of suffering. He had many external reasons *not* to be joyful, but he wanted to show the Philippians that rejoicing is an internal choice we can make that has nothing to do with our current circumstances.

> According to Hebrews 12:2, what did Jesus model for us during trying circumstances? How does this relate to today's key verse?

Paul had experienced a slew of hardships — shipwrecks, persecution, and starvation, to name a few (2 Corinthians 11:24-28) — that he could have used as reasons to grumble or give up. If anyone should have been devastated, forlorn, frustrated, and cynical, it was Paul.

> Yet in Romans 5:1-5, what did Paul "*boast*" in? How can we do the same?

All of the New Testament teaches us to trust in Christ's perfect fulfillment of the law and emphasizes that our lives are to be shaped by that trust. To truly live in Christ, death to self is necessary. As Charles Ellicott explains, "The Christian life is a dying life. If we are in any real sense joined to Christ, the power of His death makes us dead to self and sin and the world."[2]

> In Galatians 3:27, Paul said believers are *"clothed with Christ,"* and in Galatians 2:20, he also said *"Christ lives in me."* Why do you think it's important that Paul used both *inside* and *outside* imagery to describe how Jesus transforms us?

> Hebrews 11:6 says *"without faith it is impossible to please God."* But what is promised for those who believe?

Because Jesus gave everything for us, we now live with certainty that we are saved. By faith we depend upon God and His mercy, forgiveness, and undeserved kindness in every situation, for now and for eternity.

If there is one thing that can seem elusive and hard to hold on to in this life, it's joy. The fallen state of this world and the havoc that sin has wreaked upon humankind is weighty. Jesus Himself taught, *"In this world you will have trouble"* (John 16:33, NIV). There are seasons of plenty and seasons of need. We have good days and hard days.

Like us, Paul and the early Christians at Philippi were not immune to these highs and lows. Yet in the first five words of Philippians 4:4, Paul declared a powerful command that we can cling to whatever comes our way: *"Rejoice in the Lord always."*

GALATIANS 3:23-24 (LAW)	GALATIANS 2:20 (FAITH)
People were *"under the law"* (held down, trapped).	Now we are *"with Christ"* (united, connected, supported).

God gave His law to Moses in the Old Testament, including the Ten Commandments in Exodus 20. Before that, God also made covenants with men like Abraham and Noah, and they proved their trust in God through exercising faith: For example, Abraham was willing to sacrifice his son, believing God could bring him back from the dead if necessary (Genesis 22:1-18; Hebrews 11:19). Noah was willing to build an ark to save a remnant of humanity from God's flood of judgment (Genesis 6-9). Faith has always been the basis of following God: *"Abram believed the LORD, and he credited it to him as righteousness"* (Genesis 15:6). And through the rituals and moral and ceremonial commands God gave the Israelites, they exhibited or measured their faith through obedience in covenantal relationship with Him. The law was their standard.

But in the New Testament, Jesus changed *how* and *why* we obey the law. Intellectual belief was not enough to save people, nor was the law by itself. Instead, God reveals that faith is a personal response to Him and a divine gift bestowed by His grace, made possible through Jesus.

> According to Romans 7:6, what held us captive that we are now released from? How does *"we have died to what held us"* relate to being *"crucified with Christ"* (Galatians 2:20)?

DAY 24

GALATIANS 2:20

PAUL WROTE THAT BELIEVERS LIVE BY FAITH IN THE SON OF GOD, WHO LOVES US.

According to *Merriam-Webster*, "faith" can be defined as "sincerity of intentions" or "allegiance to duty or a person." Another definition is "complete trust." Belief combined with trust in whatever or whomever we are believing in will produce a life of loyalty or obedience to that thing or person.[1]

To instruct the believers of Galatia about what a life of faith meant, Paul wrote them a letter during a time when their beliefs about God were immature and in some ways misguided. Because many were still adhering to the requirements of Mosaic Law as though it was the source of their salvation (Galatians 2:13-14), Paul clarified how faith in Christ is different from a life of ritualistic behaviors. He also said living by faith is God's command for both gentile and Jewish Christians.

Paul backed up this command with his own personal testimony: *"I live by faith in the Son of God"* (Galatians 2:20). Paul was once a persecutor of Christians who lived under the law as a Pharisee and instructed others to do the same — until his eyes were opened and he was saved on the road to Damascus. As the Holy Spirit revealed to him the Truth about Jesus Christ, Paul's years of attempting to gain righteousness through obedience to the law were rendered meaningless (Acts 9:1-31).

> Read Galatians 3:23-24. Before faith came, what did the law do for God's people? Use the chart on the next page to contrast this passage with today's key verse (we've filled in the first row to get you started).

JUSTIFICATION	SANCTIFICATION	GLORIFICATION
GOD HAS SAVED BELIEVERS FROM THE PUNISHMENT FOR SIN (ETERNAL DEATH).	GOD IS SAVING BELIEVERS FROM THE POWER OF SIN OVER US.	GOD WILL SAVE BELIEVERS FROM EVEN THE PRESENCE OF SIN IN ETERNITY.
Justification describes how God declares sinners righteous through our faith in Christ. We are freed from the penalty of eternal death and given new life.	Sanctification is the process by which the Holy Spirit transforms us and makes us holy. We shed the old, sinful flesh and become more Christlike.	Glorification will occur when believers are reunited with God at the second coming of Christ. All sin will cease to exist, and believers will be fully reconciled with God and made perfect.
2 Timothy 1:9 says, *"he has saved us"* — a past event that took place when Jesus rescued us from the penalty of sin and separation from God. By grace through faith, the righteousness of Christ was given to us, and we were justified or made right before God. Our guilt has been removed because of what Jesus did on the cross. **VERSES FOR DEEPER STUDY:** · Ephesians 2:8-9. · Titus 3:5. · Romans 3:23-25.	1 Peter 1:2 refers to *"the sanctifying work of the Spirit"* as an ongoing process of renewing our hearts and minds. As we cooperate with the Holy Spirit and live out a life of faith and obedience, God continues to change us and make us more and more holy like Himself. **VERSES FOR DEEPER STUDY:** · Philippians 2:12. · James 1:21-22. · 2 Corinthians 3:18. · Colossians 3:10. · 1 Peter 2:2.	Hebrews 9:27-28 declares that Jesus died once and for all to redeem us from sin, and He will also return for us *"a second time, not to bear sin, but to bring salvation to those who are waiting for him."* He will restore order to the earth and completely eradicate sin. In eternity, we will be made completely whole and brand-new. **VERSES FOR DEEPER STUDY:** · 1 John 3:2. · 1 Thessalonians 5:23. · Romans 8:29-30. · Colossians 3:4. · Philippians 3:20-21.

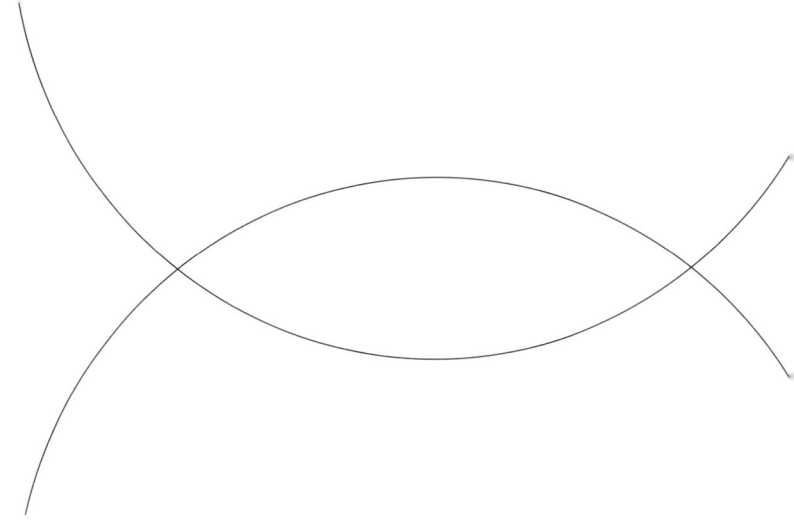

THREE STAGES OF SALVATION

When we accept Christ as our Savior, we immediately *are saved* and gloriously welcomed into God's family! At the same time, we are also *being saved* through the work of the Holy Spirit in our hearts, making us more like Jesus from now until eternity. One day, all things will be restored to what the garden of Eden was meant to be — and better! We will live in perfect, eternal communion with God (1 Corinthians 15:51-53). Until then, we live with a holy hope and confidence that we are "*being renewed day by day*" (2 Corinthians 4:16-18).

LET'S LOOK AT THE THREE STAGES OF OUR SALVATION JOURNEY ACCORDING TO SCRIPTURE.

So even our salvation is credited to Him as a "consequence of what is in God's heart, not what is in our heart."[2] While we may naturally feel compelled to make things right and "fix" our own sins, we cannot accomplish this with self-righteousness. Only *"through the washing of regeneration and renewal **by the Holy Spirit**"* (v. 5, emphasis added) can we become spiritually pure and made new.

As we live out our faith in response to all God has done, as we love Him with all of our heart, mind, soul, and strength, we can do so knowing He has saved us. *"Works of righteousness,"* as mentioned in Titus 3:5, then find their rightful place: flowing from a faithful heart and not from a driving compulsion or attempt to scrub what God has already washed clean.

In 1 Timothy 1:13-16, Paul described his own life before salvation, when he was formerly a persecutor of Christians. What gifts from God did he list that made his new life and salvation possible? How and why did he *"receiv[e] mercy"* (v. 16)?

Paul wrote his letter to Titus, who was ministering to churches on the Greek island of Crete, because he wanted the believers there to understand that no one can ever repay the price for sin by their own works. Not even by being "religious," performing rituals, or trying to do enough "good deeds." This was especially important to emphasize in Crete because a Jewish sect known as *"the circumcision party"* was *"ruining entire households"* there by falsely teaching that gentile Christians had to be circumcised according to Jewish law in order to be truly saved by faith in Jesus (Titus 1:10-11).

According to Old Testament scriptures like Ezra 6:21 and Isaiah 52:1, how did Jewish people associate uncircumcised gentiles with uncleanness?

What does Titus 3:5 teach us about what it means to be *truly* clean? (Who cleans us? Is it outward or inward cleansing, or both?)

Through the Holy Spirit's regeneration and because of what Christ did on the cross in obedience to God the Father, we can be washed, cleansed, and transformed. We didn't earn it, whether through circumcision or anything else. But by God's mercy and grace, we can rest in Christ's righteousness instead of our own. God's grace flows out of His goodness, generosity, and compassionate love for humankind.

DAY 23

TITUS 3:5

PAUL WROTE THAT GOD SAVED US ACCORDING TO HIS MERCY.

Yesterday we learned that our salvation is initiated and secured by God's love for us. Paul's teaching takes it a step further in today's key verse from the book of Titus, deepening our understanding of that love, teaching us that mercy is God's motivation for His gracious gifts.

This is known as "divine causality": the theological principle that all things start and end with God, including our salvation. Titus 3:5 emphasizes that *"he saved us"* through Jesus because God is filled with mercy. And what good would this gift be if it was not freely given?

> Read Romans 6:23. What is the penalty or *"wages"* for sin and disobedience to God? What is the *"gift"* from God, and how does this demonstrate His mercy?

The word *"mercy"* in today's key verse comes from the Greek word *eleos*, which also means "compassion" and "clemency." *Strong's Lexicon* further explains that this word "refers to the compassionate treatment of those in distress, especially when it is within one's power to punish or harm … this term encompasses both the feeling of compassion and the action that results from it."[1]

Sin had separated us from God, and we earned His punishment, but His love and mercy initiated a reboot and a divine reset. Not only did He *feel* kindness toward us, but God *took action* and made a way to bring us back to Himself through the life, death, and resurrection of Jesus. Another way to put it is that we needed cleansing, or *"washing of regeneration"* (Titus 3:5), and God's mercy poured out.

When we consider all God has done out of His great love for us, we see ourselves rightly as those whose sin debt has been paid by Christ and the sacrifice He made. No amount of good deeds on our part can ever repay the precious gifts of grace and faith, but because God initiated grace toward us, we now have new life in Christ — and our gratitude and love for Him is what motivates us to do good works.

> According to 1 Peter 5:6 and James 4:10, as we live with humble faith before God, what can we expect God to do in due season?

Yet when we read today's key verses, it might seem like Paul's theology of *"faith ... not from works"* (Ephesians 2:8-9) is at odds with the Apostle James, who taught that good works are an expression of our faith and said that without works, our faith is dead (James 2:26). Actually both are true: Paul was simply highlighting that the only way we can even believe in Jesus in the first place is by the goodness of God alone. All of our best efforts to somehow repay Jesus for *"God's gift"* of salvation would be futile (Ephesians 2:8). Works cannot save us, nor can they fulfill the debt we owe to God; belief in Jesus and our confession of faith do.

Read Ephesians 2:10. Though works cannot *save us*, what does this verse teach us about what God created us to do *once we are saved* by faith?

How does receiving salvation as a gift encourage us to give generously to others, without expecting repayment? What's one situation where you can be generous toward someone in your life this week (whether with your resources, time, words, etc.)?

Consider a recent situation or relationship you have not approached with a generous spirit. Below, write a prayer asking the Lord how you can show more grace, remembering His gift of grace to you.

DAY 22

EPHESIANS 2:8-9

PAUL WROTE THAT WE ARE SAVED BY GRACE THROUGH FAITH, NOT BY WORKS.

Ephesians is a small but powerful letter Paul wrote to Christians in Ephesus to deepen their understanding of the gospel. Perhaps because the Ephesian church was known for acts of service and labor for God's Kingdom (Revelation 2:1-3), Paul emphasized the generous gift of God that makes salvation possible — in contrast to a false, works-based idea of faith.

In all six chapters of his letter, Paul instructed the believers about how to live their new lives in Christ, and in today's key verses, Paul went to the heart of the matter and exhorted them to remember the foundation upon which their identity was built: *"For you are saved by grace through faith, and this is not from yourselves ..."* (Ephesians 2:8).

These simple words express a powerful truth in which the Ephesians and all Christians can find confidence and hope. There is no amount of striving or good deeds we can do to earn salvation. And the beauty is we don't have to! We receive salvation by faith, and we rest in the grace God has generously poured out. This gift is undeserved yet freely given to us — by God's own initiative — through the sacrifice of His Son.

> Read Jeremiah 9:23-24 alongside Ephesians 2:9. What did the Old Testament prophet Jeremiah say about boasting or celebrating that is similar to Paul's teaching in the New Testament?

Faith is best understood as active trust in the covenant grace of God and the personal lordship of Christ. True faith is belief plus trust — *receiving* the gospel and *giving* our lives to Jesus.[1] Those who live by faith in this way have *"the right to be children of God"* (John 1:12).

Like Matthew wrote in today's key verses, the Apostle Paul taught in his letter to Timothy that believers are meant to live in gospel community and relationship. Whether across the street or abroad, we are each commissioned to make disciples and lead others in how to follow Christ.

> Think of a person you know who needs to hear the Good News or who has heard the gospel but doesn't yet believe. Also think of someone who has recently received salvation or is newer in their faith than you are. Write their names here:

> What practical steps can you take to live out the Great Commission in these people's lives?

As we proclaim the Messiah's death and resurrection, we fulfill the Scriptures and reveal His Kingdom on earth. What a joy to be witnesses and ambassadors of the gospel! Through our lives of obedience to God and His Word, others will have the opportunity to come to know our Savior. As we share the hope we've found in Christ, the results are up to Him.

Evangelism was the unifying theme of the early Church. This is also why God imparted the gift of the Holy Spirit in Acts 2, empowering all believers to boldly and powerfully proclaim salvation to the world. The Church is an integral part of God's plan to reach those separated from Him because of sin and to reconcile humanity back to Himself. Making Jesus known and offering the hope of salvation to others is an incredible calling we get the privilege of sharing.

> Look up Romans 10:13-15. Who "*will be saved*"? How do unbelievers get the opportunity to receive and believe in Christ? (Also note that "*preacher*" doesn't necessarily refer to vocational Christian ministry — the Greek word here can simply mean "one who proclaims or announces.")

Jesus came for all who will believe. Every nation. Every tribe. And all who call Him Savior also become His representatives and ambassadors, equipped to share the Good News. Being an ambassador means we have both the honor and the responsibility to bring His message of reconciliation to everyone who will listen.

And Jesus not only tells us to proclaim the gospel but to "*make disciples*" who *"observe everything I have commanded"* (Matthew 28:19-20). Salvation is a one-time event, but following Jesus is a lifelong journey. This is where discipleship is critical.

> Read 2 Timothy 4:2. What five things are Christ followers instructed to do? How does this relate to the Great Commission and the ongoing process of disciple-making?

DAY 21

MATTHEW 28:19-20

JESUS DIRECTED HIS DISCIPLES TO SHARE THE GOOD NEWS AND OBEY HIM.

The life of a Christ follower is one of obedience and action, and today's verse is filled with great purpose for all Christians. Known as the Great Commission, the four commands Jesus gave His disciples soon after His resurrection are also our calling as individuals and as the family of God.

Matthew 28:19-20 teaches us to:
1. Go.
2. Make disciples.
3. Baptize believers.
4. Teach Christ's commandments.

But in a world filled with confusion about God's Truth, evangelism can seem daunting, tempting us to live the Great Omission instead of the Great Commission. Verses like Mark 6:11 warn that not everyone will receive the message of eternal life, and sometimes this feels like a reason not to share the gospel. Even in Matthew 28:17, with the risen Jesus standing right in front of His disciples, *"they worshiped, but some doubted."* Yet He called them — and us — to keep sharing the Truth to reach those who *will* believe!

> Jesus spoke to His 11 disciples (the 12 minus Judas Iscariot) in Matthew 28:19-20, but now read 2 Corinthians 5:18-20. To whom does Jesus give the rights and privileges of sharing the gospel in this passage?

WEEK 5
SURE OF WHAT WE'RE DOING

JENNY WHEELER

NOTES

NOTES

PRAYER

Father, thank You for the new identity You've given us in Christ. Forgive us for the times we've defined ourselves by our performance, our problems, or other people's opinions rather than by Your Truth. Help these realities move from our heads to our hearts — from concepts we understand to convictions we live by.

Spirit of God, make these truths come alive in us. Remind us that we are not condemned even when shame whispers otherwise. Help us function as the body of Christ, using our gifts while honoring others'. Fill us with supernatural hope when circumstances suggest despair. Enable us to pursue unity even when it's difficult. And empower us to be Your witnesses in the everyday moments of our lives.

Lord Jesus, You have given us a new identity that can't be earned or lost. May we live securely in who You say we are, not swayed by the shifting voices around us or within us. And as we embrace our true identity, use us to help others discover who they are in You. In Jesus' name, amen.

WEEK 4
WEEKEND REFLECTION AND PRAYER

As we wrap up this week exploring our identity in Christ, let's take a moment to reflect on how these truths transform our everyday lives. We've discovered that in Christ, we are free from condemnation, united as one body with diverse gifts, filled with supernatural hope, called to unity despite differences, and empowered as witnesses to God's grace. These aren't just theological concepts to file away — they're meant to change how we see ourselves and navigate our world.

When shame whispers that you're defined by your failures, remember: There is no condemnation in Christ (Romans 8:1).

When you feel isolated or insignificant, remember: You're a vital member of Christ's body with gifts given by grace (Romans 12:4-5).

When circumstances seem hopeless, remember: You're indwelled by the Spirit of the God of hope (Romans 15:13).

When differences threaten unity, remember: What joins you to other believers is far greater than what separates you (1 Corinthians 1:10).

And when you feel inadequate for God's calling, remember: You're empowered to obey Christ by the same Spirit who raised Him from the dead (Acts 1:8).

Take a few moments to consider which aspect of your identity in Christ you most need to embrace right now. What would change if you truly lived from that identity today? Let's pray.

NO CONDEMNATION

"There is now no condemnation for those in Christ Jesus ..." (Romans 8:1)

ONE BODY

"in the same way we who are many are one body in Christ and individually members of one another."
(Romans 12:5)

GOD OF HOPE

"Now may the God of hope fill you with all joy and peace as you believe so that you may overflow with hope by the power of the Holy Spirit." (Romans 15:13)

UNITED IN CHRIST

"Now I urge you, brothers and sisters, in the name of our Lord Jesus Christ, that all of you agree in what you say, that there be no divisions among you, and that you be united with the same understanding and the same conviction." (1 Corinthians 1:10)

EMPOWERED WITNESSES

"But you will receive power when the Holy Spirit has come on you, and you will be my witnesses in Jerusalem, in all Judea and Samaria, and to the ends of the earth." (Acts 1:8)

STEP 3
CONDEMNATION INVENTORY & TRUTH DECLARATION

In the left-hand column below, list a few specific areas where you feel condemned (by yourself, others, or what you perceive as God's judgment).

Now, in the right-hand column, use the language of Romans 8:1-11 to proclaim God's Truth over each condemning thought on your list. Write out a declaration like "no condemnation" or "set free by the Spirit," or if another scripture comes to mind, write that down!

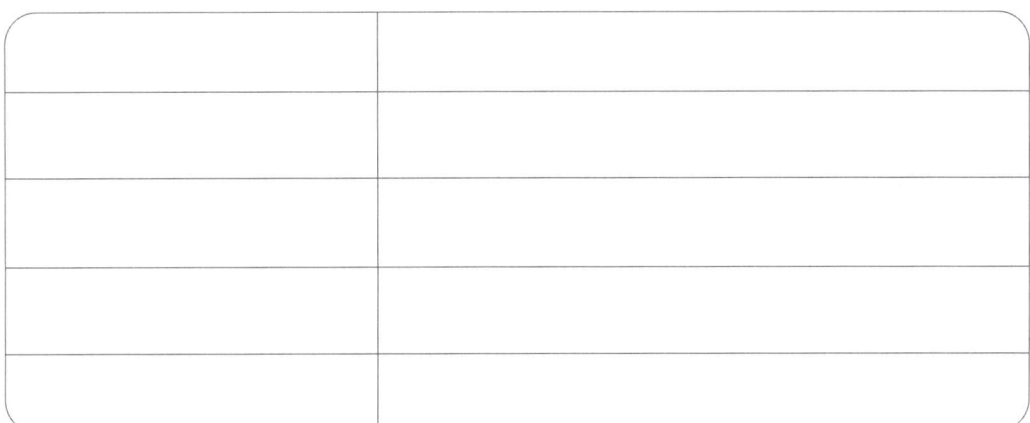

STEP 4
SCRIPTURE MEMORY

When old insecurities creep back in, when criticism cuts deep, or when failures make you question your worth, those are the very moments when knowing who God says you are makes all the difference. And one important way we can receive God's assurance is to remember His Word.

Consider cutting out the cards on the next page to carry scriptures with you throughout the day and help you memorize a few key New Testament promises about your identity in Christ.

STEP 1
IDENTITY BASELINE ASSESSMENT

On a scale of 1-10, how much do you believe that ...

- You are completely free from condemnation? _____

- You have a vital role in Christ's body? _____

- Supernatural hope is available to you daily? _____

- Unity with other believers is possible? _____

- You are empowered as Christ's witness? _____

After recording your answers here, consider revisiting them at the end of this study, or use them as prayer or journaling prompts to talk to God today. Consider the prayer in Mark 9:24: *"I do believe; help my unbelief!"*

STEP 2
TRUTH MEDITATION

Slowly read Romans 8:1-11 three times. You might even try reading it in different Bible translations each time. Ask the Holy Spirit to draw your attention to specific words He wants you to notice, and write in the space below what stands out to you.

TAKING YOUR NEXT STEP

Some truths take time to really sink in. This week, we began exploring some life-changing realities, learning from Jesus that we're not defined by our performance, our past, or other people's opinions. We started unpacking what it means to be a new creation. But if you're anything like us, you might be thinking, *I understand this in my head. It's my heart that still struggles to believe it.*

We get that! That's exactly why we're continuing this conversation. Becoming sure of who we are in Christ isn't a one-week journey — it's a lifelong process of letting God's Truth transform our deepest thoughts about ourselves.

Below are four steps to help you build a framework on the foundation of your identity in Christ. Beyond just knowing the Truth *about Him*, He invites you to live securely *in Him* day by day, moment by moment.

Jesus outlined an expanding scope for witnessing *"in Jerusalem, in all Judea and Samaria, and to the ends of the earth"* (v. 8). This progression pushed the cultural, ethnic, and social boundaries of the disciples' comfort zone. For instance, John 4:9 says *"Jews do not associate with Samaritans,"* but Jesus specifically told His Jewish disciples to take the gospel to Samaria. Their witnessing wasn't confined to people like them but extended to every corner of the world.

> What "Samaria" might Jesus be calling you to share the gospel with — a place or group that feels uncomfortable or outside your natural affinity? What might be holding you back?

While we may sometimes think of ourselves as passive recipients of salvation, Acts 1:8 calls us higher: We are active participants in God's mission. We're not merely saved *from* something but saved *for* something — to continue Christ's work through His Spirit living in us.

Remarkably, Jesus entrusts His message to flawed humans rather than using what the world might call more spectacular means. This divine strategy reveals both God's grace toward us and His desire to work through us. You and I are not just beneficiaries of the gospel but also stewards.

Living from this identity means recognizing that everywhere you go — your workplace, neighborhood, social circles, and digital spaces — you represent Christ. You are His witness, not because you follow Him perfectly but because you authentically experience His grace and power working in your ordinary, everyday life.

In what ways have you experienced your own limitations in living out your faith? How does Jesus' focus on God's power rather than human inadequacy encourage you?

Acts 1:8 promises power specifically *"when the Holy Spirit has come on you."* Throughout Scripture, the Spirit's presence distinguishes God's people. In the Old Testament, the Spirit came upon individuals for specific tasks, like prophets who had visions (Ezekiel 43:5; Micah 3:8; Numbers 24:2) or warriors who were empowered for battle (Judges 14:19; 1 Chronicles 12:18). But Jesus promises the Spirit to all His followers, making *every believer* a carrier of divine presence and power.

How conscious are you of the Holy Spirit's presence in your daily life? What might change if you were more aware of His power dwelling in you as you go about your day?

The purpose of this power is clear: Jesus said, *"You will be my witnesses"* (Acts 1:8). The Greek word for "witness" is *martys* (from which we get "martyr"), meaning someone who testifies to what they've seen and experienced. Our witness isn't primarily about winning arguments but about sharing Christ.

What aspects of Jesus have you personally experienced that you could share with others? How might you include personal experience in your gospel witness?

DAY 20

ACTS 1:8

JESUS TOLD HIS DISCIPLES TO BE HIS WITNESSES TO THE ENDS OF THE EARTH.

Here's an uncomfortable truth: God often calls us to do things we feel completely inadequate for. Maybe it's sharing our faith with a skeptical friend, stepping into a ministry role, or living out our Christian values in a hostile environment. But thankfully, when we feel this discomfort, we're in good company with Jesus' first disciples.

The parting words Jesus gave His disciples in Acts 1:8 reveal another crucial dimension of our identity in Christ: We are empowered witnesses carrying His message to the world. He said, *"But you will receive power when the Holy Spirit has come on you, and you will be my witnesses in Jerusalem, in all Judea and Samaria, and to the ends of the earth."*

> Where in your life or relationships do you feel inadequate right now? How does Jesus' promise of supernatural power speak to those feelings?

To understand Acts 1:8 fully, let's look at its context. Jesus had just risen from the grave, then appeared to His disciples and spent 40 days teaching them. Now one of them asked, *"Lord, are you restoring the kingdom to Israel at this time?"* (Acts 1:6). It's a revealing question. The disciples were still thinking in terms of political power and national boundaries (flip to Page 18 for a refresher on Jewish expectations for the Messiah). But Jesus gently redirected their focus from their narrow vision to God's global mission.

His promise began with *"you will receive power"* (v. 8). This suggests more than subtle influence — it means supernatural strength from God. The disciples had already demonstrated their limitations by denying, doubting, and deserting Jesus in His hour of need (Mark 14:50; Matthew 26:34), yet Jesus didn't focus on their weakness but on the power that would overcome it.

When we hear the word "*saints*" in this passage, we might think of special, super-holy Christians. But what do we learn about saints in Ephesians 2:17-20?

If all believers (including you!) are actually saints, how does this free us from comparison and competition?

Importantly, unity isn't based on our efforts but on Christ's completed work. Only Christ's sacrifice brings us together, reminding us that none of us have earned our place in God's family. This humbling truth dissolves the pride that fuels divisions.

When have you experienced unity with believers who were very different from you? What made that unity possible, despite the differences?

Living out our identity as a unified body doesn't mean avoiding all conflict or pretending differences don't exist. Paul even described *"factions"* as *"necessary"* in 1 Corinthians 11:19, which suggests some denominational distinctions, preferences, and convictions are inevitable (or at least expected). Even so, we can approach our differences with humility, love, and a commitment to preserve the Church Christ died to create. This means recognizing that what unites us — our shared Lord, shared salvation, and shared mission — is far greater than what divides us.

But notice how Paul began his appeal in verse 10 — *"in the name of our Lord Jesus Christ."* This isn't just a spiritual-sounding introduction. It's a powerful reminder of believers' shared allegiance. Before we are followers of any human leader or theological framework, we are followers of Christ. Our primary identity isn't found in a system of doctrine but in Christ Himself.

> What labels or affiliations sometimes compete with your identity in Christ? (These could be faith-based or cultural labels, roles in your family or community, job titles, etc.) How might overemphasizing these secondary identities create unnecessary divisions?

Paul's appeal for unity in the Church doesn't mean uniformity in every opinion. It means sharing *"the same understanding and the same conviction"* (v. 10) about the fundamental gospel Truth — agreeing on core values and purposes rather than having identical perspectives on every issue. Unity centers on essentials while allowing diversity in nonessentials.

> As an example, what areas can you think of where Christians might legitimately differ while maintaining essential unity?

Paul asked the Church a piercing question in 1 Corinthians 1:13: *"Is Christ divided?"* If we share the same Christ, how can we be fundamentally divided? If we're all parts of His body, separation contradicts our very nature.

Paul's emphasis on unity flowed directly from his understanding of our identity in Christ. In 1 Corinthians 1:2-3, he addressed *"those sanctified in Christ Jesus, called as saints, with all those in every place who call on the name of Jesus Christ our Lord."* Notice the *"all"* part — our shared calling and shared Lord creates a bond that transcends differences.

DAY 19

1 CORINTHIANS 1:10

PAUL URGED BELIEVERS TO AGREE AND BE UNITED IN THE NAME OF JESUS.

Let's be honest — unity is hard, isn't it? We naturally gravitate toward people who think like us, vote like us, worship like us. And before we know it, we're dividing into camps, drawing lines between "us" and "them."

The Corinthian church was no different. That's why Paul wrote to them, *"Now I urge you, brothers and sisters, in the name of our Lord Jesus Christ, that all of you agree in what you say, that there be no divisions among you, and that you be united with the same understanding and the same conviction"* (1 Corinthians 1:10). With these heartfelt words, Paul addressed perhaps one of the most challenging aspects of our identity in Christ.

> Where do you see divisions in the Church today? How might personal and cultural values shape these divisions more than biblical principles?

Corinth was a wealthy, diverse, status-conscious city where individualism thrived. It sat between two major ports, which meant constant traffic, trade, and influence from all over the Roman Empire. Picture a booming economy, flashy displays of wealth, and a culture obsessed with social climbing. Public image mattered. Eloquence and influence mattered. And winning admiration from the right people? That really mattered.[1]

It's not surprising the Corinthian church absorbed some of these cultural values — but it caused them to split into factions and claim allegiance to different leaders instead of focusing on Christ. Some said *"'I belong to Paul,' or 'I belong to Apollos,' or 'I belong to Cephas'"* (1 Corinthians 1:12). Sound familiar? Today some might say "I'm Baptist" or "I'm Presbyterian" or "I'm charismatic" or "I just follow God" … or many more answers.

Finally, abundant hope comes *"by the power of the Holy Spirit"* (v. 13), not through our own willpower or positive thinking. When life feels dark and prospects dim, we don't need to manufacture hope — we can access it through the Spirit, who lives within us.

> In what specific situation do you need to rely more fully on the Spirit's power today rather than your own resources? Write down three tangible ways you can invite the Holy Spirit to bring hope to this area (like reading Scripture before a hard conversation, asking Him for clarity about a decision, etc.).
>
> 1.
>
> 2.
>
> 3.

Our identity as hope-filled believers transforms how we face challenges. We're not defined by our circumstances but by our relationship with the God of hope. Even in suffering, uncertainty, or waiting, we can experience joy and peace anchored in God's character and promises, not in favorable conditions.

This doesn't mean denying difficulties or suppressing honest emotions. It means beneath our momentary feelings runs a deeper current of hope that sustains us through all of life's seasons. In Christ, we're continually being filled with supernatural joy, peace, and hope the world cannot explain — which also allows us to pour out the Good News we've received.

In the ancient world, many pagan gods were associated with specific domains — like war, harvest, or love. But the true God fills *all* believers and *all* domains of life to make us *"overflow with hope"* (v. 13), revealing something essential about His character. Our hope in Him isn't wishful thinking or forced optimism but confident expectation based on His faithfulness.

> How does knowing that hope is central to God's character change how you view your current circumstances? What would it look like for you to truly believe this is who God is?

Paul continued in verse 13 by asking *"the God of hope"* to fill believers with *"all joy and peace."* The word *"all"* is significant — not indicating partial or temporary emotional states but complete and enduring spiritual realities. And this fullness comes *"as [we] believe,"* connecting our active faith with our emotional and spiritual well-being.

> How is the presence of joy and peace in your life connected to what you actively believe? Where might unbelief be blocking this fullness in your life?

We see Paul's prayer building to a beautiful crescendo — *"so that you may overflow with hope"* (v. 13). The God of hope fills us so that we fill others. Our identity includes being channels of the very hope we've received.

> Who in your life needs hope right now? How might God be calling you to be a channel of His hope to that person or situation?

DAY 18

ROMANS 15:13

PAUL PRAYED THAT THE GOD OF HOPE WOULD FILL BELIEVERS WITH JOY AND PEACE BY THE POWER OF THE HOLY SPIRIT.

Genuine hope is rare in our world today. From news headlines to social media feeds, we're constantly bombarded with reasons to fear, worry, and divide. But today's scriptures remind us that our identity as believers includes access to a different reality — one marked by abundant hope that flows from God Himself.

"Now may the God of hope fill you with all joy and peace as you believe so that you may overflow with hope by the power of the Holy Spirit." This beautiful prayer in Romans 15:13 reveals more vital aspects of who we are in Christ: We're people of hope, not despair — of joy and peace, not anxiety and conflict.

> Where in your life do you most need to experience *"the God of hope"* right now? What situations seem most hopeless from a human perspective, and how can you seek Him in those situations *"as you believe"*?

To grasp the power of Romans 15:13, we need to understand its context. As we've mentioned in our study of other Romans scriptures, Paul was writing to a church experiencing tensions between Jewish and gentile believers — two groups with centuries of division between them. After instructing them to welcome one another as Christ did (Romans 15:1-7), Paul offered the prayer in verse 13 to point to their shared spiritual inheritance regardless of cultural background.

Our identity in Christ offers both security and purpose. We are secure because our belonging isn't based on our performance but on His finished work. We have purpose because He has strategically gifted us to serve the whole Church body. This communal aspect of our identity directly challenges the modern world's rampant individualism.

> How might embracing your identity as a member of Christ's body change your relationship with your local church? What practical step could you take this week to live out this aspect of your identity?

Far from diminishing your uniqueness, your identity as a member of Christ's body actually celebrates it. God never intended us all to be identical — He intentionally created us with different gifts to reflect different aspects of His nature and meet different needs within His family. That's why *"all the parts do not have the same function"* (Romans 12:4)! Together, united in Christ while honoring our differences, we display God's wisdom and glory to a watching world.

But Paul gave this familiar image a totally different meaning. In Romans 12, he wrote that *every part* of Christ's body matters *equally*. Whether rich or poor, influential or overlooked, every believer has a role to play. And instead of saying one person or one class was the head, Paul pointed to Christ Himself as the only "*head of the body, the church*" (Colossians 1:18). This was a radical idea, especially back then — the idea that real unity, real value, and real belonging come not from social status but from being connected to Jesus.[1]

> What challenges do you face in seeing yourself as genuinely connected to other believers? When you think of people in the Church who you don't feel connected to, how does it help to remember that Christ is your "head" *and theirs* too?

In Romans 12:6-8, Paul got practical about how the Church body functions through different spiritual gifts, including prophecy, service, teaching, exhortation, giving, leading, and acts of mercy. These diverse gifts are rooted in *"the grace given to us."* Our unique contributions aren't accidental — they're an intentional expression of God's grace.

> Which of the gifts mentioned do you see operating in your life? How does seeing this gift as part of your God-given identity affect how you use it?

Sometimes we struggle with feelings of insignificance — believing our gifts don't matter. Other times we battle pride — believing our gifts make us superior. Both miss the beauty of our shared identity. The concept of diversity and unity in the Church reveals something profound about our identity: We are not valuable because of what we can accomplish but because we belong to Christ and His body.

> When have you felt either "less than" or "better than" others based on your abilities or spiritual gifts? How does Paul's body metaphor speak to both of these perspectives?

DAY 17

ROMANS 12:4-5

PAUL WROTE THAT WE ARE ONE BODY IN CHRIST.

Have you ever felt like you don't quite fit in the Church? Maybe you've wondered if your particular mix of strengths, weaknesses, gifts, and quirks really has a place in God's family. In Romans 12:4-5, Paul addressed this very human concern with a powerful image: *"Now as we have many parts in one body, and all the parts do not have the same function, in the same way we who are many are one body in Christ and individually members of one another."*

This isn't just a nice metaphor — it's a fundamental truth about who we are in Christ. We're not isolated believers on individual spiritual journeys. We're connected parts of a body much bigger than ourselves.

> How might viewing yourself as part of Christ's body rather than just an individual believer change how you think about your Christian life this week?

To understand why Paul emphasizes this, let's look at where it sits in his letter to the Roman church. After 11 chapters unpacking the rich doctrines of salvation, Romans 12 begins applying these truths to daily life. First comes the call to offer our bodies as a *"living sacrifice"* (v. 1), and then immediately the following verses connect our individual surrender to our corporate identity.

The "body" language here would have resonated with Paul's Roman audience. In the ancient world, the human body was actually a common metaphor for society, with each person playing their role. Roman thinkers like Cicero and Seneca talked about this a lot, encouraging the kind of social order where everyone "knew their place." Upper-class people or rulers were seen as the "head," and everyone else — workers, servants, and lower classes — were "hands and feet." Their job? To take orders from the head and keep the system running smoothly.

Scripture doesn't say believers never sin or struggle. It does say those sins and struggles no longer define us or determine our standing with God. Our identity is now *"in Christ"* (v. 1) — a phrase Paul used repeatedly to describe our union with Jesus. His righteousness becomes ours. His relationship with the Father becomes the basis for ours.

When we truly grasp this reality, it transforms our spiritual growth. Instead of trying to earn God's approval or change *ourselves*, we can rest in *Christ's* completed work while inviting the Spirit to change us from the inside out.

Today, whatever you're facing, whatever mistakes are in your past, whatever struggles you're currently navigating — remember this core truth of your identity: In Christ, you are not condemned. From this foundation of acceptance, you can begin to live as the new creation you truly are.

> What does Romans 8:2-3 say "*God did*" to "*set you free from the law*"? How does this shape your reading of Romans 8:1 and allow you to approach spiritual growth from a position of "*no condemnation*" rather than trying to earn God's favor?

> When you think about your identity today, do you still define yourself more by your failures or by your position of righteousness in Christ? What would change if you truly lived as someone not condemned?

Notice Romans 8:1 also says *"there is **now** no condemnation"* (emphasis added) — this isn't just a future promise but your current reality. Right now, in this moment, despite the struggles you faced yesterday or this morning, there is no condemnation for you in Christ.

In Romans 8:2, Paul explained why — because *"the law of the Spirit of life in Christ Jesus has set you free from the law of sin and death."* The same Spirit who raised Jesus from the dead now lives in all believers, bringing new life and freedom (v. 11).

> Where have you experienced the Holy Spirit's power to break cycles of sin in your life? Where do you still need to invite Him to bring freedom?

DAY 16

ROMANS 8:1

PAUL WROTE THAT THERE IS NO CONDEMNATION FOR THOSE IN CHRIST JESUS.

Have you ever found yourself replaying mistakes in your mind, feeling the weight of your wrongs even long after you've asked God and others for forgiveness? How much time have you spent in that mental courtroom where you keep being found guilty?

Paul announces that for those in Christ, that courtroom is permanently closed: *"Therefore, there is now no condemnation for those in Christ Jesus."* These words in Romans 8:1 are some of the most liberating in all of Scripture. Think about it for a moment: *"no condemnation."* Not "less condemnation" or "temporary relief from condemnation." **No condemnation** ever again.

> When you hear *"no condemnation"* in Romans 8:1, what areas of your life do you immediately think about? Where do you most struggle to believe this truth applies to you?

In Romans 7, Paul had just finished describing that internal struggle we all know too well — wanting to do right but still failing. Romans 7:18b says, *"For the desire to do what is good is with me, but there is no ability to do it."* How relatable is that? Then comes the *"therefore"* of Romans 8:1, introducing the solution to this universal struggle.

The Greek word for *"condemnation"* in our key verse, *katakrima*, describes a judicial verdict with severe consequences. In Rome, where Paul originally sent this letter to the Church, legal condemnation could have meant loss of property, liberty, or even life. But for those in Christ, the ultimate guilty verdict for our sin has been permanently overturned.

WEEK 4
SURE OF WHO WE ARE

CAILAH GARCIA

NOTES

NOTES

PRAYER

Jesus, thank You for blessing us in every way imaginable. It is easy to lose sight of the truth that we are new creations in You. But as Paul reminds us, we have redemption through Your blood and are lavished with grace and forgiveness. Thank You, Jesus. As Paul prayed, we now pray "that the eyes of [our] heart may be enlightened so that [we] may know what is the hope of his calling, what is the wealth of his glorious inheritance in the saints, and what is the immeasurable greatness of his power toward us who believe, according to the mighty working of his strength" (Ephesians 1:18-19). In Jesus' name, amen.

WEEK 3
WEEKEND REFLECTION AND PRAYER

If you were reading magazines or spending time online in the early 2000s, you might have taken more than a few quizzes to identify "who you are." They were everywhere: *What animal are you? What color are you? Which movie character or member of this popular band are you?* Today, new versions of personality tests also rise to popularity every year. While these tests can be fun, they ultimately don't tell us much about who we really are. And if they do, within 10 years of living and learning about ourselves, we might find even our own answers change.

Yet the Bible reveals truths about us that *never* change. Our identity as believers is locked in, affirmed, and secured by Christ. Paul may have summarized it best when he wrote his letter to the church in Ephesus. Ephesians 1:3-13 answers the question that modern quizzes never really could: *Who are you?* Scripture describes exactly who we are in Christ Jesus. Spend some time reading Ephesians 1:3-13, and in the box below, write down everything it says you are in Christ (the list is long!).

In this past week of studying the New Testament, we've actually just scratched the surface of who we are — and there's another whole week of study on this topic to come. So let's pray the Lord continues to ground us in the Truth of His Word and reveal to us who He has created us to be.

Read each passage below, and note in the right-hand column what else you learn about the Holy Spirit and His roles in the lives of believers.

VERSE	WHAT ROLES DOES THE SPIRIT PLAY?
John 14:26	
Romans 8:26	
Galatians 5:22-23	
2 Corinthians 3:17	
Romans 15:13	

On top of being saved, cleansed, made into new creations, and baptized, we have been given the Holy Spirit. With Him, there is freedom and hope — what a gift He is.

WHAT IS BAPTISM IN THE NEW TESTAMENT?

While all major Christian traditions affirm the importance of baptism, believers may understand and practice baptism differently depending on church denomination, biblical interpretation, and conviction. Some denominations, like Roman Catholic, Eastern Orthodox, Lutheran, and many Reformed traditions, view baptism as a means of grace — an outward sign through which God works inwardly — and baptize infants of believing families. This is seen as a continuation of God's covenant with His people, somewhat parallel to Old Testament circumcision. Others, such as Baptists and many Evangelicals, see baptism primarily as a symbolic act of obedience and personal faith, typically reserved for those who have made a conscious confession of faith.

Practices vary as well: Some immerse fully in water while others pour or sprinkle. Some Eastern churches even immerse infants. Some denominations, like Quakers, do not baptize with water at all but stress an inward spiritual baptism. Despite these differences, the worldwide Church is unified in recognizing baptism as tied to the message of Jesus' burial and resurrection. In Jesus' own words, "Go, therefore, and make disciples of all nations, baptizing them in the name of the Father and of the Son and of the Holy Spirit" (Matthew 28:19).

Based on Acts 2:38 and the scriptures above, there seems to be a chain of events that leads a person to baptism. How would you describe it?

The *Christ-Centered Exposition Commentary* puts it like this: "One must repent and believe in order to be saved. This faith is expressed through baptism, a public declaration of one's faith in Christ."[1] God's grace is what starts this chain of events. We see this in Acts 2:37 as people heard the gospel and were *"pierced to the heart"* by the Truth and grace of Jesus — next, they asked, *"What should we do?"* Baptism was the answer.

John Piper describes that for anyone who has trusted in Christ, "our old self of unbelief and rebellion and idolatry died. And our new identity, a person of faith and submission and treasuring Christ, came into being—all of that through faith. And that's what we confess, and that's what we symbolize when we go down into the water, as though we were being buried with Christ, and then come up out."[2]

Reading Acts 2:38 again, what did Peter say will happen once believers are baptized?

It's important to note that baptism *itself* does not save us or fill us with the Holy Spirit. In Acts 10:44-48, for instance, we see that gentiles who believed in the gospel *"received the Holy Spirit"* *before* they were baptized — because faith alone in Christ alone is what saves us! Yet we also see that these believers followed through with baptism soon afterward, publicly demonstrating their love of Christ and obedience to Him. This is what Peter called *"those who accepted his message"* to do in Acts 2:38-41. And by promising *"the gift of the Holy Spirit"* after baptism, Peter was teaching that the Holy Spirit wasn't just a special gift for the apostles but for **all believers**.

Earlier in Acts 2, the Spirit had descended to dwell within believers for the first time, which had miraculous effects! The Spirit even gave the apostles power to *"speak in different tongues"* (v. 4), which allowed people to hear the gospel in their own diverse languages. And that is just a snapshot of the Spirit's power!

DAY 15

ACTS 2:38

PETER TOLD THE PEOPLE TO REPENT AND BE BAPTIZED IN THE NAME OF JESUS CHRIST.

The New Testament has a lot to say about our identity. So far this week, we've learned a few truths regarding who we *are* in Christ compared to who we *were* without Him. We were lost sinners, but now we have been saved, cleansed of our sin, and made into a new creation. And as an outward sign of this transformation, the New Testament also tells us to be baptized. This is an ordinance given to all believers and was modeled by Jesus Himself — an event recorded in all four Gospels (Matthew 3; Luke 3; Mark 1; John 3)!

Today's key verse was spoken by Peter, one of Jesus' apostles, to a crowd of people gathered at Pentecost. After the Holy Spirit descended to dwell within followers of Jesus, Peter preached the gospel and said to those who believed, *"Repent and be baptized, each of you, in the name of Jesus Christ for the forgiveness of your sins, and you will receive the gift of the Holy Spirit"* (Acts 2:38).

Look at each of the passages below. What do they say about baptism?

VERSE	WHO SAID IT?	WHAT DOES IT TEACH ABOUT BAPTISM?
Matthew 28:19		
John 3:5		
Mark 16:16		
Romans 6:3-4		

Contextually, Christianity was considered a "new" religion when Paul wrote Romans 1:16 — the Church had been around for fewer than 50 years. Many people rejected Jesus and His resurrection, and Christianity also caused political and social controversy in Rome. Keep in mind this is the same city where Paul was eventually martyred — tensions were high between Christians and the Roman regime, which was threatened by the growth of God's Church. Still, in the face of all those tensions, Paul taught that "the preacher of the cross of Christ will be mocked by the ignorant, [but] he is not to be ashamed. For if the Son of God bore the shame of the cross on our behalf, how could it not be out of place for us to be ashamed at the Lord's suffering for us?"[5]

Paul was **proud** of the sacrifice of Christ. Why? Because the gospel *"is the power of God for salvation to everyone who believes"* (Romans 1:16). The Greek word for *"power"* here is *dunamis,* which is where we get our English words "dynamite" and "dynamic."[6] Yes, the gospel is that explosively powerful!

> Read Ephesians 2:8-9. What else does this teach us about salvation through Christ? How does it encourage us to have unashamed faith?

Through *faith* we come to salvation. Those who are ashamed … those who are angry or skeptical … those who think they are "just fine" without Christ … we all only need to have faith in Him to experience redemption and trade our shame for glory.

That is the power of the gospel. It is like the roaring floodwaters of divine mercy and justice meet to wash us clean. Because of Christ's sacrifice, it is so for those who believe. We are saved.

Knowing this about the environment of Rome, what cities might be similar today? What kinds of tensions might a diverse church face in a city like this?

In a time of social upheaval and shifting identities, Paul's words were of critical importance for the diverse church in Rome. Not only did Paul remind individual believers of their identity and mission, but he also united believers as a whole. This Truth of God permeates through the bounds of time and remains equally important today. The unifying message that Paul wrote about *"to everyone who believes"* is the gospel (Romans 1:16).

And Paul's declaration of the gospel began strongly in this verse: He said, *"I am not ashamed."* The implication here is that he was speaking to people who *were* struggling with shame, uncertainty, or hesitation around their faith.

When you think of shame, what comes to mind? What actions or experiences in your own life have you felt ashamed of?

Why do you think Paul began his declaration like this? If a preacher or teacher were to say this from a pulpit today, what might be some reasons why?

DAY 14

ROMANS 1:16

PAUL WROTE THAT HE WAS NOT ASHAMED OF THE GOSPEL, WHICH SAVES EVERYONE WHO BELIEVES.

The book of Romans is arguably the most familiar Pauline letter for many Christians today. Some might even say it is one of the most popular books of the Bible! John Piper suggests "Romans is the most important theological, Christian work ever written." And theologian J.I. Packer once said, "All roads in the Bible lead to Romans, and all views afforded by the Bible are seen most clearly from Romans, and when the message of Romans gets into a person's heart there is no telling what may happen."[1]

Those are some big claims about this small letter! It strongly focuses on one thing: the importance of salvation in Christ. The whole book of Romans centers on "God's judging and saving righteousness in the Gospel of Jesus Christ … God judges sin and yet at the same time manifests his saving mercy."[2] And today's key verse testifies that this merciful salvation comes from the gospel itself — *"because it is the power of God"* (Romans 1:16).

When Paul wrote this in his letter to Rome, the church there was struggling with division between Jewish and gentile believers. Around this time, the Roman government had sent away Jews from Rome for about five years because their faith was causing disruptions among citizens. They were allowed back after this brief exile, but when Jewish Christians rejoined the church in Rome, which was now predominantly gentile, many tensions and disagreements arose. So Paul wrote his letter as an encouragement *"to the Jew, and also to the Greek"* to be sure of their shared identity in Christ (v. 16).[3]

Outside of the church, the culture of Rome was also fractured. Rome had incredible military power, was economically advanced, and set a kind of social blueprint as a "city of the world," but scholars note that the Roman government was also "pitiless" to its citizens, who suffered at the expense of these advancements in a variety of ways.[4]

The ESV translation of our key verse says God has always been *faithful* and *just* to forgive. You can trust that truth because it is based on His proven character. Numbers 14:18, echoing Exodus 34:6 and many other Old Testament scriptures, says God is *"slow to anger and abounding in faithful love, forgiving iniquity and rebellion."* And in the New Testament, the sacrifice of Jesus Himself assures forgiveness of our sins: "Because Christ has taken [our] punishment and has promised [us] his righteousness, this forgiveness and cleansing is the just and faithful thing for God to do."[4]

There is nothing too big, too bad, or too scary to confess to Him. Even if we feel like it is. God will receive His children's confessions, and He will cover us with His love (1 Peter 4:8). And then we will be cleansed *"from all unrighteousness"* (1 John 1:9).

> As believers, we practice ongoing confession, not just a one-time admission of sin when we first trust in Jesus. In what ways do you need to practice confession today? Start by writing down a prayer to the Lord, confessing to Him what comes to your heart. And then take peace in knowing that the Lord covers you in His love.

John was attempting to dismantle a way of thinking that was prevalent in the society he wrote to: People were saying they followed Jesus but were living in sin at the same time. Yet as one scholar puts it, John established that "a lifestyle characterized by ongoing, unrepented sin proves one is not converted."[2] Believers certainly aren't perfect, and we all struggle with sin as long as we're alive on this earth; however, the life of a Christ follower is not characterized by *habitual*, *hidden*, or *unapologetic* sin. It is characterized by repentance.

In response to John, some said they could not be counted as unrepentant because they did not sin at all (v. 8)! But this self-deception is no better than the first, and John responded with today's key verse: *"If we confess our sins, he is faithful and righteous to forgive us our sins and to cleanse us from all unrighteousness"* (v. 9).

> This verse doesn't specifically mention **who** we "*confess our sins*" to, but other scriptures can offer insight. What do Psalm 32:5 and James 5:16 teach us about who is to hear our confessions?

> When was the last time you confessed sin to God? To others? How did you experience God's faithful and just forgiveness?

As the early church father Andreas of Caesarea says, "If we acknowledge our sin and confess it, he will forgive it, and not only that one but all our sins."[3] God is quick to forgive. And God's people have vouched for this deliverance not only in the New Testament but throughout biblical history.

> Read Psalm 32:1-7. How did the psalmist feel when he kept sin unconfessed? How did he feel when he confessed?

DAY 13

1 JOHN 1:9

JOHN WROTE THAT IF WE CONFESS OUR SINS, GOD FORGIVES AND CLEANSES US.

For some people — maybe for most — confession of sin can feel like the last thing on our minds. Often we turn on "autopilot" and go about our day: Get the kids to school, go to work, pick up groceries, make dinner, etc. Rinse and repeat. Acknowledging that we are also sinning daily doesn't necessarily make the checklist.

To really sit down to look at our sin is *hard*. It takes time. It's uncomfortable. And confessing those sins to the perfect Creator of the universe, or even to those we love? That's even harder.

Today's reading is all about confession, and we find it in a letter written by John to the church in Ephesus. This is believed to be the same John who wrote the Gospel of John; as we learned in the first week of this study, he was one of the 12 disciples and an eyewitness to Christ's resurrection, which occurred roughly 50 years before John wrote today's key verse.[1] John's hope was to communicate the love and salvation of Christ to his readers.

To lay the foundation for his letter, John first set up two claims in 1 John 1:5-9 that act as pillars holding up the Truth of the gospel. Each begins with an *"if we say"* statement introducing a hypothetical *false* claim, which is then followed by a *true* assurance.

Read 1 John 1:6 and verse 8. What are the two *"if we say"* claims John shared?

1.

2.

Read 2 Corinthians 5:15 and verse 21. How do these verses say we should live as new creations?

The Truth of the gospel changes everything. It changes how we see the world, the Lord, our own actions, our own motivations, ourselves, and others. As the early church father Augustine says: "Let us *forget* the whole past and, like citizens in a new world, let us *reform* our lives, and let us consider in our every word and deed the dignity of Him who *dwells within us*."[4] May we do just that — in the power, forgiveness, and love of Christ.

Read Psalm 51:10-13, and spend a couple of minutes praying this psalm to God. Feel free to write your prayer or thoughts in response to these verses below:

Today's key verse says those in Christ are *"a new creation; the old has passed away, and see, the new has come!"* (v. 17). This really is great news. And the people of God had been anticipating this for hundreds of years!

> Read Isaiah 43:18-19, a prophecy where the Lord said what He would do in ancient Israel. How do Paul's words in 2 Corinthians 5:17 echo this prophecy and show its fulfillment in Christ?

Christ fulfilled the prophecies, but in some ways, as scholars note, "the old age would continue steamrolling right alongside the new."[2] See, when Paul said *"the old has passed away"* (v. 17), he was speaking to the Church — people who were already in Christ. Yet the old temptations and habits of sin had not vanished into thin air, never to tempt them again. No, temptation remained right alongside the church in Corinth, and the same is true today. To fall back into the old, into our sin, is frightfully easy. But 2 Corinthians 5:17 declares that our sin is not *who we are* anymore. We have a new identity.

The roots of this truth go even deeper in Scripture than just Paul and Isaiah. The word for "*creation*" in today's key verse is the same Greek word Mark 10:6 uses to describe God's creation of humanity. Paul was saying that when we accept Christ and are made new, "humanity is created a second time."[3] Talk about defeating sin and death! Jesus really transforms us as human beings.

> Corinthian believers struggled with judging others by *"what is seen"* instead of trusting the Holy Spirit and focusing on *"what is unseen [and] is eternal"* (2 Corinthians 4:18). This is one of the ways they slipped into the old self. What old ways do you find yourself slipping into?

DAY 12

2 CORINTHIANS 5:17

PAUL WROTE THAT IF ANYONE IS IN CHRIST, THEY ARE A NEW CREATION.

It changes everything. You know that moment — the hesitant confession from a friend about a way they've been suffering, the phone call with bad news about a loved one, the seconds after an accident (or narrowly avoiding one). But there are other moments, too — turning in your last assignment to graduate college, deciding you are finally *done* with something that has been hurting you, the moment your baby is born.

Some moments in life feel like they change everything, from how you perceive the world to how your life flows. For better or worse, nothing is the same.

> When you read the phrase "it changes everything," what moment in your life first comes to mind? What impacts did it have?

In today's passage, Paul described the biggest, most world-shifting, life-altering change we can ever experience: salvation in Christ. 2 Corinthians 5:17 tells us that not only does our perspective shift, but we *ourselves* change when we follow Jesus.

For context, Paul had been struggling with the church in Corinth. The believers were stumbling back into the patterns of their lives before Christ and questioning Paul's authority and leadership.[1] In his letters to the Corinthian church (which we know as 1 and 2 Corinthians), Paul was aiming to restore their relationship with him — and more importantly, with Jesus. That meant reminding them of their identity in Christ.

Paul had two names — sort of. "Saul" was his Hebrew name, and "Paul" was the Greek version, which he used predominantly when ministering to gentiles. Despite popular belief, God didn't necessarily *change* his name from Saul to Paul (though God did change the names of some other biblical figures, like Abraham in Genesis 17:5).[1]

Paul spent three years in Arabia before his public ministry (Galatians 1:17). Some scholars believe he spent this time studying Scripture and preparing for the missionary work God would give him.

Paul wrote 13 letters to churches that are part of the New Testament.

Paul went on four major missionary journeys where he planted a dozen or more churches, performed miracles, and preached the gospel.

Not everyone considered Paul a great speaker. Some said, "*His letters are weighty and powerful, but his physical presence is weak and his public speaking amounts to nothing*" (2 Corinthians 10:10). Yet his ministry was really about God's Word, not his own!

Paul's profession, outside of being a missionary and evangelist, was tentmaking (Acts 18:3).

While **Paul's death** is not recorded in the Bible, church history reports that he was eventually martyred under Emperor Nero, who began persecuting Christians after the Great Fire of Rome around 64 B.C.[2] Paul wrote several of his last letters from prison in Rome before his death.

WHO WAS THE APOSTLE PAUL?

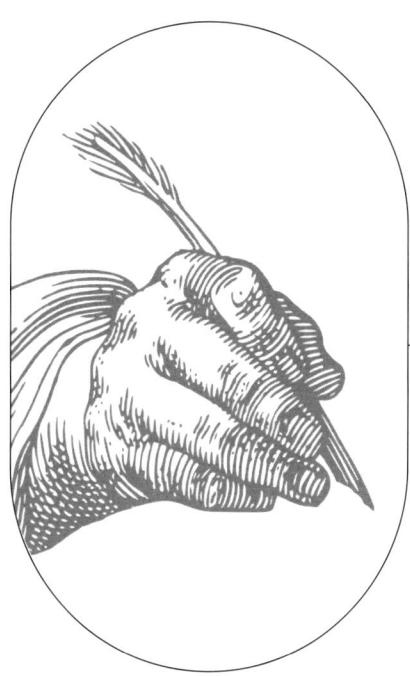

As you continue in this study, you are going to hear the name "Paul" quite often. Whether this is your first time reading about Paul or your thousandth, here are some key facts about his life:

Paul was a Pharisee — which means he studied and taught the Old Testament Jewish law strictly. Paul described himself as zealous and even "*blameless*" in terms of the law (Philippians 3:4-6).

As a Pharisee, he directly opposed the gospel of Jesus. He spent much of his time persecuting Christians and was not only present but "*stood there giving approval*" of the stoning of Stephen, the first Christian martyr after Christ Himself (Acts 22:20).

Paul's conversion to Christianity was dramatic — Jesus appeared and spoke to him, and Paul became blind for three days afterward (Acts 9:1-19)! After this, Jesus opened his eyes and gave him a mission to spread the gospel to gentiles.

Scholars believe Paul was born shortly after Jesus, and his conversation with the risen Messiah was likely only a few years after His death and resurrection.

Read Acts 17:32-34. What was the response to Paul's sermon?

Hughes explains the crowd's mixed reaction like this: "Everything is fine as long as we remain theoretical, but when we call for action, men begin to shift their posture and look at their watches. Seeing their accountability to the true God makes many uncomfortable."[5]

However, some people stayed. Some asked questions. Some surrendered what they knew and repented to receive the gospel. Verse 34 says *"some people joined [Paul] and believed, including Dionysius the Areopagite,"* and church history reveals that this Dionysius became the first Christian bishop in Athens.[6]

Who we are is much bigger than our past or even our ongoing struggle with sin. In Christ, we are not our sin, and that shift in our identity starts here: acknowledging our wrongdoing and turning away from it with a new focus on Him.

> Has the call to accountability for your sin ever made you uncomfortable? How does a testimony like Dionysius' encourage you to push past this discomfort toward repentance, obedience, and faith?

In Acts 17:30-31, today's key verses, what was God's command in response to people's idolatry, and why?

Pastor R. Kent Hughes says idolatry occurs when people set "anything above God as the object of their time, thought, energy, or life, [as] they are worshiping the work of their hands and are thereby degrading God and themselves."[2] Thinking about your day-to-day life, where do you spend most of your time, thought, energy, or focus? What are you tempted to idolize?

The call *"to repent"* in verses 30-31 would have struck both fear and hope in Paul's listeners. Their *"times of ignorance"* toward God had passed. Jesus had now come, died, and risen, and He promised to *"judge the world."*

God is not only the Lord of the Jews but the God of *all* — so *all* are called to repent before Him. The *Christian Standard Commentary* on Acts says, "The egalitarian nature of this command is clear: all people everywhere need to turn from their idolatry and serve God."[3] In fact, Paul repeated the Greek word *panta*, meaning "all" or "every," six times in this short sermon! This is a point he wanted to drive home to the Athenians — and us. God may have left the sins of idolatry unpunished in previous eras (Romans 3:25), but the gospel of Jesus started a new era.

So what did all of this mean for the Athenians? What does it mean for us as we struggle with our own idolatrous ways today?

Well, Paul declared humanity's crisis and the only cure: We are sinners in desperate need of repentance. Pastor and author Tyler Staton defines sin as "trusting yourself or anything else before God."[4] This, friends, is our nature. Apart from Christ, we trust ourselves before God all the time. We trust our anger, our limited perspective, our financial status, our reasoning and logic … but the good news is we are not alone, abandoned, or unloved even in our sin. Acts 17:31 calls attention to the One who loved us with such intensity that He died for us while we were still in sin (Romans 5:8).

DAY 11

ACTS 17:30-31

PAUL DECLARED THAT GOD HAD OVERLOOKED TIMES OF IGNORANCE, BUT NOW HE COMMANDS ALL PEOPLE TO REPENT.

When you think of great speeches, what comes to mind? Maybe it's Martin Luther King's "I Have a Dream" during the American Civil Rights Movement, or perhaps it's Winston Churchill's "We Shall Fight on the Beaches" during World War II. Or maybe you're a fan of Samwise Gamgee in *Lord of the Rings*: "I can't carry it for you, but I can carry you." Each of these speeches declared something crucial to its listeners that hugely impacted history (or fictional history).

The Apostle Paul delivered his own famed speech in Acts 17, which is widely regarded as one of his greatest sermons in the Bible. Today's verses are in some ways the pinnacle of this speech: Acts 17:30-31.

Paul was speaking at the Areopagus, otherwise known as Mars Hill, which was a religious center and place of political council in ancient Greece. Philosophers there *"spent their time on nothing else but telling or hearing something new"* (Acts 17:21), and Paul was invited to share the gospel! Keep in mind the Areopagus was down the road from the Acropolis in Athens, otherwise known as "the birthplace of democracy." Paul was at the center of the intellectual world at this time in history.

> Read Acts 17:22-23. What problems did Paul identify in the city? What stumbling blocks can you infer this audience was struggling with?

After his words in verse 23, it may have seemed to the Athenians like Paul was attempting to add another idol for them to worship; however, Paul instead attempted to dismantle their entire idolatrous religious system by revealing that there is only *one* true God.[1]

WEEK 3
SURE OF WHO WE ARE

MICHAELA ROSCOE

NOTES

NOTES

PRAYER

King Jesus, we stand in awe of Your perfect plan. You came not to be served but to serve and give Your life as our ransom. What the enemy meant for evil at the cross, You transformed into our salvation. Thank You for breaking into our reality with Your Kingdom. Help us to live as citizens of this Kingdom — turning from sin, turning to You, and believing the Good News with our whole hearts.

As we face uncertainty in our daily lives, anchor us in these certainties: You reign supreme, You have set us free, You can reverse our darkest moments, and You will return as conquering King. Until that day, may our lives reflect the confident hope we have in Your high and holy name. In Jesus' name, amen.

WEEK 2
WEEKEND REFLECTION AND PRAYER

As we reflect on our study this week, let's remember the certainties we have in Christ. In a world of constant change, these truths remain steadfast:

JESUS IS KING, AND HIS KINGDOM IS HERE.

Jesus declared, *"The time is fulfilled, and the kingdom of God has come near"* (Mark 1:15). This wasn't a promise of something distant but an announcement that with His arrival, God's Kingdom has broken into our reality.

JESUS CAME AS A RANSOM.

Christ turned kingship upside down when He said, *"The Son of Man did not come to be served, but to serve, and to give his life as a ransom for many"* (Mark 10:45). Jesus' sacrifice on the cross demonstrated the highest form of love. He paid the price to free us from our enslavement to sin and our imprisonment by the enemy.

JESUS SECURES THE DEFEAT OF THE ENEMY.

The rulers of this age thought crucifying Jesus would ensure their victory; instead, they unwittingly participated in God's plan for their defeat (1 Corinthians 2:8). What was meant for evil, God transformed into the greatest good.

JESUS' RESURRECTION AND ASCENSION CONFIRM HIS VICTORY.

The resurrection isn't just a nice ending to the story — it's the cornerstone of our faith. And Christ's victory over sin and death was completed at His ascension, that glorious "exclamation point," when He was seated at the right hand of the Father (Luke 24:51).

JESUS HAS PROMISED TO RETURN.

The ascension also gives us confidence about Christ's return. The angels promised, *"This same Jesus, who has been taken from you into heaven, will come in the same way that you have seen him going into heaven"* (Acts 1:11). When Christ returns, He will do so as the conquering King to judge evil once and for all.

As we navigate the uncertainty of our lives, let's commit to fix our eyes on these unshakable truths.

Write out a personal prayer that captures the hope of Jesus' ascension for you:

We could summarize it all this way:

Jesus has ascended.
Jesus sits on a throne of judgment.
The evil forces of the world will face the judgment of Christ.
Believers are judged righteous by faith in Christ and will be reunited with Him forever.

As we consider the ascension of Christ, we are reminded of the power of Christ, the Kingship of Christ, and the all-encompassing reign of the King on earth and in heaven.

> How does the reality that Christ is currently seated at the right hand of the Father, having put all dark forces on notice, impact your perspective on suffering, evil, and injustice in the world today?

Jesus' ascension is also important because the way He ascended is how He will return. The disciples who watched Christ rise into the heavens received this promise:

"While he was going, they were gazing into heaven, and suddenly two men in white clothes stood by them. They said, 'Men of Galilee, why do you stand looking up into heaven? This same Jesus, who has been taken from you into heaven, will come in the same way that you have seen him going into heaven'" (Acts 1:10-11).

As the disciples lifted up their eyes and watched Christ ascend, angels reminded them that He will not be gone forever. He will come back — not as the suffering servant but as the conquering King of heaven and earth. As Christ was raised into the heavens, above evil powers that are subjugated to Him, He will return to judge and sentence those evil powers to destruction once and for all. We can be confident of this.

> How does this dual nature of Christ as both a servant and conquering King influence how you relate to Him in prayer and worship?

DAY 10

LUKE 24:51

LUKE WROTE THAT JESUS PARTED FROM EARTH AND WAS CARRIED UP INTO HEAVEN.

Imagine someone asking a Christian, "What exactly did Jesus accomplish?" The believer may respond, "Jesus accomplished victory over sin and death through His death, burial, and resurrection." This is a common way to describe the work of Christ. We often find ourselves saying it without even really thinking, almost like muscle memory.

This statement is true and accurate; however, it is somewhat incomplete — because there's one more thing Jesus did right after His resurrection that is crucial to His victory. Christ is the Savior who has *ascended*.

The ascension of Christ is a woefully neglected doctrine, yet it is the glorious exclamation point that punctuates Christ's inauguration as King of the cosmos! We see Luke's account of Jesus' ascension in today's key verse: *"And while he was blessing [His disciples], he left them and was carried up into heaven"* (Luke 24:51).

At this moment, Christ put the dark forces of the world on notice: His ascension started the divine judgment clock, declaring that it is only a matter of time until the enemies of God are fully and eternally vanquished (1 Corinthians 15:23-26).[1] Dr. Patrick Schreiner makes this important observation regarding Christ's victory over dark powers: "While Paul ties this action to the work on the cross, the work of the cross was only a triumph after the resurrection and ascension."[2]

> How does acknowledging Jesus' ascension change or deepen your understanding of His complete work? How might a greater focus on Christ's victorious ascension affect your daily walk with God?

And all of this is incredibly good news for us. Because we who put our trust and faith in Christ Jesus will receive what He has received. What is true of Christ will be true of us. We will also be risen and seated with Christ in eternity (Romans 6:3-11; Galatians 2:20; Ephesians 2:1-6; Colossians 2:12; Colossians 3:1-4). Of this, friend, we can be sure.

> As you reflect, what does it mean to you personally to know that you will be risen and seated with Christ? How does this future hope impact your present challenges?

> As today's study of Ephesians 1:20 affirms the certainty of Jesus' resurrection, what other aspects of your faith do you feel certain about? In which areas do you still wrestle with questions? How might Jesus' resurrection help you navigate uncertainties in other areas?

Read the following Old Testament scriptures, and note *who* is sitting and *why*:

- **1 Kings 1:46:**

- **Psalm 9:7:**

- **Psalm 29:10:**

- **Psalm 47:8:**

- **Psalm 99:1:**

Jesus is King. For Him to take a seat in heaven is a royal enthronement. How does understanding Jesus as the enthroned King change your approach to following Him in your daily life?

TWINS THEORY

A fringe theory proposes Jesus had a twin brother, and this twin just switched spots with Jesus. There is no evidence or historical data to suggest this. And it would have been the easiest to disprove because people who knew this twin would have noticed his disappearance and reappearance as "Jesus."

Some may reject the idea of resurrection outright as a natural impossibility: Dead people don't come back to life. But if God is the all-powerful Creator who dwells *"in the heavens,"* what on earth could stop Him from *"exercis[ing] this power in Christ by raising him from the dead"* (Ephesians 1:20)? Additionally, how can you make sense of all of the eyewitnesses? Further, why would many followers of Jesus die horrific deaths as martyrs in order to protect a lie?

This leaves us with one conclusion: **Jesus resurrected from the grave.** We can be confident in Christ, the risen One.

> What objections have you heard from unbelievers about Jesus' resurrection? How might you respectfully respond to someone who doubts this central Christian claim?

> How does the historical evidence for the resurrection strengthen your personal faith? In what ways might you use this evidence when discussing your faith with skeptics or seekers?

In Ephesians 1:20, Paul gives us hope in the gospel because we can rely on the power of God. It was God who worked in Christ by raising Him from the grave. And who is Christ but God Himself? Therefore, it is fitting that Christ is both raised and seated at the *"right hand"* of the Father.

DAY 9

EPHESIANS 1:20

PAUL WROTE THAT GOD'S POWER RAISED CHRIST FROM THE DEAD.

If there was one thing that could ever single-handedly confirm Jesus was a fake, it would be proof that His resurrection was a hoax. That the resurrection never happened. That it was perhaps a figment of the imagination of people who were struck with extreme grief. Yet 2,000 years later ... Christianity is alive, well, and growing because we can be sure that Jesus *did in fact rise* from the grave. As Ephesians 1:20 says, God *"exercised this power in Christ by raising him from the dead."*

Skeptics have suggested various theories over time to deny Christ's resurrection, including:

SWOON THEORY

Some suggest Jesus just passed out on the cross. But the Romans were literally experts at killing people by crucifixion — so they definitely would have known the difference between a dead Jesus and an unconscious Jesus. And the fact that *"one of the soldiers pierced his side with a spear, and at once blood and water came out"* (John 19:34) is evidence that the spear likely punctured His heart. Jesus was dead.

STOLEN BODY THEORY

Others suggest Jesus' disciples stole His body from the grave. But the Roman soldiers guarding Christ's tomb were the best of the best — the equivalent of Navy Seals today (Matthew 27:65-66). We really think those guards fell asleep, then stayed asleep while a whole group of people tried to roll the rock away? Plus, the rock in front of the tomb could have weighed anywhere between 2-4 tons.[1]

HALLUCINATION THEORY

Another theory is that everyone who saw Jesus alive after His death on the cross — including *"over five hundred brothers and sisters at one time"* (1 Corinthians 15:6) — were actually hallucinating. The problem is this would mean hundreds of people all had the *same* hallucination across a variety of times and places. That is not how hallucinations work.

Today when we fear how plans will work out, or even when we doubt the work of God, we can turn to the cross and remind ourselves that what the enemy planned for evil, God reversed for an ultimate good. *"None of the rulers of this age knew this wisdom, because if they had known it, they would not have crucified the Lord of glory"* (1 Corinthians 2:8).

> As you reflect on this truth, consider Genesis 50:20, Romans 8:28, and the scripture right after today's key verse — 1 Corinthians 2:9. In what specific situation in your life do you need to trust God's ability to bring about this kind of reversal?

Today's key verse about Jesus also recalls an earlier ancient story: that of Haman and Mordecai in the book of Esther. Haman, an evil ruler in Persia around 480 B.C., went out of his way to construct a gallows to hang Mordecai, a man of God. However, in an ironic reversal, Haman was hanged on the very gallows he built in Esther 7:9!

> What other biblical examples of divine reversal can you think of, and how do they strengthen your faith when you face challenges?

> How does the cross — the ultimate divine reversal — change your perspective on suffering or difficulties you're currently experiencing?

In the same way Haman built his gallows, the rulers, authorities, and dark powers of this world sent Jesus to the cross, thinking that as He hung there, so would the hope of humanity. As Christ died, so would God's promises. Little did they know that when they sent Jesus to the cross, they were securing their own ultimate death and defeat.

As Jesus hung on the cross, the hope of humanity was *established*. Christ's enemies and ours spiritually hung in defeat as their plans came crashing down, overturned by the resurrection and ascension of the risen King Jesus.

The enemy loved the cross at first because it was the ultimate symbol of loss, horror, and utter defeat. The Roman statesman and philosopher Cicero once said, "Whenever we crucify the guilty, the most crowded roads are chosen, where the most people can see and be moved by this fear."[1] Satan thought the cross would be the perfect place to display the death of God Himself. But the cross was in fact the very plan and path God used to bring about the enemy's defeat.

DAY 8

1 CORINTHIANS 2:8

PAUL WROTE THAT EARTHLY RULERS DID NOT UNDERSTAND GOD'S PLAN, OR THEY WOULD NOT HAVE CRUCIFIED JESUS.

Uno is a favorite family card game. It's simple but can get super competitive quickly. Sometimes small family rivalries, like fights between siblings, are revealed through specialty cards in the deck that can skip someone's turn, give them more cards, or reverse the direction of play.

The reverse card has to be played just right — the best is when you reverse on someone who is about to win. Just when they think they can call "uno" and walk off in triumph, they get the reverse card, and all their triumph turns into a tragic moment.

In 1 Corinthians 2:8, we get a divine reversal. Paul tells us *"the rulers of this age"* had a plan to destroy Jesus, seemingly undermining the plan of God to reunite humanity to Himself. They thought by sending Christ to the cross, they would ensure their own victory. But while we may be tempted to doubt the plan of God, this verse reminds us we can be sure of *"this wisdom"* that *"none of the rulers of this age knew"*: Their plan to use the cross as a symbol of defeat would backfire completely. In the ultimate reversal, the crucified Christ would rise from the grave.

> When have you experienced a divine reversal in your own life, where something that initially seemed negative or destructive ultimately worked for good?

> In what areas of your life might God be working right now to transform apparent defeat into victory, even if you can't yet see the full picture?

CONTINUITY OF THE OLD & NEW TESTAMENTS

ELLEN ADKINS

Some people see the Old Testament as ancient history — interesting but not really essential for our faith today. But the truth is we can't fully grasp the beauty and depth of the New Testament without the Old Testament. It is the first 75% of the story! Think about if you only read the last book in a series like *The Lord of the Rings*. You might walk away entertained or even inspired ... but you'd miss so much of the story. How much more must this be true when we read Scripture?

The Bible is not just a story about heroes to admire or rules to follow. It's first and foremost about God and His plan for redemption of all things. The overarching story can be summarized in four movements: 1) Creation, 2) Fall, 3) Redemption, and 4) Consummation. In short, God created the world and everything in it, but humans chose sin, which corrupted and destroyed everything in and around us. God, however, has set forth a plan to redeem all things and reclaim His people for Himself. He was and is making everything new.

So the Old Testament is the foundation we need to understand God's character, His covenant love, His pursuit of His people, and His promises that Jesus came to fulfill. Jesus didn't come out of nowhere — He stepped onto a stage that had been perfectly set. In fact, *everything* in the Old Testament points toward Jesus.

Jesus Himself understood this: In Matthew 5:17, He said, *"Don't think that I came to abolish the Law or the Prophets. I did not come to abolish but to fulfill."* The New Testament does not do away with the Old Testament, but rather everything in the Old Testament points to the New Testament, and everything in the New Testament shows the fulfillment of the Old Testament.

So the next time you read through Levitical law, for instance, and you're tempted to dismiss it as irrelevant ... consider how God created us to live in fellowship with Him, and though we all sinfully desire independence from God, in His mercy, He gave His people a sacrificial system so they could experience His presence and forgiveness. All of this pointed toward the day when Jesus Himself would fulfill the law and be a perfect sacrifice so we might have life forever with Him (Hebrews 9).

You will notice that much of this study guide through the New Testament also points us back to scriptures from the Old Testament. As we engage with God's Word, let's allow the overarching narrative to inform our understanding of who Jesus is, who we are, what we're doing, and where we're going.

This is what Jesus was getting at in His parable of the strong man in Mark 3:27: *"No one can enter a strong man's house and plunder his possessions unless he first ties up the strong man."* Jesus did just this on the cross. In the most unexpected redemptive reversal, the death of Christ is the very ransom that actually binds the strong man (Satan and dark forces) by defeating death *through* death. So now the *"plunder"* or the prisoners of war — people like us — are set free by Christ! We can be sure that redemption and restoration are guaranteed for all who trust in the ransom of Christ's sacrifice on the cross and His resurrection from the grave.

And one final detail: What Jesus did on the cross was also a continuation of God's liberating work in the Old Testament. The Greek verb for *"ransom"* (*lytroo*) was also used in the Septuagint to describe God redeeming His people from Egyptian slavery in scriptures like Exodus 6:6 and Deuteronomy 7:8. When Jesus gave His life as a ransom, He did so to rescue us from a much greater enemy than Egypt and Pharaoh. He forever rescues us from the grip of sin and death. Of this we can be certain.

> How does seeing Jesus' sacrifice as part of the story of God's liberating work, connecting to Exodus and the Old Testament, deepen your appreciation for what He has accomplished? What does this tell you about God's consistent character throughout Scripture?

How might you need to turn your own expectations upside down to follow Jesus' example of servant leadership?

Jesus' servanthood gives us an assurance of His deep love. It is love that sent Christ to the cross as a ransom for the lost. An interesting detail about the word "*ransom*" (or *lytron* in Greek) in today's key verse is that it was used in secular Greek to refer to purchasing freedom for a slave or a prisoner of war. In the Greek version of the Hebrew Bible (the Septuagint), we see this in Leviticus 25:51-52, which said a slave *"must pay his redemption price"* to be freed.

Think about that for a second. As humans, apart from Christ, we are in fact enslaved to sin. And because of this enslavement, we are prisoners of our enemy, Satan.

Which of these metaphors (slave to sin or prisoner of the enemy) speaks most powerfully to your personal experience, and why?

Christ's sacrifice frees us from both sin and the enemy's power. What does it personally mean to you to be set free by Christ? How has this freedom manifested in your daily life and relationships?

DAY 7

MARK 10:45

JESUS SAID HE CAME AS A SERVANT WHO WOULD GIVE HIS LIFE FOR MANY.

One popular theme in suspense movies is kidnapping — a situation where someone dearly loved is taken captive. The captors typically ask for some kind of ransom in exchange for a safe return, and the movie builds tension by emphasizing the plight of the victim's family. What parent wouldn't do whatever it took and pay whatever the cost to get their child back?

In Mark 10:45, Jesus invites us into the purpose of His earthly life and ministry: *"For even the Son of Man did not come to be served, but to serve, and to give his life as a ransom for many."* You and I can be sure of the truth that Christ came to serve because the ultimate act of service was giving His own life for us.

In yesterday's study, we talked about how we can be sure of Jesus as King, and that will be a running thread through the rest of this week's study. Take a moment and think about how unlikely Jesus' words in Mark 10:45 would have seemed to those first followers who had also heard Him speak Mark 1:15. If Jesus was a **King**, shouldn't He **be served**?

Yet Jesus turns the entire concept upside down. The purpose of the incarnation was for Christ to act as the ultimate servant, becoming the ransom for the rescue of the family of God.

> In what specific areas of your life have you experienced Christ's "ransom" power breaking chains that once held you captive? In which areas do you struggle to fully embrace this freedom?

kind of evil. Thankfully, Jesus came to break that cycle and to lead His people in true obedience.

> In what areas of your life do you find it most difficult to live as though Jesus is truly King? What might true repentance look like in those areas?

> To *"repent and believe"* in Jesus (v. 15) involves more than intellectual knowledge. How would you describe the difference between *knowing* about Jesus as King and *living* with Him as your King?

Notice the flow of Jesus' teaching in our key verse: He wants us to be confident in His Kingship and Kingdom. Because of this confidence, He then summons us to live in accordance with the Truth. Faith requires a commitment to depend on God and to live in alignment with the King's desires.

And, friend, all of this is *"good news"* (Mark 1:15). It is worthy of proclamation. It should fill our hearts with hope because we know the King and His Kingdom are breaking into our very reality, which means the fullness of the Kingdom — and all the good that comes with it — is well on the way!

You and I today can be sure of these two things:

JESUS IS ALREADY KING OF HEAVEN AND EARTH.

This is not a new truth but a preexisting and eternal truth: *"The Lord has established his throne in heaven, and his kingdom rules over all"* (Psalm 103:19).

JESUS' KINGDOM IS HERE NOW AND IS ALSO STILL COMING.

Theologians refer to this as the "already but not yet" of His Kingdom. The "not yet" refers to the future culmination of the new heavens and new earth, where sin will be no more and God's people will live in His full presence and glory for eternity.

> How does understanding God's Kingdom as "already but not yet" change your perspective on your current challenges and future hope?

> How might your priorities and decisions change if you consistently viewed yourself as a citizen of God's Kingdom rather than merely a citizen of this world?

What does the glorious news of Christ's Kingship mean for us? Jesus tells us in the second half of Mark 1:15: *"Repent and believe the good news!"*

The concept of repentance is rooted in the Old Testament Hebrew word *teshuvah*, which has a double meaning. To repent is to turn away from evil and also to turn toward God.[2] The problem with ancient Israel was they would turn away from evil ... but then they would turn to a different

DAY 6

MARK 1:15

JESUS PROCLAIMED THAT THE KINGDOM OF GOD HAS COME NEAR.

Anticipation is a tension to be managed. On the one hand, we are eager to receive what we look forward to. On the other hand, the waiting is often less than ideal.

Imagine the anticipation of the Israelites in the Old Testament, who must have felt like they were in a constant holding pattern. They kept hearing stories of a future king who would come from the line of David, a Messiah or Anointed One who would bring redemption and usher in a restored Kingdom, but for generation after generation ... He was nowhere to be seen.

Then Jesus declared in Mark 1:15a, *"The time is fulfilled, and the kingdom of God has come near."*

What are the implications of such a statement? First, there could be no Kingdom without a King. This is what Christ *"fulfilled"* — Jesus established Himself not only as the *"King of the Jews"* (Mark 15:2; Mark 15:26) but of all heaven and earth (Matthew 28:18).

When Jesus says God's Kingdom *"has come near"* in Mark 1:15, or in some translations, *"is at hand"* (ESV), the Greek word conveys the meaning "has arrived."[1] Christ invites us into a brilliant truth: His Kingdom is not something far off that will only come *someday* but is a reality breaking into earth *today*. This is exactly why Jesus also teaches us to pray, *"Your kingdom come. Your will be done on earth as it is in heaven"* (Matthew 6:10).

> In what specific ways could you pray for God's Kingdom to break into your family, workplace, or community this week?

WEEK 2
SURE OF WHO JESUS IS

DR. JOEL MUDDAMALLE

NOTES

NOTES

PRAYER

Jesus, thank You that You are who You say You are. No one compares to You. Not only are You different from other leaders, teachers, "gods," or prophets, but You are so much better than anyone or anything else we could ever worship. As we keep studying the New Testament, let us be more and more amazed by how You exceed our greatest expectations, relieve our heaviest burdens, and replace our deepest doubts with assurance of Your love and Truth. In Jesus' name, amen.

WEEK 1
WEEKEND REFLECTION AND PRAYER

Maybe it's been a while since you played "spot the difference" — but you might remember these puzzles from kids menus, magazines, or the ubiquitous Magic Eye book in the orthodontist waiting rooms of yesteryear. The idea is that two similar images are printed on side-by-side pages. At a glance, they look identical, but a keen eye can pick out a few subtle distinctions. A change of color. A shift in position. Something that wasn't there before.

If we look at Jesus at a glance, we might think He looks a lot like other wise teachers or religious figures in history — people who had good morals, promoted love, and tried to help others. But looking at Him closely, we can spot more than a few crucial differences.

Jesus was different from any other godly men who came before Him — because He is the perfect God-man (John 1:14; John 20:31). He had different ideas about work and power, leading with a gentle heart instead of an iron fist (Matthew 11:28-30). He had a different relationship with sinners, seeking to *"save the lost"* instead of bringing immediate judgment (Luke 19:10). He gave different instructions about how to draw near to God, saying clearly and compassionately, *"No one comes to the Father except through me"* (John 14:6).

And as Bible scholar Hank Hanegraaff points out, the ultimate evidence of Jesus' uniqueness is His resurrection: If Jesus is "merely one more person in a pantheon of pretenders, His proclamations can easily be pushed aside," but a Messiah who has conquered death "does not stand in a line of peers."[1] Friend, we can be certain there is only one resurrected Savior. And He is the only One we need.

JOHN 6:35:

"I am the _____ of life..."

JOHN 10:11:

"I am the good _____."

Some people who question Jesus' divinity suggest that His followers claimed He was God, but Jesus Himself never actually did. However, Scripture clearly reveals that Jesus proclaimed His divinity many times. These proclamations also reference Old Testament imagery associated with the God of Israel, further proving that Jesus is one with Yahweh.

"The Lord [who] is my light and my salvation" in Psalm 27:1 is Jesus.
"The Lord [who] is my shepherd" in Psalm 23:1 is Jesus.
Indeed, He is the great *I Am*.

JOHN 8:12a:

"I am the _____ of the world."

JOHN 11:25a:

"I am the _____ and the life."

JOHN 10:9:

"I am the _____. If anyone enters by me, he will be saved…"

JOHN 14:6a:

"I am the _____, the _____, and the life."

JESUS IS THE GREAT *I AM*

Jesus once told a group of Jewish religious leaders, *"Before Abraham was, **I am**"* (John 8:58, emphasis added). Then they tried to execute Him for blasphemy.

Not only was Jesus claiming to be eternal like God — existing before Abraham, who had lived on earth about 40 generations earlier — but He was claiming to *be God*. When Jesus said *"I am,"* His words echoed the sacred, covenantal name the Lord revealed to Moses in Exodus 3:14: *"I AM WHO I AM"* (or in Hebrew, "Yahweh"). This sacred name of God was so highly revered among Jews that even priests refrained from fully speaking it aloud or writing it down.

Yet Jesus boldly used *"I am"* to identify Himself — and not just once!

Using the images and scriptures below, fill in the blanks of Jesus' seven "*I am*" statements in the New Testament. (Or try to do it from memory if you're familiar with the verses!)

JOHN 15:1:

"I am the true _____, and my Father is the _____."

When Israel went through the Red Sea, God miraculously parted the waters to deliver them from Egyptian slavery (Exodus 14:16). When Israel went through the wilderness, they had disobeyed God and deserved His wrath, but still He patiently led them to the promised land (Deuteronomy 2:7). With God, "through" means there are no shortcuts or alternate routes to His will. It means endurance. It means transformation. Sometimes it means suffering. It also means redemption. It means trusting Him. "Through" is how God has always guided His people, and *"no one comes"* to Him by any other path (John 14:6).

When we read today's key verse, it may seem harshly exclusive that Jesus claims to be the *only way* to salvation. But through Him, the door to heaven is actually open wider than ever — not only for Israel but for anyone who believes in His name.

> Jesus Himself went *through* false accusations, then *through* death itself, to emerge victorious on the other side and prove that He is *"the truth, and the life."* How does this encourage you to accept His invitation to come to the Father (v. 6)? How can you encourage others to do the same?

If you could ask Jesus any three questions today, what would they be?

1.

2.

3.

If you asked Him these questions and *"Jesus told [you], 'I am the way, the truth, and the life'"* (John 14:6), would His answer be enough for you? Take a 60-second pause to imagine this before you answer below, explaining why or why not.

Right after Jesus identified Himself as the way to eternal life, another of His disciples said, *"Show us the Father, and that's enough for us"* (v. 8).

In other words: "Thanks for the answer ... sort of. But we're still confused." The disciples thought they needed to see more *from Jesus*. What they really needed was to see more *of Jesus*. And here's another nuance that's more than just semantic: Jesus said, *"No one comes to the Father except **through** me"* (John 14:6, emphasis added).

> "Through" is one of the most important prepositions in Scripture. Based on the psalms below, what did God bring His people *through* in the Old Testament? (If you can think of more examples, list them here too!)
>
> **Psalm 66:12:**
>
> **Psalm 136:16:**
>
> **Psalm 23:4:**

DAY 5

JOHN 14:6

JESUS SAID HE IS THE WAY, THE TRUTH, AND THE LIFE.

Have you ever tried to learn a new language? Maybe you've traveled to another country and tried to order a glass of water at dinner, but fumbling over unfamiliar words, you accidentally requested "a glass *in* water" or "a glass *under* water." While we can laugh at what gets lost in translation, these struggles make us appreciate the power of even the smallest words.

Let's study today's key verse with this same eye for linguistic detail: *"Jesus told him, 'I am the way, the truth, and the life. No one comes to the Father except through me'"* (John 14:6).

First, the phrase "*told him*" reveals that Jesus was responding to someone here. What did His disciple Thomas ask in John 14:5? (Consider that this conversation took place at the Last Supper, with Jesus' crucifixion impending.)

When Thomas heard Jesus' answer, do you think it was what he expected? Why or why not?

For anyone else but the Savior of the world, saying "*I am the way*" (v. 6) would be a grammatical error. We'd need a different verb. Someone might *know* the way or *show* the way from one place to another, but a person typically cannot *be* the way. Yet Jesus did not misspeak. Thomas asked "where" and "how" questions, and Jesus gave a "who" answer — an instruction based on His identity.

With complete certainty, we can trust the One who labors alongside us. Instead of a cruel or indifferent overseer driving us to do His bidding and hold His bags, Jesus is a friend who shares our burdens. "*I am lowly and humble in heart,*" He says, more than willing to yoke Himself to us as a co-worker (v. 29).

> How does the New Testament further illustrate this idea in 1 Corinthians 3:9 and Colossians 3:23? How can you serve and thank Jesus as your co-worker today?

More than a master who commands us to carry Him, Jesus is a teacher who invites us to *"learn from"* Him (v. 29). He has no use for our usefulness. He desires our surrender. He lightens our load.

Jesus promises our overloaded souls: "*I will give you rest*" (v. 28). In other words, He does not see us as beasts of burden. He has no desire to exploit us for how far we can go or how much we can carry — nor would He have any reason to do that. For the God who holds the entire universe in His hand (Psalm 95:4-5; Jeremiah 32:17), how could there be any burden He needs our help to bear? Instead of heaviness, He offers us lightness.

At the same time, it's interesting to note what Jesus *does* call us to carry: "*Take my yoke upon you ... for my yoke is easy*" (vv. 29-30).

> Look up a definition of the word "yoke" (and/or use a Bible concordance to see where else it's used in Scripture). How does this relate to the animal imagery in Matthew 11:28-30?

> What tensions do you see between Jesus' invitation to rest and His invitation to work under His yoke? How is it possible to do both?

At first, this might not seem like a solution. Jesus tells us to stop laboring ... so that we can labor? But there's actually a beautiful nuance here: Rather than calling us to abandon all work, Jesus redefines work so that it no longer exhausts us. In the Kingdom of Christ, we all have responsibilities and assignments, but our work is also worship. Instead of a grueling daily grind, it's a labor of love. In fact, it's a labor *with love* Himself: We are yoked to Jesus, not chained to a desk or tangled up in worldly fears and pressures of productivity that would crush our souls to "harness our potential."

Jesus used a similar redefining logic earlier in Matthew 11, teaching His disciples not to complain "*like children*" (v. 16) yet also teaching that God *"ha[s] hidden [true] things from the wise and intelligent and revealed them to infants"* (v. 25). In other words, there's a difference between being *childish* and *childlike*. And there's also a difference between working for the world and working for Jesus.

DAY 4

MATTHEW 11:28-30

JESUS INVITED THOSE WHO ARE WEARY TO COME TO HIM FOR REST.

Some of the first domesticated animals in the Ancient Near East were donkeys. Able to carry loads up to 30% of their body weight, donkeys were especially useful for farming and transportation because they could cart heavy baggage (like food, water, equipment, and items for trade) across long distances. Ancient caravans often travelled with dozens or hundreds of donkeys, and historical evidence suggests that even as early as 1900 B.C., "not having a donkey was a sign of dire poverty."[1]

So what does this have to do with Jesus? In today's key verses, while teaching crowds in Galilee, Jesus used the familiar image of a pack animal: a creature *"weary and burdened"* from hard labor (Matthew 11:28). Like Jesus' original listeners would have done, we can picture a donkey saddled and struggling to stand under the backbreaking weight of other people's stuff.

> Take a moment to picture this vividly in your mind. In what ways does this imagery resonate with burdens or baggage you've carried in your own life?

> What does Jesus say He will do for all *"who are weary and burdened"* in Matthew 11:28-30? What does He call *us* to do?

Then through His resurrection and ascension, Jesus finished the work of salvation He came to accomplish! No matter how hopelessly lost we feel, we can be found by Him. By simple faith, all we have to do is what Zacchaeus did: *"He quickly came down and welcomed [Jesus] joyfully"* (Luke 19:6).

How can you joyfully welcome Jesus as your Savior today? Start by writing a prayer below:

Instead, Jesus said He *"has come to seek and to save"* people exactly like Zacchaeus — those who are "*lost*" (v. 10).

> Jesus also told parables about lost things in Luke 15:8-10 and Matthew 18:12-14. How does this help us understand Luke 19:10?

The Greek word for "*lost*" in our key verse derives from *apollumi*, which means more than just misplacing something or taking a wrong turn. It also refers to ruin, demise, or destruction.[1] In Matthew 8:25, for example, when Jesus' disciples were in a raging storm and said *"we're going to die,"* they used the word *apollumetha*.

> Now read Matthew 27:20, where another form of *apollumi* is translated as "*execute*." Who was to be executed? What does this reveal about how Jesus saves the lost?

Apart from God's grace, we're all like Zacchaeus once was: confused, perishing, and lost in every sense of the word. His fellow Jews called Zacchaeus a *"sinful man"* (Luke 19:7) … and the thing is, they were right. But that didn't stop Jesus from seeking this lost tax collector. And He seeks us just the same.

How can we be sure? Because Jesus **became** *apollumi* — and He **overcame** *apollumi* — for you and me. To seek the lost, He came down from heaven and lived among the lost on earth. To save us from being destroyed by our sins, He subjected Himself to destruction on the cross. Just days after He called Zacchaeus down from his treetop hideout, the Son of Man was nailed to a tree as a sacrifice for our sins (2 Corinthians 5:21).

DAY 3

LUKE 19:10

JESUS SAID HE CAME TO SEEK AND SAVE THE LOST.

For the past few days, our study of John's Gospel has helped us answer the question: *Who is Jesus?* With certainty, we can say He is the Messiah who came to earth as God Himself in human flesh. Now, as we turn to Luke's Gospel, let's continue with an important follow-up question that might be on our minds: *Why did Jesus come?*

How does Luke 19:10 answer this question?

For context, also read the first nine verses of Luke 19. Who was the speaker of verse 10? Who was spoken to?

In some Bibles, today's key verse may be printed in red ink to show that this is a line of dialogue straight from Jesus' mouth. When He said *"Son of Man"* in verse 10, He was talking about Himself, and He was talking to Zacchaeus, a tax collector in Roman-occupied Israel. This meant Zacchaeus was essentially a professional political traitor, taking money from his own people on behalf of the Roman regime and often overcharging to line his own pockets in the process. Understandably, the people in Zacchaeus' community resented his selfishness and corruption, and they expected Jesus to do nothing less.

Who Jesus Is NOT: ARIANISM AND DOCETISM

The New Testament Church spent a lot of time combatting heresies, or wrong beliefs and teachings about Jesus — and among the earliest of these was **Docetism**. In the first century, this false doctrine suggested Jesus took on a human *appearance* but not a true human *nature* in His incarnation. In other words, Jesus only seemed to be human.

This may sound like a small discrepancy, but it has huge implications. As one early church father wrote, "That which He has not assumed, He has not healed." If Jesus wasn't really human, then He couldn't really save human sinners like us. Hebrews 2:17 confirms, *"He had to be like his brothers and sisters in every way, so that he could become a merciful and faithful high priest in matters pertaining to God, to make atonement for the sins of the people."*

Other early Christians were misled by the heresy of **Arianism**, which taught that Jesus was *created* by God. However, this idea directly contradicts John 1:1-3: *"In the beginning was the Word, and the Word was with God, and the Word was God ... All things were created through him."* If God created Jesus, it would mean that Jesus is not God — that He is not eternal or self-existent and is not equal with the Father and the Holy Spirit in the divine Trinity. And if Jesus was anything less than fully God, His promise to give us *"life in his name"* (John 20:31) would not be fully reliable.

Wrong beliefs about Jesus — including versions of these same heresies from thousands of years ago — continue to stir up confusion in our culture today. But the more we know the biblical Truth about Christ, the more we can tell each other and the world who He really is: our fully human and fully divine Savior.

Interestingly, as pastor Barry Cooper observes, the word *mashiach* in the Old Testament does not always refer exclusively to Jesus: "Anyone whom God had anointed for a particular purpose could be called a (small-c) 'christ' or 'messiah.' Prophets, priests, and kings in the Old Testament were all said to be 'anointed' or chosen by God for these roles—they were 'christs' ... But there would one day be an infinitely greater liberation, enacted by an infinitely greater Christ."[2]

For example, King Saul was called *"anointed"* in 1 Samuel 24:6, and so was King Cyrus in Isaiah 45:1 ... but only Jesus is the King of kings (Revelation 19:16).

> How does this illuminate John's claim that "*Jesus is **the** Messiah*" (John 20:31, emphasis added)? What makes Jesus different from the lowercase "messiahs" before Him?

When we look to small-c christs, we may find wisdom, encouragement, or inspiration, but we won't find salvation. This is also true if we treat Jesus Himself as a small-c christ — viewing Him merely as a good teacher, for instance. Whether we reject Jesus outright or more subtly try to renegotiate His identity on our own terms, both are unbelief.

Thankfully, God is kind and patient even in our flawed faith. He graciously gives us not only the New Testament but all of Scripture to tell us who Jesus truly is so we can trust Him with certainty. In fact, that's the whole reason *"these are written"* (John 20:31)!

> How does John 20:31 emphasize the importance of reading Scripture to know Jesus and *"have life in his name"*? What practical habits help you prioritize time in God's Word, or what new habits could you start today?

James 2:19 says, *"You believe that God is one. Good! Even the demons believe—and they shudder."* How does this show that mere belief in God's existence is different from the belief in Jesus that John 20:31 describes? What is the difference between faith that *saves* and faith that only *"shudder[s]"* before God?

Today's key verse tells us that true, redeeming faith means believing *"Jesus is the Messiah,"* or in some translations, *"Jesus is the Christ"* (ESV). The Greek word here — and in more than 500 other New Testament scriptures about Jesus — is *christos*. Like the Hebrew word *mashiach* in the Old Testament, it means "Messiah" or "Anointed One."

Let's look at a few key passages in the Old Testament about God's *mashiach*, then compare them to Jesus Christ:

PROPHECIES ABOUT THE MESSIAH	JESUS CHRIST
"Then I will raise up a faithful priest for myself. He will do whatever is in my heart and mind. I will establish a lasting dynasty for him, and he will walk before my anointed one [mashiach] *for all time"* (1 Samuel 2:35).	What does Hebrews 7:26-28 say about Jesus?
"You come out to save your people, to save your anointed [mashiach]. *You crush the leader of the house of the wicked ..."* (Habakkuk 3:13).	What do Acts 4:12 and Romans 16:20 say about Jesus?
"Now I know that the LORD *gives victory to his anointed* [mashiach]; *he will answer him from his holy heaven with mighty victories from his right hand"* (Psalm 20:6).	What do Mark 14:61-62 and Acts 2:32-33 say about Jesus?

DAY 2

JOHN 20:31

JOHN WROTE SO WE MAY BELIEVE JESUS AND HAVE LIFE IN HIS NAME.

According to recent survey data, about 9 in 10 people in the United States today believe Jesus was a real person who lived on earth. About 6 in 10 Americans even say they've made a personal commitment to Jesus — which is certainly a hope-filled statistic!

But at the same time, only 5 in 10 say they believe Jesus is God. And only 3 in 10 believe Jesus is perfect, without sin.[1]

If we do the math, these numbers reveal a troubling truth: Many people who profess faith in Jesus lack crucial knowledge of who He really is. Even if many identify as Christian, not all know the true identity of Christ — all the fullness of God in the form of a sinless man.

This makes today's key verses especially relevant for us! John said he wrote his Gospel to correct misunderstandings about Jesus and clarify the truth. Because it's only when we *"believe that Jesus is the Messiah, the Son of God"* that we *"have life in his name"* (John 20:31).

> What are some common misconceptions or false beliefs about Jesus you've encountered in your community? (See Page 37 for two examples from the early Church.)

Jesus is both perfect and personal. He is exalted and embodied. He is "*from the Father*" and "*among us*" (John 1:14). This has all kinds of beautiful implications for our lives, but let's conclude with this: Because Jesus has experienced humanity fully, there is no doubt that He fully understands us. He doesn't have 50% sympathy for our struggles or partial comprehension of our pain.

> How do these certain truths about Jesus' identity reassure you today? How do they increase your desire to know Him even more?

Now let's consider *"his glory, the glory as the one and only Son from the Father"* (John 1:14). What does God say about His glory in Isaiah 42:8 and Isaiah 48:11?

If we believe Scripture when it says God does not share His glory with anyone, yet *"we observed his glory"* in Jesus (John 1:14), then that can only mean one thing: **Jesus is God.** The Almighty made it possible for human eyes to see His glory — and even more amazingly, He humbled Himself to see us through human eyes of His own! This is what it means that *"the Word became flesh"* (v. 14). **Jesus is a person.**

It's hard to overstate how radical this really is. It astonished Jewish religious leaders so much that in John 10:33, they threatened to stone Jesus *"for blasphemy, because you—being a man—make yourself God."*

How does John 1:14 prove the opposite is actually true? Why is it important that Jesus is God who became human — not a human who became God?

The Jews who rejected Jesus' divinity thought they were defending Old Testament scriptures like Numbers 23:19, which says *"God is not a man."* But in reality, Jesus' incarnation is not a contradiction of this truth — it's a progression of how God planned all along to reveal Himself to the world. John 1:1-4 clarifies that God has always existed in a nonhuman, spiritual form since time immemorial, but something new happened when He *"dwelt among us"* (John 1:14). Without *subtracting* from His divinity, Jesus *added* humanity to Himself.

God also foretold this long ago. In Isaiah 9:6-7, for instance, what language or imagery points to the incarnation of a *human and divine* Savior? How does this show John 1:14 was always God's plan, not just an unannounced "surprise" in the New Testament?

DAY 1

JOHN 1:14

THE APOSTLE JOHN WROTE THAT JESUS IS THE WORD OF GOD
WHO BECAME FLESH AND DWELT AMONG US.

Usually when we first meet someone, we introduce ourselves by name so they know what to call us. Next we might say something about our job, our family, where we live, or how we like to spend our time.

The Gospel of John introduces Jesus like this: *"The Word became flesh and dwelt among us. We observed his glory, the glory as the one and only Son from the Father, full of grace and truth"* (John 1:14).

Talk about a handshake and hello! John knew Jesus well — arguably better than anyone else on earth. Not only did they spend years doing ministry side by side, but of the 12 disciples, John was Jesus' closest friend, *"the one Jesus loved"* (John 20:2). There was perhaps no one more qualified to write a firsthand account of Jesus' life, death, and resurrection, and when John began his Gospel, he started with some key facts about Jesus' identity.

Interestingly, before he ever used Jesus' first name (John 1:29), John described Him as *"the Word"* who possesses and reveals the *"glory"* of God (John 1:14).

Read John 1:1-4 to find out more about the Word:

- When was the Word? (Or since when — how long has He existed?)

- Where was the Word?

- Who was the Word?

- What did the Word do?

WEEK 1
SURE OF WHO JESUS IS

CLAIRE FOXX

WEEKS 7-8: SURE OF WHERE WE'RE GOING

DAY 31   3 JOHN 4
John had no greater joy than to hear that believers were walking in the truth.

DAY 32   PHILEMON 6
Paul prayed for effective faith resulting in the full knowledge of every good thing in Christ.

DAY 33   2 JOHN 8
John warned believers to watch ourselves so we can receive a full reward.

DAY 34   HEBREWS 10:24-25
The author of Hebrews urged believers to encourage one another as the great Day approaches.

DAY 35   JUDE 24-25
Jude praised the God who is able to present us blameless in His glorious presence.

DAY 36   REVELATION 21:4
John wrote that God will wipe away every tear.

DAY 37   JAMES 1:12
James wrote that believers who endure will receive the crown of life.

DAY 38   1 PETER 1:3-5
Peter praised God for giving believers new birth into a living hope kept in heaven for us.

DAY 39   2 PETER 3:13
Peter said believers are waiting for new heavens and a new earth.

DAY 40   1 THESSALONIANS 4:16-17
Paul wrote that the dead in Christ will rise first and that living believers will meet the Lord in the air.

WEEKS 5-6: SURE OF WHAT WE'RE DOING

DAY 21   MATTHEW 28:19-20
Jesus directed His disciples to share the Good News and obey Him.

DAY 22   EPHESIANS 2:8-9
Paul wrote that we are saved by grace through faith, not by works.

DAY 23   TITUS 3:5
Paul wrote that God saved us according to His mercy.

DAY 24   GALATIANS 2:20
Paul wrote that believers live by faith in the Son of God, who loves us.

DAY 25   PHILIPPIANS 4:4
Paul reminded believers to rejoice in the Lord.

DAY 26   2 THESSALONIANS 3:11-13
Paul wrote to encourage believers not to grow weary in doing good.

DAY 27   EPHESIANS 4:1-3
Paul urged believers to be eager to maintain unity.

DAY 28   COLOSSIANS 3:12-14
Paul wrote that believers should forgive one another as the Lord forgives us.

DAY 29   1 TIMOTHY 4:12
Paul wrote to Timothy to set an example in speech, conduct, love, faith, and purity.

DAY 30   2 TIMOTHY 3:16-17
Paul wrote that all Scripture is inspired by God to equip us for every good work.

WEEKS 3-4: SURE OF WHO WE ARE

DAY 11   ACTS 17:30-31
Paul declared that God had overlooked times of ignorance, but now He commands all people to repent.

DAY 12   2 CORINTHIANS 5:17
Paul wrote that if anyone is in Christ, they are a new creation.

DAY 13   1 JOHN 1:9
John wrote that if we confess our sins, God forgives and cleanses us.

DAY 14   ROMANS 1:16
Paul wrote that he was not ashamed of the gospel, which saves everyone who believes.

DAY 15   ACTS 2:38
Peter told the people to repent and be baptized in the name of Jesus Christ.

DAY 16   ROMANS 8:1
Paul wrote that there is no condemnation for those in Christ Jesus.

DAY 17   ROMANS 12:4-5
Paul wrote that we are one body in Christ.

DAY 18   ROMANS 15:13
Paul prayed that the God of hope would fill believers with joy and peace by the power of the Holy Spirit.

DAY 19   1 CORINTHIANS 1:10
Paul urged believers to agree and be united in the name of Jesus.

DAY 20   ACTS 1:8
Jesus told His disciples to be His witnesses to the ends of the earth.

MAJOR MOMENTS

WEEKS 1-2: SURE OF WHO JESUS IS

DAY 01   JOHN 1:14
The Apostle John wrote that Jesus is Word of God who became flesh and dwelt among us.

DAY 02   JOHN 20:31
John wrote so we may believe Jesus and have life in His name.

DAY 03   LUKE 19:10
Jesus said He came to seek and save the lost.

DAY 04   MATTHEW 11:28-30
Jesus invited those who are weary to come to Him for rest.

DAY 05   JOHN 14:6
Jesus said He is the way, the truth, and the life.

DAY 06   MARK 1:15
Jesus proclaimed that the Kingdom of God has come near.

DAY 07   MARK 10:45
Jesus said He came as a servant who would give His life for many.

DAY 08   1 CORINTHIANS 2:8
Paul wrote that earthly rulers did not understand God's plan, or they would not have crucified Jesus.

DAY 09   EPHESIANS 1:20
Paul wrote that God's power raised Christ from the dead.

DAY 10   LUKE 24:51
Luke wrote that Jesus parted from earth and was carried up into heaven.

inseparable truths: Because Christ's body has been raised, so will ours be if we have received the gift of salvation through Him. Paul addressed this issue head-on, dismantling illogical thinking and redirecting believers to the person and deity of the risen Christ.

Not only did Paul point out the fallacies of unbelief, but he taught that *right thinking* about Christ's resurrection is linked to *right living* in His Kingdom. 1 Corinthians 15:1-4 shows that orthopraxy (acts or practices of faith) and orthodoxy (faith or doctrine itself) both hinge on the resurrection:

"The gospel I preached to you, which you received, on which you have taken your stand and by which you are being saved ... [is] that Christ died for our sins according to the Scriptures, that he was buried, that he was raised on the third day ..."

As theologian Matthew Henry summarizes, "Christ's death and resurrection are the very sum and substance of evangelical truth. Hence we derive our spiritual life now, and here we must found our hopes of everlasting life hereafter."[5]

In the Gospels, we'll see that even some who witnessed Jesus' miracles were skeptical, asking, *"Who is this man ... Who can forgive sins but God alone?"* (Luke 5:21). The incarnation settles this question. Who is man? Jesus. Who is God? Jesus. Who forgives sins? Jesus — precisely because He is the God-man.

In His humanity, Jesus can *"sympathize with our weaknesses"* because He *"has been tempted in every way as we are, yet without sin"* (Hebrews 4:15). In His divinity, *"God was pleased to have all his fullness dwell in [Jesus], and through him to reconcile everything to himself"* (Colossians 1:19-20).

And the more we are enthralled by this remarkable Redeemer, the more we realize being enthralled is only the beginning. When we are sure of who Jesus is, we will surely trust our whole hearts to Him.

GOD RESURRECTED

Another core tenet of Christianity is the truth that Jesus, the Son of God, sinless and spotless, sacrificially died for our sins. But without His resurrection three days later, Christ's death on the cross would be meaningless. As Paul wrote to the Corinthian church, *"If Christ has not been raised, your faith is worthless; you are still in your sins"* (1 Corinthians 15:17).

The resurrection reveals Christ's power over death, publicly declaring His redemptive work is fully accomplished — and believers will be raised with Him (1 Corinthians 15:54; Ephesians 2:6). Because of His resurrection, we have hope and victory in the present as well as the future, making our purpose sure!

In his letter to Corinth, Paul challenged believers to examine all aspects of their lives through the lens of this gospel Truth. Because Corinth was a Greek city near Athens, people's ideas about the body, death, and resurrection were influenced by Greek philosophy — including dualism, which taught that all matter (what we can see, touch, and taste in the world) was evil and that only the spirit was good. Dualists believed bodies could not rise from the dead because the body was evil.

But Jesus *did rise bodily* from the dead!

Still, early Christians sometimes put Jesus in a separate, unique category and denied that their own bodies would be raised from the dead (1 Corinthians 15:12). They separated their belief in Jesus' resurrection from belief in a personal resurrection. Yet Paul taught that these are

GOD INCARNATE

Who is Jesus? There are many possible answers to this question — almost as many as there are people on earth. For example, below are just a few different perspectives from about the last century of Western thought:

- An encyclopedia definition of "Jesus" describes Him simply as "a religious leader revered in Christianity, one of the world's major religions."[1]

- British intellectual and atheist H.G. Wells describes Jesus as "irrevocably the very center of history."[2]

- American fiction writer Flannery O'Connor calls Jesus "a wild ragged figure motioning [us] to turn around and come off into the dark where [we] might be walking on the water and not know it."[3]

- The renowned German scientist Albert Einstein once called Jesus "the luminous figure of the Nazarene."

In fuller context, Einstein said in a 1929 interview: "I am a Jew, but I am enthralled by the luminous figure of the Nazarene … No one can read the Gospels without feeling the actual presence of Jesus. His personality pulsates in every word. No myth is filled with such life."[4]

We'll see throughout our study of the New Testament that this is certainly true. Jesus is luminous. He is also a revered religious leader. He is the center of history. He does wildly beckon us toward the miraculous. But most importantly … **Jesus is the incarnate Son of God.**

From Latin root words meaning "in the flesh," the word "incarnation" itself does not appear in the Bible, but Christians use it to describe a core tenet of our faith. Jesus took on a *human form* and a *human nature* to live on earth, all while remaining *fully God* in nature, power, and essence, just as when He dwelled in heaven throughout eternity past.

This means Jesus isn't just "human on the outside" and "God on the inside." Nor is He sometimes human and other times divine. Jesus is God *and* human. Both at once. Both fully and flawlessly. To use another theological term, His divinity and humanity coexist in *hypostatic union* — almost like a perfect marriage, two natures forever covenanted as one, unmixed yet inseparable.

Still, even the analogy of marriage can only go so far in describing this miraculous mystery. The best way for us to understand the incarnation — to understand Jesus — is to read His Word and experience His actual presence. Which is exactly what we're doing in this study!

TWO KEY TRUTHS ABOUT JESUS

GOD INCARNATE • GOD RESURRECTED

CLAIRE FOXX AND JENNY WHEELER

WHY THIS MATTERS FOR YOUR STUDY

As we begin this 40-day journey through the New Testament, it's helpful to keep the first-century context in mind. Understanding the political pressures, religious divisions, and cultural shifts of the time helps us see why Jesus' message was so radical, why the early Church faced so much opposition, and ultimately how God ensured that the gospel Truth spread powerfully despite every obstacle.

Knowing this, we can be all the more confident that this same gospel still changes everything — starting with us.

But not everyone had the same idea of what the Messiah would look like:

- Some expected a warrior-king like David, who would lead an army against Rome and restore Israel's political independence.

- Others looked for a spiritual leader who would renew worship and reform the religious system.

- Some, like the Essenes, anticipated an apocalyptic figure who would usher in the end of the age.

Jesus fulfilled these prophecies in ways no one expected. Instead of leading a military rebellion, He preached love and forgiveness. Instead of overthrowing Rome, He established a Kingdom *"not of this world"* (John 18:36). Instead of defeating enemies with a sword, He conquered sin and death through the cross.

Because of this, many rejected Him. He didn't fit their expectations. But for those who recognized Him as the true Messiah ... everything changed.

GREEK CULTURAL INFLUENCE

HELLENISM

Even though Rome was in charge, Greek culture dominated the way people thought and communicated. This influence, known as Hellenism, had been spreading ever since the conquests of Alexander the Great, shaping everything from education and philosophy to architecture and entertainment.[7]

For instance, one of the most significant impacts of Greek culture was linguistic: Koine Greek became the common tongue, allowing ideas to spread across the Roman empire. That's why the New Testament was written in Greek, making it widely accessible.[8]

Greek philosophy also shaped how people approached truth and wisdom. Ancient thinkers like Plato and Aristotle had introduced ideas about the human soul, morality, and the nature of reality. Christian evangelists like Paul, who was well-versed in Greek thought, would use this cultural touchpoint to connect with Greek audiences, like in Acts 17:22-31 when he referenced their own poets to introduce them to the true God. Jesus and His followers engaged with the Greco-Roman cultural backdrop to present the gospel in a way both Jews and gentiles could understand.

JEWISH RELIGIOUS LIFE

A DIVIDED FAITH

While Rome ruled politically, Jewish leaders still had significant influence over religious life in Israel. But instead of being united, Jews were divided into different groups, each with its own perspective on what faithfulness to God should look like.[4]

- PHARISEES

  Passionate about upholding God's Old Testament law, the Pharisees went to great lengths to ensure obedience — even adding extra rules to "help" people avoid sin. Pharisees were respected in society but were often judgmental of those they saw as lawbreakers. Jesus challenged them because they didn't practice what they taught and they valued their traditions over the spirit of God's law (Matthew 23:3; Mark 7:9).

- SADDUCEES

  These were elite, wealthy priests who served in the temple in Jerusalem. They cooperated with Rome, and their influence was political as much as religious. They saw Jesus as a threat to their control and rejected true doctrines like resurrection and the afterlife (Mark 12:18-27; Matthew 22:23).[5]

- ESSENES

  Instead of engaging with Roman rule or temple politics, the Essenes withdrew from society altogether. They lived in isolated desert communities, focusing on purity, strict discipline, and the study of Scripture. Many scholars believe they wrote the Dead Sea Scrolls (which you can learn more about on Pages 187-189!).

- ZEALOTS

  This group wasn't interested in patience or diplomacy — they believed armed rebellion was the way to restore Israel's kingdom and overthrow Rome. Simon the Zealot, one of Jesus' disciples, came from this movement, showing how Jesus brought together people from vastly different backgrounds.

JEWISH EXPECTATION OF THE MESSIAH

For centuries before the New Testament, the Jewish people had clung to the promise of a Messiah — a divinely anointed leader who would restore Israel's glory, bring justice, and establish God's Kingdom on earth. This expectation was woven throughout Old Testament prophecy and only intensified under Roman rule.[6]

STEP INTO THE WORLD OF THE NEW TESTAMENT

CAILAH GARCIA

Now that we've laid the groundwork for what the New Testament is and why we trust it, let's set the stage for what was going on in the world around the time of Jesus' earthly ministry. The New Testament wasn't written in a vacuum. It was shaped by a world of political tension, deep religious traditions, and cultural influences that impacted everything from daily life to how people understood the promise of a coming Messiah.

We can even imagine ourselves stepping into these places where Jesus walked, the apostles preached, and the early Church began to grow against all odds ...

THE POLITICAL LANDSCAPE

ROMAN RULE

At the time of Jesus' birth, Rome was in control of much of modern-day Europe, Asia, and northern Africa, and life under Roman rule was a mix of order and oppression.[1] Thanks to the Pax Romana (a period of relative peace across the empire from about A.D. 27-180), travel was safer than ever before, and a vast network of well-built roads made it easier to spread ideas, eventually including the gospel.[2] The Romans also established a legal system that allowed for some justice, though it was not always fair, especially for those on the margins of society.

For God's people in Israel, Rome's presence was a daily reminder that they were not politically free. Heavy taxation weighed on families, soldiers enforced laws with violence, and leaders like Herod the Great (king of Judea) ruled with paranoia and cruelty during the time of Jesus' birth. For instance, the census that forced Jesus' earthly parents to travel to Bethlehem in Luke 2:1-5 wasn't just an inconvenience; it was a stark example of how much control Rome had over people's lives.[3]

Many Jews longed for a deliverer who would free them from Rome's grip — but Jesus came offering a freedom far greater than political independence.

EYEWITNESSES

In a court of law today, eyewitness testimony remains one of the most crucial forms of evidence. The credibility of an eyewitness who directly observed an event is often considered irrefutable. And if one eyewitness is good, two is exponentially better! The New Testament is informed by *many eyewitness testimonies* all repeating the same overall account of the life, death, and resurrection of Jesus Christ.

The Apostle John affirmed this in 1 John 1:1-3, emphasizing that he and others reported *"what we have seen with our eyes, what we have observed and have touched with our hands, concerning the word of life."* The Bible offers more eyewitness testimony for Jesus' resurrection than what is often required to convict criminals in our world's best court systems, where sometimes no eyewitness testimony is required.[4]

Here we've only scratched the surface of the persuasive evidence for biblical authentication, but even this brief overview shows that when we read the Bible, we are not simply reading a book among many. And still the *primary* persuasive work is that of the Holy Spirit in our hearts. When we read with faith, we experience Scripture as *"living and effective and sharper than any double-edged sword, penetrating as far as the separation of soul and spirit, joints and marrow. It is able to judge the thoughts and intentions of the heart"* (Hebrews 4:12).

In other words, when we read the Bible, it also reads *us*. For the believer, it resonates with our hearts and minds in a way no other book does. God Himself speaks to our deepest needs and questions, shows us His nature and our nature, and brings conviction and comfort. Through the working of His Spirit, the Bible is the primary way God calls people to Himself. (See Hebrews 1:1-2, John 17:17, Isaiah 55:11, Romans 15:4, and Matthew 4:4.)

While there are many compelling reasons to trust the Bible, we ultimately trust it by a miracle of God. Praise the Lord! May our faith in Him and His Word increase day by day.

UNITY

The Bible is *extraordinarily unified* in its message, especially when we consider its diverse authorship. The Old and New Testaments were written:

- Over approximately 2,000 years.

- By at least 40 different authors from various backgrounds (including shepherds, kings, fishermen, and scholars).

- In three languages (Hebrew, Aramaic, and Greek).

- In, across, and from various continents (Asia, Africa, and Europe).

Yet the Bible conveys a single, unified message: God created the world good, but humanity fell into sin that separates us from God. The tragic reality of sin includes terrible consequences — namely, death. Yet we have hope because God, in His love, sent the Messiah, Jesus Christ, to pay the penalty for sin through His death on the cross and defeat death by rising from the grave. Through faith in Christ, anyone who turns to Him receives eternal life.

The Bible's coherence and harmony about this message is nothing short of miraculous. No mere human effort could have produced such a unified book across such a span of time and geography.

PROPHECY

The Bible also contains hundreds of prophecies that have been fulfilled with remarkable accuracy — giving us confidence that any as yet unfulfilled will surely be completed in the future. Take the prophecy in Isaiah 53, written around 700 B.C., which vividly describes the suffering and sacrifice of Jesus Christ. The details in this prophecy align with the gospel with striking precision, down to the tiniest detail like Jesus' burial in a rich man's tomb (Isaiah 53:9; Matthew 27:57-60). This is just one example of how fulfilled prophecies throughout Scripture reinforce the divine origin and authenticity of God's Word.

Why Do We Trust the Bible? INSPIRATION & INTERNAL EVIDENCE

ERIC GAGNON

As we've already learned in this study guide, there are great logical reasons to trust the Bible. With approximately 6,000 ancient Greek New Testament manuscripts still in existence, as well as 10,000 Latin manuscripts and 9,300 manuscripts in other languages,[1] the Bible is the world's most well-preserved ancient text.[2] The historical accuracy of the Bible and the alignment of archaeological discoveries with biblical narratives also continue to confirm the Truth of God's Word.

But as Christians, our trust in the Bible stems not just from its historical accuracy or its textual reliability — Scripture proves itself to us as God grants us divine understanding about His own words. In verses like Psalm 119:18 and Luke 24:45, we see that God Himself opens hearts and eyes to receive the Truth of Scripture. 1 Corinthians 2:13-14 reveals that believers are *"taught by the Spirit, explaining spiritual things to spiritual people."*

Because Scripture is divinely inspired, we can be confident that God in His infinite wisdom has preserved the Bible throughout history exactly as He intended, accomplishing all He desires to accomplish. Christians sometimes talk about this in terms of the "doctrine of inerrancy," which affirms "the God-breathed Scriptures are wholly true in all things that they assert in the original autographs and therefore function with the authority of God's own words."[3]

Reading God's Word is the way to truly and deeply know Him on this side of heaven! So let's consider three ways the Bible proves itself to us through some of its own internal evidence.

Now for another significant question: If we're meant to obey it, how can we be sure that the New Testament is both authoritative and accurate?

Let's first ask this: How can we trust that Homer wrote the *Iliad* and the *Odyssey* or that Shakespeare penned *Romeo and Juliet*? It's based on evidence, right? Well, here is a fascinating detail about ancient New Testament manuscripts: We have more significant evidence for the validity and historicity of the New Testament than the vast majority of ancient writings. When it comes to the New Testament, we have close to 6,000 manuscripts in Greek alone.[8] Some of the early manuscripts we have were copied within 25-150 years of the original writings. A conservative estimate leaves us with roughly 124 manuscripts that were meticulously copied within 300 years of the New Testament's original composition.[9]

Let's consider how this stacks up with other ancient writings. Based on the manuscripts available to scholars, the earliest copies of many ancient texts were created roughly 1,000 years after their original composition — like Herodotus' *The Histories* or Demosthenes' *Speeches*. And we only have roughly 12 or fewer fragmentary or partial manuscripts of these books. Take all of this and compare it with the Bible: We have so much more in terms of quantity and quality of manuscripts! It truly is an "embarrassment of riches," as many scholars say.

So where does this leave us? It leaves us with overwhelming evidence for a reliable New Testament canon that was authoritatively used for teaching in the early Church — and this builds our confidence and assurance in the Word of God we have in our hands today.

> *To learn even more about New Testament manuscripts, turn to Pages 187-189 for a comparison of some of the most important ancient manuscripts in existence today.*

In A.D. 325, the church historian Eusebius may have been the first to mention the seven general epistles (James; 1 and 2 Peter; 1, 2, and 3 John; and Jude) as an authoritative collection.[1] As early as A.D. 367, Athanasius of Alexandria famously wrote down the traditional 27-book New Testament canon.[2] This grouping of books was presented and authoritatively affirmed by the Third Council of Carthage in A.D. 397.[3] New Testament scholar Donald Hagner clarifies what took place at this council: "When later church councils did declare decisions about canon, in effect they put their stamp of approval only on books that already enjoyed that status."[4]

Eusebius (the church historian) also gives us a glimpse into the criteria used to affirm the New Testament canon:[5]

1. **Each book contains truth that matches the regula fidei (rule of faith), meaning it is consistent with the full counsel of God's Word.** Several church fathers (e.g., Ignatius and Irenaeus) pointed to 1 Corinthians 15:3-11 as a summary of the core truths we believe as followers of Jesus; therefore, any book that contradicted these tenets was excluded.

2. **Each book demonstrates genuine apostolic authorship and inspiration from the Holy Spirit.** This means each book had to be written by either an apostle of Jesus or a direct associate of that apostle (think of Luke, who was a historian and also a travel partner of the Apostle Paul).

3. **Each book or letter had preexisting authority, widely recognized among Christian churches.** The church father Augustine said, "Among the canonical Scriptures he will judge according to the following standard: to prefer those that are received by all the catholic churches to those which some do not receive."[6] (Note that "catholic" here just means "universal," indicating the *whole* Church.)

In summary, the New Testament did not come into existence sometime in the fourth century because of Constantine, Rome's first Christian emperor. There was a *gradual approval and authorization* process that started with the apostles and continued into the early Church era until councils eventually *affirmed* the canon.

Interestingly, the English word "canon" is rooted in the Greek *kanon,* which referred to "a reed used in making measurements."[7] We might say the 27 books of the canon are the books that have always "measured up." *Kanon* is also used in the New Testament in the context of how we should conduct or "*measure*" ourselves as believers (2 Corinthians 10:13). So the New Testament in a way establishes the standard of conduct for the Christian life.

Digging Deeper:
THE ORIGIN AND RELIABILITY OF THE NEW TESTAMENT

DR. JOEL MUDDAMALLE

If you asked someone how we got the New Testament in our Bibles, you could easily get one of two responses.

First: "I have no clue. Does anyone?"

Second: "Oh, that's easy. I read about this in *The Da Vinci Code*. The Roman Emperor Constantine came up with the New Testament we now have."

You may be shocked by the latter response, but when Dan Brown's novel was published in 2003, it made waves with over 82 million copies sold, all suggesting we got our New Testament sometime in the fourth century.

But here's the problem: This is simply not true. Since the first century, churches have been teaching and referencing New Testament writings in an authoritative manner, recognizing them as God's Word.

Groups of Christians who met in official church councils *confirmed* the New Testament as we know it today. But these church fathers were compiling what was *already widely circulated* among believers ever since the first Gospel accounts were written around A.D. 40.

Knowing this background about where the New Testament came from and how the early Church trusted it helps to lay a foundation for our confidence in the Scriptures today. So let's dig a little deeper.

AUTHORSHIP

- The Author of all Scripture is God! His Holy Spirit inspired every New Testament writer (2 Timothy 3:16; 2 Peter 1:21). There are at least eight confirmed human authors: Matthew, Mark, Luke, John, Paul, James, Peter, and Jude.

GENRE AND LANGUAGE

- The books of the New Testament include several genres of writing, including historical narrative, epistle, apocalyptic writing, parable, poetry, and prophecy. The New Testament was written in Koine Greek, which was the most commonly spoken language in the eastern parts of the Roman Empire. As opposed to literary Greek, *koine* means "common."

DATES OF WRITING

- The New Testament was written from about A.D. 45-100. Some suggest 1 Thessalonians was the first book to be written, and Revelation was likely the last.

EARLY USE IN THE CHURCH

- By about A.D. 100, most early churches were using the Gospels and Paul's letters in their teachings and relying on these scriptures to live their new Christian faith.

- For the next 100 or so years, Christians came under persecution in the Roman Empire, but when the Edict of Milan (A.D. 313) legalized Christianity, the Church was able to openly assemble its Scriptures.

- By the end of the fourth century, the Church formed councils to help decide in a formal, official way which books would be part of the New Testament. Keep reading to learn more about this process on the next page!

Here are some more facts about this important section of Scripture:

STRUCTURE

THE GOSPELS (FOUR BOOKS)

- Matthew, Mark, Luke, and John recorded the life and teachings of Jesus from their own perspectives.

- Matthew and John were among Jesus' original 12 disciples, and Luke was a physician who later came to faith in Christ and documented Jesus' life based on reliable testimonies from His apostles. Mark was a companion of the Apostles Peter and Paul.

- Matthew, Mark, and Luke are called the "Synoptic Gospels" because they share a similar chronological structure tracing Jesus' life. John's Gospel focuses more on Jesus' divinity and other theological concepts.

ACTS OF THE APOSTLES (ONE BOOK)

- In the book of Acts, Luke also recorded the history of the early Church as a "sequel" to his Gospel account.

EPISTLES (21 BOOKS)

- The Apostle Paul wrote at least 13 of these 21 letters addressed to first-century churches or individuals (like pastors or church leaders) to encourage believers and address matters of doctrine and church challenges.

REVELATION (ONE BOOK)

- The Apostle John wrote Revelation, which begins like an epistle but is filled with symbolic imagery and prophecy of Christ's return and final victory.

The Big Picture:
WHAT IS THE NEW TESTAMENT?

GLYNNIS WHITWER

The writings we now call "the New Testament" were actually recognized as Scripture, copied, shared, and used by the first followers of Jesus for hundreds of years before they were formalized into the Bible. Believers for generations guarded these precious teachings so you and I can experience the Good News of Jesus just like the first Christians did.

The Apostle John explicitly says this is the reason he wrote his Gospel account: *"Jesus performed many other signs in the presence of his disciples that are not written in this book. But these are written **so that you may believe that Jesus is the Messiah**, the Son of God, and that by believing you may have life in his name"* (John 20:30-31, emphasis added).

Although the **27 books** that comprise the New Testament are sometimes different in content and style, they are unified in these significant ways:

- The **central focus** is Jesus — His life, teachings, and ministry; His death, resurrection, and ascension; and the promise of His future return.

- They were written by people who either knew Jesus personally when He walked the earth or who gathered **firsthand testimony** from those who walked with Him (2 Peter 1:16).

- They are **inspired** by the Holy Spirit (2 Timothy 3:16).

- They contain **consistent theology** and doctrine (1 Thessalonians 2:13).

Together we'll trace the gospel story of redemption by moving through four New Testament themes, spending two weeks, or 10 days, studying each of these ideas:

- Sure of Who Jesus Is
  FOUNDATIONAL TRUTHS ABOUT JESUS

- Sure of Who We Are
  OUR IDENTITY IN HIM

- Sure of What We're Doing
  OUR PURPOSE AS HIS FOLLOWERS

- Sure of Where We're Going
  THE FUTURE HOPE HE HAS SECURED FOR US

As we dive into the New Testament, we'll also recognize the rich connection it shares with the Old Testament; together, they tell one cohesive story of God's redemptive work through history. The Old Testament makes up roughly three-quarters of the entire Bible — about 78% of its chapters, 75% of its verses, or 77% of its total word count, depending on translation — which lays an important foundation for our understanding of the gospel and ministry of Jesus.[1]

The introductory content and bonus pages throughout this guide will further enhance your understanding of Scripture's historical and cultural context, how the books of the New Testament were written and compiled, and why we can trust them with *sure faith*. From understanding the political landscape of Rome to unpacking core doctrines of the early Church to highlighting the Holy Spirit's guidance of the biblical authors — and much more — we've included some helpful activities, research, and visuals to deepen your appreciation and confidence in God's Word.

What a blessing that studying the Bible is not just an intellectual exercise. It's an opportunity to meet with God, be transformed by His Truth, and grow in Christlikeness. Our prayer is that the next 40 days will ignite a passion for God's Word that carries you forward for days, weeks, and years to come.

WHAT YOU HAVE TO LOOK FORWARD TO IN THIS STUDY

ERIC GAGNON

Have you ever flown across the country and looked out the airplane window, watching the land stretch endlessly below? It's a remarkable experience that can change how you see the world. Those familiar streets, homes, and towns that once felt so big suddenly seem small against the backdrop of mountains, sprawling cities, and endless plains.

Flying offers a higher perspective that connects the details of everyday life to a much bigger picture. That's also what this 40-day journey through the New Testament offers: Each day we'll "fly over" the landscape of Scripture together and marvel at God's work through the life of Jesus, the power of His ministry, and the beginnings of the Church, as seen through the eyes of the people who were there "on the ground." At the same time, our goal isn't just to look at landmarks from a distance — at the end of our time together, we pray you have not only new knowledge but deeper personal relationship with the Savior who steadies our uncertainties.

As we begin, let's take a moment to explain why we chose these particular scriptures and how we will approach studying them. Every passage included in this study is carefully selected to provide a rich and systematic overview of the New Testament. By "systematic," we just mean the topics of each study day are organized theologically (not necessarily chronologically) to help us understand God and the Bible.

This arrangement could also be called "credal," generally including the subject matter of the earliest Christian creeds or confessions of faith in Christ. While each of the 27 New Testament books is represented at least once in this study, we have prioritized larger books with more passages and also arranged them to follow a thematic progression.

Nowhere is that tension more profound than in the 400 years of silence between the Old and New Testaments. No prophets spoke. There were no new words from God to His people. There was just waiting, remembering, and hoping.

But this season of silence was not void of purpose. It was filled with promise. Because it led — finally — to Jesus.

God's 400-year silence broke not with thunder but with a baby's cry from a Bethlehem stable. The long-awaited Messiah had come. Jesus *is God* and is the fulfillment of every promise *from God* (2 Corinthians 1:20). He is the suffering Servant, Messiah, and Savior. He is the One who was struck by the serpent but who then crushed the serpent's head, per Genesis 3:15, through His death and resurrection.

Every page of the New Testament points to this reality: **God did what He said He would do.**

And this is good news for us — because we're not so different from the people of old. We still find ourselves in seasons of waiting. We still wrestle with doubt, anxiety, and questions like, *What is God doing in my life? How can I be sure He's with me? Will He really come through?*

But unlike those who waited in silence, we wait with a most certain hope in Jesus. We have the full truth of His life, death, resurrection, and ascension. We wait with confident assurance, knowing He will return to redeem the world He created, forever defeat every enemy, and gather all believers to spend eternity with Him.

This is why we study the New Testament. Not just to learn facts or gather knowledge but to encounter the living proof that God keeps His promises. As we walk through these 40 days together, may our faith be strengthened, our hope deepened, and our identity and purpose confidently anchored in the One who is the fulfillment of every word God has spoken — Jesus, our Messiah.

Surely Jesus is the Savior who can settle all of our uncertainty.

IN CHRIST'S LOVE,

Cailah, Claire, Ellen, Eric, Glynnis, Joel, Jenny, Michaela, and the Proverbs 31 Ministries team

WELCOME TO OUR STUDY

Have you ever found yourself waiting for something you were *told* would happen ... but as time stretched on, your confidence began to waver? Whether you're waiting for healing, breakthrough, provision, direction, or another answer to prayer, sitting in that in-between space can feel like standing in a fog, unsure of which way is forward.

God's people know this feeling all too well. In fact, much of the Old Testament tells the story of people living in that tension between the promises of God and their fulfillment. All the way back in Genesis 3, when sin first fractured the relationship between God and humanity, God declared that one day a human being, a descendant of Adam and Eve, would crush the head of the serpent (Genesis 3:15). This first glimmer of the gospel, known as the *protoevangelium,* was the beginning of a thread of hope that would weave its way through every generation.

It continued through the promises God made to Abraham: a covenant that his family, the people of Israel, would be a blessing to all nations (Genesis 12:1-3). Prophets like Isaiah clung to this same covenant, and God revealed more and more of His plans to redeem the world through a suffering Servant and Messiah, born of a virgin, who would come through the line of David (Isaiah 7:14; Isaiah 11; Isaiah 53). All along, God's people held on to His assurances, even if the fulfillment seemed impossibly far off.

We must exchange whispers with God before shouts with the world.

LYSA TERKEURST

PAIR YOUR STUDY GUIDE WITH THE FIRST 5 MOBILE APP!

This study guide is designed to accompany your study of Scripture in the First 5 mobile app. You can use it as a standalone study or as an accompanying guide to the daily content within First 5.

First 5 is a free mobile app developed by Proverbs 31 Ministries to transform your daily time with God.

Scan the QR code to download the First 5 app on your smartphone, and create a free account!

WWW.FIRST5.ORG

40 DAYS THROUGH THE NEW TESTAMENT

KNOWING THE SAVIOR WHO
STEADIES OUR UNCERTAINTY

Written by Cailah Garcia, Claire Foxx, Ellen Adkins, Eric Gagnon, Glynnis Whitwer,
Dr. Joel Muddamalle, Jenny Wheeler, and Michaela Roscoe | Designed by Anna Twumasi
Copyright © 2026 by Proverbs 31 Ministries

All Scripture quotations are **Christian Standard Bible (CSB)** unless otherwise noted.